W9-BGT-638

Chicago

Jack Schnedler

Third Edition updated by
Michael Austin and Elizabeth Canning

Photography by Zbigniew Bzdak

COMPASS AMERICAN GUIDES
An Imprint of Fodor's Travel Publications

Chicago
Third Edition

Compass American Guides and colophon are trademarks of Random House, Inc.
Fodor's is a registered trademark of Random House, Inc.
ISBN 0-679-00841-1
Compass American Guides, 5332 College Avenue, Oakland, CA 94618

Production House: Twin Age Ltd., Hong Kong   Manufactured in China

Managing Editor: Kit Duane   Editors: Kit Duane, Julia Dillon
Creative Director: Christopher Burt   Map Design: Eureka Cartography, Berkeley, CA;
Designers: Christopher Burt, David Hurst   Mark Stroud, Moon Street Cartography,
                                                    Durango, CO

10 9 8 7 6 5 4 3 2 1

THE PUBLISHER WISHES TO THANK Elizabeth Canning and Mike Austin for their work updating this third edition of the guidebook. Thanks are also due to Beth Burleson and Cheryl Koehler for help editing the third edition of the guide. We also want to thank Jeff Johnson for his essay on Chicago blues, pages 81-85; Henry Kisor for reading this manuscript for factual accuracy; and the following institutions for the use of their photographs and illustrations: Chicago Historical Society pp. 22, 27, 30, 33, 35, 40, 44, 93, 113, 212; Chicago Sun-Times pp. 50, 147, 150, 178; Chicago Transit Authority p. 232; Kogan Collection p. 44,; Library of Congress pp. 61, 140; National Baseball Library Archive pp. 96, 97; Phyllis Kind Gallery p. 141; Ragdale Foundation p. 225; Times, Munster, Indiana p. 203; Underwood Photo Archives pp. 5, 36, 39, 48, 62, 90, 100, 142; University of Chicago Archives p. 190; University of Illinois, Jane Addams Memorial Collection pp. 41, 43; Wilmette Historical Society p. 23. Thanks to Ron Brown for photos on pp. 103 and 135 (bottom).

To Marcia and Martha

ACKNOWLEDGMENTS

I WANT TO THANK ALL THE PEOPLE who've helped me understand and appreciate Chicago since I arrived as a wide-eyed 17-year-old from Missouri to attend Northwestern University in 1960. My colleagues at the old *Chicago Daily News* from 1965 to its death in 1978 gave me the broadest and most liberal education about the city that has become my home. There are too many to name them all, but a number of bosses who taught me a lot stand out: M. W. Newman, Ray Sons, Edward S. Gilbreth, Robert G. Schultz, Robert Signer. *Chicago Sun-Times* book editor Henry Kisor, a friend I cherish deeply, has inspired me by his recent zeal in writing wonderful books. And I'd know a lot less about Chicago without the unpredictable input of another bosom friend, Robin Robinson. The *Sun-Times* has permitted me to slip away from my travel editor's duties just enough to make this book possible, while assorted colleagues have contributed facts and ideas. The paper's own *Metro Chicago Almanac*—written by wizard reporters Don Hayner and Tom McNamee—has served as a rich lode of leads. Many other published works have launched me in rewarding directions, and many folks I've met out and around have fleshed out bare details.

From Compass American Guides, I've received the sturdy support any tremulous first-time book author needs—thanks to Christopher Burt, Kit Duane, Julia Dillon, Tobias Steed, and others. Collaborator Zbigniew Bzdak has lent valued encouragement while making me hope my verbal images can be half as vivid as his photographs.

I do wish that my father, Kurt Schnedler, could have lived to see this effort of a son in whom he invested so much care and love. Martha Schnedler continues to be the finest mother a son could want. Marcia Schnedler, wife and fellow traveler, can't imagine how much she means to me—in this project and the rest of life.

The powers that be salute author Jack Schnedler's work.
(Underwood Photo Archives, San Francisco)

C O N T E N T S

Maps

Literary Extracts

Topical Essays

CHICAGO OVERVIEW & NEIGHBORHOODS

CHICAGO FACTS

CITY HISTORY:

Name Derivation:	*Checaugou*, Potawatomi for swamp grass
First European Arrivals:	Marquette and Joliet, 1673
First Permanent Resident:	Jean-Baptiste Point du Sable, 1779
Incorporated:	1837

CITY STATISTICS 2000:

Area:	228 square miles
City Population:	2,896,016

"Other Race", "White Hispanic" and "Two or More Race" may comprise the Hispanic population, but this is not statistically defined.

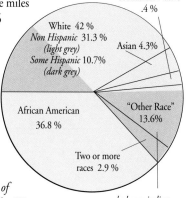

American Indian or Alaskan Native .4 %

White 42 %
Non Hispanic 31.3 %
(light grey)
Some Hispanic 10.7%
(dark grey)

Asian 4.3%

African American 36.8 %

"Other Race" 13.6%

Two or more races 2.9 %

dark grey indicates likely source of remaining 15.3% of population reporting Hispanic heritage.

NOTES OF INTEREST:

The 2000 Census saw the first increase in Chicago's population since the 1950s.

Chicago has the second largest population of Polish people (937,000) in the world—after Warsaw, Poland.

CLIMATE

Hottest Day	Coldest Day	Heaviest Rainfall	Heaviest Snowfall
106° F	-27° F	9.5 inches	18.6 inches
July 13, 1995	Jan. 20, 1985	July 26, 1968	Jan. 2, 1999

HOW WINDY IS IT?

Chicago's nickname, the Windy City, derives from the "windbag" reputation of civic boosters who hustled to land the 1893 world's fair. But Chicago is windy: on April 14, 1984, the city was pummeled by 69 m.p.h. winds.

Chicago's magnificent skyline seen from the Shedd Aquarium looking north along the Lake Michigan shoreline.

CHICAGO

*H*og Butcher for the World,
Tool Maker, Stacker of Wheat,
Player with Railroads and the Nation's Freight Handler;
Stormy, husky, brawling,
City of the Big Shoulders:
They tell me you are wicked and I believe them, for I have seen your
     painted women under the gas lamps luring the farm boys.
And they tell me you are crooked and I answer: Yes, it is true I have
     seen the gunman kill and go free to kill again.
And they tell me you are brutal and my reply is: On the faces of women
     and children I have seen the marks of wanton hunger.
And having answered so I turn once more to those who sneer at this my
     city, and I give them back the sneer and say to them:
Come and show me another city with lifted head singing so proud to
     be alive and coarse and strong and cunning.
Flinging magnetic curses amid the toil of piling job on job, here is a tall
     bold slugger set vivid against the little soft cities;
Fierce as a dog with tongue lapping for action, cunning as a savage
     pitted against the wilderness,
          Bareheaded,
          Shoveling,
          Wrecking,
          Planning,
          Building, breaking, rebuilding,
Under the smoke, dust all over his mouth, laughing with white teeth,
Under the terrible burden of destiny laughing as a young man laughs,
Laughing even as an ignorant fighter laughs who has never lost a battle,
Bragging and laughing that under his wrist is the pulse, and under his
     ribs the heart of the people,
          Laughing!
Laughing the stormy, husky, brawling laughter of Youth, half-naked,
     sweating, proud to be Hog Butcher, Tool Maker, Stacker of
     Wheat, Player with Railroads and Freight Handler to the Nation.

—Carl Sandburg, 1916

*(previous pages) A dramatic evening view looking south from the
observatory of the Hancock Building.*

O V E R V I E W

CHICAGO RESIDENTS AND FREQUENT VISITORS often speak glowingly of the treasures their city has to offer. A top list would, most certainly, include the following (in no particular order):

Magnificent Mile
Art Institute of Chicago
Field Museum of Natural History
Shedd Aquarium
Architecture and Sculpture in The Loop
Navy Pier
Lincoln Park
Museum of Science and Industry
Blues clubs

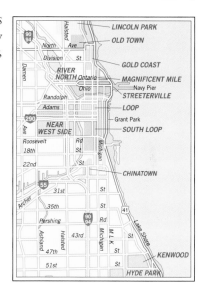

THE LOOP AND SOUTH OF THE LOOP
pages 104-131

The area referred to as "The Loop" is the heart of Chicago's business and finance world. Strictly speaking, the Loop is bounded by Lake Street to the north, State Street to the east, Van Buren to the south, and Wells to the west. Striking public sculptures accent the district's important architecture: a tour of the Loop amounts to a walk along the timeline of architecture (and architectural theory) from the mid-18th century to the present.

Grant Park and the widely renowned Art Institute of Chicago border the eastern edge of the Loop. Grant Park extends south along the lakeshore, where the majestic Field Museum of Natural History and Shedd Aquarium are the grand finale. Directly south of the Loop lies an area that has been extensively redeveloped in recent years; the gigantic McCormick Convention Center is its centerpiece. Walk farther south to reach Chicago's thriving Chinatown.

SOUTH TO HYDE PARK
pages 132-143

Well to the south of the city center is Hyde Park, home to the University of Chicago, one of America's leading academic institutions. Also in this neighborhood is the Museum of Science and Technology, billed as Chicago's number one tourist attraction. Frank Lloyd Wright's famous Robie House draws design disciples. Just north is Kenwood and its many historic mansions.

NEAR WEST AND RIVER NORTH   *pages 144-159*

Located just across the Chicago River's south branch from the Loop, the Near West side is home to the Chicago campus of the University of Illinois and has traditionally been the heart of Little Italy and Greektown. Just across the Chicago River north of the Loop, the River North neighborhood is dominated by the giant Merchandise Mart. Many restaurants, nightclubs, and galleries also make the Near North their home.

MAGNIFICENT MILE THE GOLD COAST   *pages 160-183*

The Magnificent Mile refers to the mile long stretch of Michigan Avenue from the Chicago River to Lakeshore Drive. This broad avenue is the greatest shopping street in the city

with a concentration of hotels within several blocks to the east and west.

Streeterville, a narrow strip of land just off the southeastern end of Michigan Avenue, runs to the waterfront. At the end of this strip is the Navy Pier, Chicago's Disneyland and summer playground for locals and tourists alike.

The once exclusive residential neighborhood often referred to as the "Gold Coast" —just north of the end of Michigan Avenue and bordering South Lakeshore Drive up to North Avenue—is lined with the fabled mansions of Chicago's elite.

LINCOLN PARK & NEAR NORTHWEST
pages 184-215

Lincoln Park and the Near Northwest encompass the collection of neighborhoods north of North Avenue where German, Polish, and Ukrainian immigrants originally settled. The area includes the neighborhood along Lincoln Avenue, one of the best "new" neighborhoods in the city. Chicagoans most popular playgrounds, lakefront Lincoln Park, and the sports arena of Wrigley Field, are also in this area. An area known as Old Town has a collection of good restaurants, historic house, and interesting shopping opportunities.

THE SUBURBS *pages 216-233*

Like all of America's great cities, Chicago is ringed by dozens of suburbs, some of which will be of interest to a variety of visitors. West of downtown Chicago, Oak Park is home to the world's largest trove of buildings designed by Frank Lloyd Wright. The town is also the home to the Ernest Hemingway Museum, the town having been his birthplace. North of the city are the very affluent suburbs of Highland Park and Lake Forest. In nearby Evanston can be found the campus of Northwestern University, the Chicago Botanic Garden, and the landmark Baha'i House of Worship.

INTRODUCTION

NEARLY 1,800 DAYS OF GLOBETROTTING as the travel editor for a Chicago newspaper gradually converted me into a rabid advocate for my own city, whose rough-hewn assets I'd often undervalued until I started spending so much time away from home. Now this guidebook may serve as a soapbox to spread the chauvinistic sermon that salts my conversational sallies among newly met strangers from Paris to Phuket: if you want a crash course in what the United States is all about, there's no better place to begin than Chicago.

"Only in the most indifferent does Chicago fail to awaken an ardent curiosity," was the 1919 bouquet tossed by Henry Justin Smith, managing editor in the *Chicago Daily News'* literary heyday, when Carl Sandburg even tried his hand (not so memorably) as silent-movie critic. Nelson Algren, who simultaneously adored and despised his hometown, said that living in Chicago "is like being married to a woman with a broken nose: There may be lovelier lovelies, but never a lovely so real." Norman Mailer, declaiming from the dust raised by the head-busting 1968 Democratic National Convention, pronounced Chicago "perhaps the last of the great American cities." Studs Terkel wrote that Chicago "is America's dream, writ large." Jan Morris, after a 1988 visit, waxed somewhat doubtful, recalling that Chicago once "was the heart of America in all its strength, violence, avarice, homeliness and absurdity." Now, she lamented, "Even Chicago's celebrated self-regard, itself a kind of metaphysical monument, has inevitably lost its power." Nobody today would greet a foreign visitor, as did a 19th-century train conductor, with: "Sir, you are entering the Boss City of the Universe."

Indeed, the last Big Boss—Mayor Richard J. Daley—has been dead and gone since 1976. His son Richard M. Daley, a resourceful politician but hardly a figure to inspire fearful awe, became mayor in 1987. But the power equation continues to shift. The traditional rivalry between North Siders and South Siders is less relevant today than the jockeying among whites, African-Americans, and Hispanics. Two of Chicago's best-known citizens are indomitable civil-rights activist Jesse Jackson and equally indefatigable talk-show wizard Oprah Winfrey.

Jan Morris may not be entirely wrong when she suggests that "few foreigners give a thought to Chicago from one year to the next." But my own travel encounters indicate that the city's image is improving in one regard: the most famous Chicagoan in far-flung corners of the world is no longer Al Capone. That movie-made mobster was displaced on the marquee of global awareness by basketball's supreme maestro, Michael Jordan. No question—a slam dunk is a step up in style from a rat-a-tat-tat.

Visitors and residents amble Chicago to savor the celebrities, the architecture, the lakefront, the museums, the neighborhoods, the dining, the shopping, and the other obvious allures. With a bit of on-the-street effort, those from out-of-town can share the insights and humor of ordinary Chicagoans; despite the thickening of big-city calluses, people here remain more open to strangers than in many another metropolis. With luck, you'll leave Chicago more cheerfully inclined than Rudyard Kipling, who wrote a century ago, "Having seen it, I urgently desire never to see it again. It is inhabited by savages." And you'll likely depart less befuddled than the daddy in Ogden Nash's whimsical verse: "I reel, I sway, I am utterly exhausted./Should you ask me when Chicago was founded I could only reply I didn't know it was losted."

A REAL CITY

I have struck a city,—a real city,—and they call it Chicago. The other places do not count. San Francisco was a pleasure-resort as well as a city, and Salt Lake was a phenomenon. This place is the first American city I have encountered. It holds rather more than a million people with bodies, and stands on the same sort of soil as Calcutta. Having seen it, I urgently desire never to see it again. It is inhabited by savages. Its water is the water of the Hughli, and its air is dirt. Also it says it is the 'boss' town of America.

—Rudyard Kipling, *From Sea to Sea,* 1889

(following pages) Most of Chicago's outdoor leisure activity takes place along the Lake Michigan waterfront.

H I S T O R Y

TURN BACK THE TIME MACHINE two centuries, and Chicago vanishes. It's a summer day in the early 1800s, and you're standing in a swamp beside a sluggish little river the Potawatomi Indians call "Checaugou," which probably means "wild onion" or "swamp grass." In the 21st century, you'd be dwarfed by a skyscraper forest while dodging the relentless traffic at one end of the Michigan Avenue Bridge linking the Loop and the Magnificent Mile. But here in the late 18th century, the flat landscape stretching west across the endless Great Prairie looks about as empty and primeval as when the last glacier retreated 13,000 years earlier. A canvas virtually blank of civilization, it seems an unpromising setting for the "City of the Big Shoulders" soon to be born.

■ FIRST SETTLERS

Yes, there is a log house near the north bank of the Checaugou, plus a scattering of other rough-hewn buildings. The homestead belongs to trader Jean Baptiste Point du Sable, who arrived around 1779 to become Chicago's first permanent resident. As the local Indians later would say, before the last of them were hustled westward in the 1830s, "The first white man to live here was a black man." Something of a mysterious figure who may have been born on Santo Domingo in the Caribbean, du Sable is mentioned in a British dispatch a few years after the Revolutionary War as "a handsome Negro, well educated and

Chicago's first non-Native American resident was a black man probably from Santo Domingo named Jean Baptiste Point du Sable who homesteaded on the banks of the Chicago River in 1779. (Chicago Historical Society)

This painting depicts the construction of Fort Dearborn, finished in 1804, and once called "the neatest and best garrison in the country." (Wilmette Historical Society)

settled in Eschikagou." As an ingenious and resourceful man of commerce, this First Chicagoan makes an apt progenitor for a metropolis perpetually on the make with the civic slogan "I will!" (Columnist Mike Royko once suggested that a truly honest Chicago motto would be "Ubi est mea?"—Where's mine?)

◆ FORT DEARBORN MASSACRE

In 1830, when the first town survey was plotted, the population numbered only 50. In 1837, when Chicago incorporated as a city with 4,170 residents, there were no paved streets and the tallest buildings towered all of two stories.

The Fort Dearborn Massacre, which took place at the onset of the War of 1812, stemmed from the same frontier tensions that had led to its construction in 1803 on the south bank of the Chicago River. A series of brass pavement markers around the Michigan Avenue-Wacker Drive intersection marks the site of the unprepossessing log fort. It stood directly across the river from the old du Sable homestead, which was bought in 1804 by an irascible silversmith named John Kinzie. Long known as "The Father of Chicago" by those who preferred to ignore the black man at the root of the city's family tree, Kinzie was a survivor of the Indian attack along with his nine-year-old son, John (destined to be the loser of Chicago's first mayoral election in 1837).

More than 500 warriors ambushed a procession of some 100 soldiers, women, and children who were trying to evacuate the isolated fort on August 15, 1812. Fifty-three Americans died in the massacre along the lake about two miles south of the outpost, which the Indians burned to the ground the next day. One of the four stars in Chicago's flag symbolizes Fort Dearborn, rebuilt on nearly the same site in 1816 and demobilized in 1836 after the Indian threat had evaporated. The successor fort was demolished like much of the city's heritage, but logs salvaged when it was torn down in 1857 have been fashioned into a section of blockhouse wall at the Chicago Historical Society. Touch that timber, and you are reaching about as far back into Chicago's tangible past as it is possible to go.

◆ PLACE OF LOW, FILTHY HUTS

Illinois became a state in 1818, but straggling Chicago lay almost unnoticed on its wilderness fringe far from the southern population centers along the Mississippi and Ohio Rivers. William H. Keating, a University of Pennsylvania mineralogist who visited Chicago in 1823 wrote, "The village presents no cheering prospects, as, not withstanding its antiquity, it consists of but few huts, inhabited by a miserable race of men, scarcely equal to the Indians from whom they are descended," wrote the non-visionary Keating.

*T*heir log or bark houses are low, filthy and disgusting, displaying not the least trace of comfort.... As a place of business, it offers no inducement to the settler, for the whole annual shipment of the trade on the lake did not exceed the cargo of five or six schooners.... The dangers attending the navigation of the lake, and the scarcity of harbors along the shore, must ever prove a serious obstacle to the increase of the commercial importance of Chicago.

■ SPECULATIVE MANIA

The Erie Canal completed in 1825, opening a new Great Lakes water route from the East to Chicago, and opportunity was in the wind. Entrepreneur Mark Beaubien, who arrived from Detroit in 1826 to visit his brother stayed to erect the city's first frame building. It housed some of Beaubien's 23 children, as well as a tavern and Chicago's first hotel, the Sauganash. Beaubien, who played the violin with passion and favored a swallow-tail coat with brass buttons on festive occasions, once declared that he "kept tavern like hell." With jolly souls like him

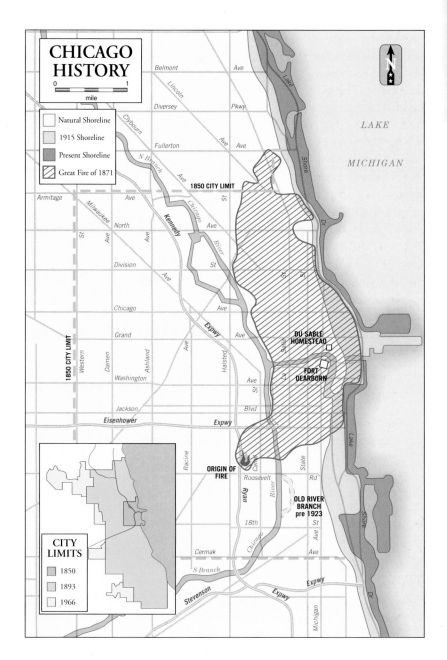

CHICAGO HISTORY

0 _____ 1
mile

Natural Shoreline
1915 Shoreline
Present Shoreline
Great Fire of 1871

1850 CITY LIMIT

LAKE MICHIGAN

DU SABLE HOMESTEAD

FORT DEARBORN

ORIGIN OF FIRE

OLD RIVER BRANCH pre 1923

CITY LIMITS

1850
1893
1966

in a location ideally suited to profit from America's impending westward boom, Chicago was poised to explode onto the national landscape.

Chicago's original plat, which straddled the river's three branches, covered only three-eighths of a square mile in a simple rectangular grid—setting a basic pattern that led one visitor to call this "the most right-angle city in the United States." There was more than ample land for the 1830 population of roughly 50, and $100 was the highest price paid in the initial auction of lots that year. Then the speculators swooped in, and barely born Chicago found itself at the vortex of "the most intense land speculation in American history," as historian William Cronin called it in his 1991 *Nature's Metropolis*. Those $100 lots of 1830 were selling for as much as $100,000 by 1836 in a frenzy fed mainly by visions of wealth from the I&M Canal—which, as events transpired, wasn't completed until 1848.

It was as if "some prevalent mania infected the whole people," wrote British traveler Harriet Martineau. The scene presaged the impression of a Swedish visitor 15 years later: "It seems as if on all hands, people come here merely to trade, to make money, and not to live." Some speculators quickly became leading citizens, among them William R. Ogden, who won Chicago's first mayoral election in 1837 and amassed a big enough real-estate fortune to build a mansion on a full block of city land. The new city adopted as its motto *Urbs in Horto*—City in a Garden—although the prevalent motif on the unpaved streets was mud deep enough to swallow a horse.

The last Native Americans vanished from the Chicago area after the 6,000 remaining Potawatomis in northern Illinois were forced to sign two treaties in September 1833, ceding all their land east of the Mississippi River to the white man. The closing of the second Fort Dearborn in 1836 symbolized the end of Chicago's frontier era, even if residents were still hunting wolves that year within earshot of downtown.

◆ URBAN FIRSTS—*FAST*

Emerging hallmarks of urban life included the city's first newspaper (launched in 1833 as the *Chicago Democrat*), the first brewery (opened in 1836 by German immigrants William Haas and Konrad Sulzer), and the first paid policeman (hired in 1839, by which time there were so many saloons that temperance activist John Hankins lamented, "I have never seen a town which seems so like a universal grog shop").

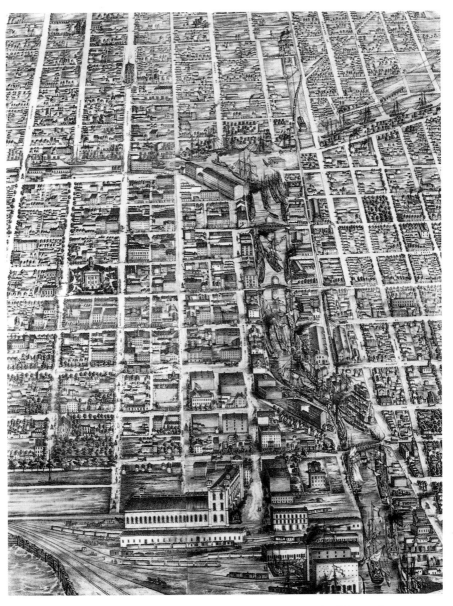

By 1857, when this engraving of the cityscape was made, Chicago had blossomed into a major city in only 20 years thanks to the railway and a canal connecting Lake Michigan with the Mississippi. (Chicago Historical Society)

Chicago's knack for architectural innovation, which would make it the cradle of the skyscraper at the end of the century, manifested itself in a new kind of construction designed to meet the sudden population surge of the 1830s. The balloon frame, devised by Augustine Taylor to build St. Mary's Church in 1833, was ideally suited for rapidly growing communities. A house could be erected in a week, and the balloon-frame method—thin plates and studs running the full length of the building and held together only by nails, later called simply "Chicago construction"—spread across the nation. Except for the balloon frame, the *New York Tribune* concluded in 1855, "Chicago and San Francisco never could have arisen, as they did, from little villages to great cities in a single year."

Joseph Jefferson, destined to become a distinguished actor for whom Chicago's annual theater awards are named, visited the fledgling community by steamboat in 1837 and recorded a whirl of impressions:

> People hurrying to and fro, frame buildings going up, board sidewalks going down, new hotels, new churches, new theaters, everything new. Saw and hammer—saw, saw, bang, bang—look out for the drays!— bright and muddy streets—gaudy-colored calicos—blue and red flannels and striped ticking hanging outside the dry-goods stores—barrooms— real-estate offices—attorneys-at-law—oceans of them!

The speculative boom went bust that very year during the Panic of 1837, which ushered in one of the nation's early economic depressions. Chicago lot prices sank back to $100 by 1840, most local businessmen landed flat on their financial backs, and work on the I&M Canal stopped after Illinois defaulted on its debt obligations. But canal construction resumed in a couple of years, and the city began to regain its breath.

■ IMMIGRANTS AND RAIL ROADS

One of its first ethnic neighborhoods sprang up around the canal's eastern end, populated by Irish laborers digging the waterway. Originally known as Hardscrabble, it was Bridgeport by the time Chicago annexed the area in 1863. A font of Irish-American heritage—and Irish-American politicians—for more than a century, Bridgeport is most famous as the lifelong home of the late Mayor Richard J. Daley.

By 1848, the Pioneer and other locomotives were whistling along the Galena and Chicago Union line. And the Chicago Board of Trade was newly open to broker the array of agricultural and other commodities that would flow into the world's prime rail hub in the decades ahead. The city limits encompassed only a fraction of modern Chicago, but the advent of horse-drawn street railways by the end of the 1850s boosted the growth of suburbs later absorbed within the municipal boundaries (like Lake View, Hyde Park, and Blue Island), as well as others that remain separate entities (like Evanston, Oak Park, and Lake Forest). German and Scandinavian immigrants, along with the Irish, were swelling the population of a once-again boomtown where a strong back virtually ensured employment.

♦ RAISING THE CITY ABOVE THE MUD

A lot of that muscle between 1855 and the Civil War went into levitating the city—physically lifting most buildings from the mire by as much as a dozen feet to match newly raised street grades. Like the reversal of the Chicago River to flow out

The famous Baldwin "4-2-0" puffer-belly on display at the Chicago Historical Society helped build the city's first railway in 1848.

of Lake Michigan four decades later, it was a marvel of civic engineering—and a necessity if urban growth was to continue. Because Chicago occupied a swamp, the streets at their natural level were quagmires most of the year. Citizens "were begot in mud, born in mud, and bred in mud," an early Chicagoan recalled. Whimsical signs marked the most treacherous passages with such warnings as "Team Underneath" and "Stage Dropped Through," while a hat plopped on the mud in one spot was labeled "Man Lost." After the elevation, strolling the streets no longer guaranteed a mud bath. The legacy of the occasional contrarian who refused to jack up his property can be seen today in neighborhoods near the Loop where a few old houses squat in yards sunk a half-dozen feet below the sidewalk.

In its early days the city was so mired in mud that its buildings had to be literally raised to match its new paved streets, as illustrated here in the raising of the Briggs Hotel in 1857. (Chicago Historical Society)

◆ Rival Rail Roads Puff into the City

By 1856, Chicago was the hub for 10 rival rail lines and steaming mightily toward one of the brawny titles bestowed by Carl Sandburg: "Player with Railroads and the Nation's Freight Handler." The arrival of passenger service from New York the following year cut travel time between the cities to just two days from the three weeks it had taken in the 1830s. Riding high as the nation's rail capital, Chicago saw its population soar from 4,470 in 1840 to 28,000 in 1850, 110,000 in 1860, and 300,000 in 1870. By 1890, with 1.1 million residents, it had passed Philadelphia to become America's Second City—a status grudgingly surrendered to Los Angeles in 1990.

■ Abraham Lincoln Nominated in Chicago

The web of 15 railroads converging on Chicago by 1860 made the self-styled Queen City of the Lakes a likely candidate to host the nominating convention of the infant Republican Party, a coalition that included most anti-slavery forces in a nation on the brink of bloody rupture. By then the ninth largest U.S. city, Chicago boasted the world's biggest train station, seven first-class hotels (where a luxurious room cost $2.50 a night), 50 more hotels at $1.50 a night, and 100 at $1. Meanwhile, the raising of the city continued. As Ida Tarbell wrote decades later in her Life of Lincoln:

> The audacity of inviting a national convention to meet there, in the condition in which Chicago chanced to be at the time was purely Chicagoan. No other city would have risked it... When the invitation to the convention was extended, half the buildings in Chicago were on stilts; some of the streets had been raised to the new grade, others still lay in the mud.... A city with a conventional sense of decorum would not have cared to be seen in this demoralized condition, but Chicago perhaps conceived that it would but prove her courage and confidence to show the country what she was doing.

The City Council, led by Republican Mayor "Long John" Wentworth, appropriated funds for a jerry-built pine-board convention hall with a capacity of 10,000 at Lake and Market streets, on the northwest fringe of today's Loop. People called it the "Wigwam," and the Republicans nominated Abraham Lincoln for president there on the third ballot. "Without attempting to convey an idea of the

POLITICAL CONVENTION CAPITAL

It took Chicago 28 years after the 1968 Democratic debacle that showed the world an ugly set of images: barbed wire and bayonets ringing the International Amphitheatre, angry chants of "Dump the Hump," the crunch of police nightsticks on the skulls of protesters and reporters, the stench of tear gas and stink bombs, the twisted face of Richard J. Daley cursing Sen. Abraham Ribicoff's attack on "Gestapo tactics in the streets of Chicago." But this brawny city securely retains its title as the capital city of national political conventions, those quadrennial circuses of the Donkeys and the Elephants. Chicago has hosted 25 Democratic and Republican conventions, starting on a high note with the 1860 GOP gathering that nominated Abraham Lincoln in the Wigwam, a jerry-built wooden arena at what is now Lake Street and Wacker Drive. Baltimore runs a distant second with 10 conventions.

As the nation's premier railway and then airline hub, Chicago has always been an obvious choice for the two major parties. And some of the most memorable conventions have been staged here. William Jennings Bryan delivered the famous "Cross of Gold" speech that swept him to the 1896 Democratic nomination in the first Coliseum, at 63rd and Harper. Republican regulars beat back the "Bull Moose" insurgents of ex-President Theodore Roosevelt to nominate William Howard Taft in 1912 at a newer Coliseum on Wabash Avenue between 14th and 16th streets. (And Roosevelt's Progressive forces held their own rump convention here later that summer.) In 1920, GOP bigwigs huddled in the original smoke-filled room at the Blackstone Hotel to swing a stalemated Coliseum convention to Warren Harding. Newly nominated Franklin D. Roosevelt broke a century of precedent in 1932 by flying to Chicago to accept the first of his four Democratic nominations in person at Chicago Stadium (where basketball's Bulls played before the United Center was built).

The last truly contested national convention saw Republican partisans of Dwight Eisenhower out fight Robert Taft's conservatives at the International Amphitheatre in 1952. Although a total of 10 U.S. presidents have been nominated in Chicago, Ike turned out to be the only winner among the five men chosen at the Amphitheatre, which sits on the edge of the old stockyards district at 43rd and Halsted. Adlai Stevenson came up a loser in 1952 and 1956, as did Richard Nixon on his first presidential bid in 1960. And Hubert Humphrey never recovered from the 1968 bloodletting where the whole world was watching. The twenty-first century was nearly at hand before the planet got a chance to watch Chicago's twenty-fifth national political convention—when the Democrats met at the new United Center in 1996.

delirious cheers, the Babel of joy and excitement, we may mention that strong men wept like children," reported the *Chicago Press and Tribune.* Lincoln became America's most revered president, and Chicago went on to host another 24 major-party nominating conventions—including the bruising Democratic gathering of 1968, when the whole world was watching.

■ POWERHOUSE OF COMMERCE

The meatpackers of Chicago took no Christmas holiday in 1865. They were busy that December 25 with the formal opening of Union Stock Yards, destined to become one of the city's most famous—and aromatic—landmarks, as well as its largest employer for more than half a century. Writers already had branded Chicago "The Great Bovine City of the World," thanks in part to its major role in supplying beef for Union troops during the recently concluded Civil War. It was also called "Porkopolis," having processed enough hogs in 1863 to stretch in curly-tailed single file all the way to New York. Now a consortium of nine railroads and

Longhorns, once a symbol of the settlement of the Plains, await their fate at the Union Stock Yards in 1903. (Chicago Historical Society)

a half-dozen meatpackers was consolidating slaughterhouse operations on a square mile of land south of 39th Street and west of Halsted, beyond that era's city limits.

Carl Sandburg portrayed the city "half-naked, sweating, proud to be Hog Butcher." The yards did have their darker sides, memorably exposed in 1906 by Upton Sinclair's *The Jungle,* including the revolting neglect of sanitation and the abysmal conditions under which immigrant laborers toiled.

Meatpacking, which finally faded from Chicago with the closing of Union Stock Yards in 1971, formed merely one sinew of the city's commercial and industrial prowess as the nation moved into the post-Civil War era of the Robber Barons. Chicago ranked as the world's largest grain handler and the premier North American lumber market. The huge McCormick plant, on the north bank of the river between Pine and Sands streets, dominated the trade in reapers and other farm machinery around the globe. George Pullman built his prototype sleeping car in 1864, and the North Chicago Rolling Mills turned out the nation's first steel rails the following year. In 1869, the 13,730 vessels docking at Chicago Harbor exceeded the combined commercial traffic for the ports of New York, Philadelphia, Baltimore, Charleston, Mobile, and San Francisco.

◆ WORKING CLASS SUFFERS

While Chicago's newly wealthy came to shop along Lake and State from their mansions to the west and north, the city's working-class majority suffered the indignities of the industrial revolution. "Unable to get away from the noise and odor of packing houses, tanneries and distilleries, the bulk of them huddled in modest pine cottages on small lots without the benefit of paved streets or sewers," according to Mayer and Wade's, Chicago: Growth of a Metropolis. More than 200,000 Chicagoans "were jammed into these frame jungles. City fathers and visitors alike might take pride in the fact that few tenements were built and that 'thrifty workmen own the houses they live in' or can 'rent a whole house,' but filth, disease, vice and privation were the constant companions of those living in poor neighborhoods."

Cholera and typhoid, which did not spare those better off, struck with regularity because the rapidly growing city fouled its Lake Michigan drinking water with raw sewage and industrial offal carried along by the increasingly polluted Chicago River. Only by standing nature on its head and permanently reversing the river's flow at the turn of the century did health officials finally vanquish the waterborne diseases.

Pullman's rail carriages were the ultimate in late-19th-century travel luxury, as this Pullman club car with barber's chair demonstrates. (Chicago Historical Society)

■ GREAT FIRE OF 1871

In fact, more prosaic forces touched off the October 8-10 conflagration, which remains the most indelibly mythic event in the city's history. Chicago in 1871 was a densely packed community of 300,000 built principally from wood; more than two-thirds of its 60,000 structures were entirely wooden; the sidewalks were mainly wooden; most streets were paved with tar-swathed wooden blocks; and the numerous lumberyards and grain elevators were torches waiting to ignite. Meanwhile, lengthy drought had turned the city tinder-dry. Into this kindling box, as one commentator described it, Lucifer threw his match.

The prime suspect, familiar to generations of schoolchildren, was a cow—not one of those hapless beef cattle waiting to meet its steak-maker at Union Stock Yards, but a milk cow belonging to Irish immigrants Patrick and Catherine O'Leary. It is a well known tale that Mrs. O'Leary went to the shed behind the family's West Side cottage on that fateful Sunday night, and that the cow kicked

Prudish souls declared that the Great Chicago Fire of October 8-10, 1871, was holy retribution for the city's "wickedness." (Underwood Photo Archives, San Francisco)

over the lantern while she was trying to milk the creature. But Mrs. O'Leary and her Bossie likely got a bum rap, as Don Hayner and Tom McNamee suggest in the breezy *Metro Chicago Almanac:* "The fire almost undoubtedly started in the family barn, but there is little evidence that Mrs. O'Leary was milking her cow at the time. To the contrary, in the only two interviews Mrs. O'Leary ever gave—both under oath—she said that she and her husband had gone to bed early that night. The legend of the cow may have been concocted by an imaginative newspaper reporter, and the fire's real origin remains unknown."

However ill-treated by popular legend, the O'Learys were fortunate in having their cottage escape the Great Fire, which burned its way north and east on prevailing winds through the commercial center and residential north side of the city. The death toll reached 250 or more, and 100,000 Chicagoans were left homeless by the destruction of more than 17,000 buildings. Only a handful of structures survived in the four square miles of devastation extending from Taylor Street on the south to Fullerton Avenue on the north, and from the river on the west to the lakefront *(see map page 25)*. The crenellated Water Tower, completed just two years earlier at Michigan and Chicago Avenues, became the most famous (and most photographed) survivor. It sits today, dwarfed by the Gold Coast's forest of highrises, as a talisman of the city's pluck in the teeth of adversity.

The *Chicago Tribune,* printing on borrowed presses after its supposedly fireproof building had been consumed, ran an upbeat editorial: "CHEER UP! In the midst of a calamity without parallel in the world's history, looking upon the ashes of 30 years' accumulations, the people of this once beautiful city have resolved that CHICAGO SHALL RISE AGAIN!"

The city's commercial core was back bigger and better in less than five years, with buildings erected to much more stringent fire codes. Chicago's population, buoyed by annexing a ring of suburbs in 1889, stood comfortably above a million (1,099,805) in the 1890 census, a full decade ahead of the booster's forecast.

■ QUEEN AND GUTTERSNIPE OF CITIES

Freshly crowned as America's Second City by the 1890 census, Chicago staged a world's fair in 1893 that flew directly in the face of a disastrous economic depression. The World's Columbian Exposition brought the glittering fantasy of an electrically lighted "White City" to the South Side lakefront, while a "Gray City" of unemployment and anxiety lurked beyond the fairgrounds. It was a moment that spotlighted the chasm—especially wide during the Gilded Age but always a yawning gap in Chicago's social landscape—between the grand visions professed by the powerful and the grimmer realities faced by so many others. "Chicago, queen and guttersnipe of cities, cynosure and cesspool of the world!" declaimed English journalist George W. Steevens after an 1896 visit. He surveyed the "splendid chaos" as

> . . . the most beautiful and the most squalid, girdled with a twofold zone of parks and slums; where the keen air from lake and prairie is ever in the nostrils, and the stench of foul smoke is never out of the throat; the great port a thousand miles from the sea; the great mart which gathers up with one hand the corn and cattle of the West and deals out with the other the merchandise of the East; widely and generously planned with streets of 20 miles, where it is not safe to walk at night; where women ride straddlewise, and millionaires dine at midday on the Sabbath; the chosen seat of public spirit and municipal boodle, of cut-throat commerce and munificent patronage of art; the most American of American cities, and yet the most mongrel.

This "miracle of paradox and incongruity" that amazed visitors like Steevens was wrought from a new cycle of expansion and development in the two decades following the Great Fire. The prosperity "ushered in one of the most important epochs in Chicago's history," in the words of Mayer and Wade's *Chicago: Growth of a Metropolis.* The most inspired creation of the era was the skyscraper, a distinctive urban form that has since utterly reshaped skylines from Alaska to Australia.

The same businessmen financing the fledgling skyscrapers endowed a diadem of new cultural institutions still alive today: the Chicago Symphony Orchestra, born in 1891; the Art Institute of Chicago, opened the next year, and a legacy of the World's Columbian Exposition—the massive neoclassical building that housed first the Field Museum of Natural History. The preservation of the lakefront for public pleasure, a revelation to travelers from cities less fortunate, was sanctified as public policy in Burnham's famous Chicago Plan of 1909. "Make no little plans," Burnham urged, and the sunnier side of the city's life bears the stamp of his foresight.

(opposite) Sally Rand's fan dance act during the Century of Progress Exposition landed her in court, where Judge J. B. David threw the case out declaring, "Some people would like to put pants on horses." (Chicago Historical Society)

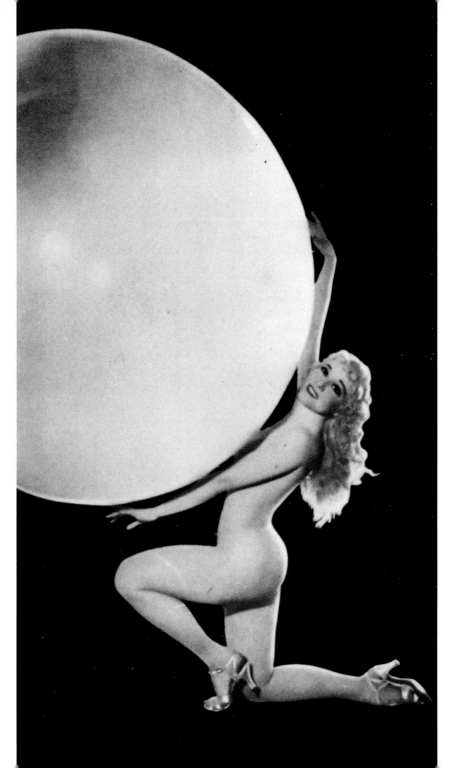

■ POVERTY AND WORKING CLASS UNREST

But the same magnates who could be so generous to the arts typically practiced the age's industrial ethos of paying their workers as little as possible for laboring 60 hours a week or longer under conditions too often satanic. Labor unrest sparked some of the city's unhappiest episodes: the Haymarket bombing of 1886, which killed eight policemen and brought death sentences to eight socialist-anarchists in a trial of very doubtful justice; and the Pullman Strike of 1894, crushed by U.S. Army troops after the sleeping-car mogul cut wages sharply in his company town on the South Side.

The advent of Hull House, where Jane Addams began her seminal work in 1889 with impoverished immigrants on the West Side, spoke to the desperate straits of a rapidly growing tenement population. Witness this 1906 Addams description of one housing block, not far from where the Chicago Fire had begun 35 years earlier:

> The streets are inexpressibly dirty, the number of schools inadequate, sanitary legislation unenforced, the street lighting bad, the paving miserable and altogether lacking in the alleys and smaller streets, and the stables foul beyond description. Hundreds of houses are unconnected with the street sewer. The older and richer inhabitants seem anxious to move away as rapidly as they can afford it. They make room for newly arrived immigrants who are densely ignorant of civic duties.

George M. Pullman, founder of the Pullman Palace Car Company, built model housing for his workers and envisioned a contented and appreciative workforce. But relations with his employees degenerated after the Pullman Strike of 1894. By the end of his life, Pullman was directing his tomb be lined with double layers of concrete and lead for fear workmen would steal what was left of him after he was buried. (Chicago Historical Society)

The lowest rung on the residential ladder was reserved for blacks, who were arriving in Chicago from the South for the first time in substantial numbers. As the city's black population rose from 3,700 in 1870 to 30,000 in 1900 and to 110,000 by 1920, segregation formed a "Black Belt" ghetto stretching along State Street from 16th Street south toward 55th. A survey of this South Side area in 1913 found only a quarter of the buildings in good repair, according to *Chicago: Growth of a Metropolis,* and one-third still had outdoor toilets. "Yet rents for Negro housing were never less than for comparable white housing and commonly ran 25 percent more." Tensions fueled by rapid expansion of the ghetto during World War I touched off a race riot in July, 1919, that left 23 blacks and 15 whites dead. The riot's six days "were the worst the city had known since the Great Fire," concluded the *Growth of a Metropolis* authors.

Jane Addams, winner of the 1931 Nobel Peace Prize for her 46 years of service to poor immigrants at Hull House. (University of Illinois at Chicago, Jane Addams Memorial Collection.)

"Mobs pulled blacks from streetcars, bands roamed neighborhoods, homes were sacked and burned. Finally the governor sent in the troops. Peace was restored, but the scars could not be easily erased, for the grim affair left deep wells of guilt and remorse, hate and bigotry. Worse still, conditions did not change, and the ghetto continued to expand and fester."

Of course, there were city departments charged with such matters as sweeping the streets and maintaining the peace. But too many officials devoted their energies to self-enrichment rather than public duties in a city redoubtably corrupt

ROSES IN CHICAGO

*I*n those early days we were often asked why we had come to live on Halsted Street when we could afford to live somewhere else. I remember one man who used to shake his head and say it was "the strangest thing he had met in his experience," but who was finally convinced that it was "not strange but natural." In time it came to seem natural to all of us that the Settlement should be there. If it is natural to feed the hungry and care for the sick, it is certainly natural to give pleasure to the young, comfort to the aged, and to minister to the deep-seated craving for social intercourse that all men feel. Whoever does it is rewarded by something which, if not gratitude, is at least spontaneous and vital and lacks that irksome sense of obligation with which a substantial benefit is too often acknowledged....

We were also early impressed with the curious isolation of many of the immigrants; an Italian woman once expressed her pleasure in the red roses that she saw at one of our receptions in surprise that they had been "brought so fresh all the way from Italy." She would not believe for an instant that they had grown in America. She said that she had lived in Chicago for six years and had never seen any roses, whereas in Italy she had seen them every summer in great profusion. During all the time, of course, the woman had lived within ten blocks of a florist's window; she had not been more than a five-cent car ride away from the public parks; but she had never dreamed of faring forth for herself and no one had taken her. Her conception of America had been the untidy street in which she lived and had made her long struggle to adapt herself to American ways.

But in spite of some untoward experiences, we were constantly impressed with the uniform kindness and courtesy we received. Perhaps these first days laid the simple human foundations which are certainly essential for continuous living among the poor: first, genuine preference for residence in an industrial quarter to any other part of the city, because it is interesting and makes the human appeal; and second, the conviction, in the words of Canon Barnett, that the things which make men alike are finer and better than the things that keep them apart, and these basic likenesses, if they are properly accentuated, easily transcend the less essential differences of race, language, creed, and tradition.

Perhaps even in those first days we made a beginning toward that object which was afterwards stated in our charter: "To provide a center for a higher civic and social life; to institute and maintain educational and philanthropic enterprises, and to investigate and improve the conditions in the industrial districts of Chicago."

—Jane Addams, *Twenty Years at Hull-House,* 1910

*The immigrants who flooded into the neighborhood of Hull House worked long hours
and lived in miserable conditions, yet, as Jane Addams wrote in her memoirs, they
often met adversity with pluck and good humor.*
(University of Illinois at Chicago, Jane Addams Memorial Collection)

even by the loose standards of the Robber Baron decades. A champion among boodlers —those who dished out the bribes—was transit wheeler-dealer Charles T. Yerkes, who finally lost his lucrative streetcar franchises at the turn of the century. Most visible among the "gray wolves," the aldermen with their hands out, were "Bathhouse John" Coughlin and Michael "Hinky Dink" Kenna, whose First Ward domain emcompassed the Loop along with the red-light district known as the Levee. Their shady legend is etched in Chicago history for the First Ward Ball they hosted each Christmas season at the old Coliseum as a Democratic fundraiser. "It's a lollapalooza," Hinky Dink said of the 1908 ball, where 10,000 magnums of champagne and 35,000 quarts of beer were consumed. "All the business houses are here, all the big people. Chicago ain't no sissy."

No sissy, indeed. This was the city that invented the smoke-filled room, that locked-door cliche of cigar-chomping politicians bent on shifty deals. It happened at the 1920 Republican National Convention, just as predicted by Warren G. Harding's campaign manager, Harry Daugherty. He had told the *New York Times* months earlier that the GOP convention would be deadlocked and eventually decided by a small group of men "sitting around a table in a smoke-filled room" at about two o'clock in the morning. That's exactly how Harding sewed up the nomination, in Suite 804-805 at the Blackstone Hotel.

Quintessential ward politicians, Johnny "De Pow" Powers (right), boss of Chicago's 19th Ward and a conniving politico often challenged by Jane Addams, is here seen with the "Prince of Boodlers," "Hinky Dink" Kenna at a Democratic party function. (Kogan Collection)

HINKY DINK DEMOCRACY

*O*n the morning of the day last December when voters were choosing between Hopkins and Swift a very prominent republican politician, who was a member of the campaign committee, went into the first ward to quietly look for frauds. He pulled up his coat-collar, drew his hat forward and loafed around the polling places just to see what was happening and not to attract attention. In the "Hinky Dink" precinct he was standing apart watching the barrel-house delegation put in enough ballots to offset the entire school-teacher vote. A man with a badge noticed him and called him aside.

"Have you voted yet?" he asked.

"No, not yet."

"Come on over and have a drink."

They went into the headquarters conducted by "Hinky Dink" McKenna [*sic*] and the man wearing the badge stood treat. The two talked for a minute or two about the weather and the probable size of the vote, and then the prominent republican began to edge toward the door. But the other man followed him.

"Here," said he, pushing a half dollar into his hand. "Don't put it off any longer, but go and vote for Hopkins."

The prominent republican was too much amazed to return the money. He began to wonder if he resembled a tramp. It was a good joke, but perhaps the joke was on him. At any rate he didn't tell the story until some time afterward.

—George Ade, collected from the *Chicago Record*, 1893-1900

■ PROHIBITION AND THE MOB

A moon-faced New York thug named Alphonse Capone hit Chicago in 1920: Prohibition had arrived the previous January along with his 20th birthday. Capone soon became the Babe Ruth of mobsters, riding the Roaring '20s tidal wave of bootleg booze to wealth and worldwide notoriety. He remains to many, alas, Chicago's most famous denizen—almost a half-century after he died of syphilis following eight years in Alcatraz for income tax evasion. In fact, he survives larger than life: introduce yourself as a Chicagoan, almost anywhere from Buenos Aires to Bangkok, and the response may well include a pantomimed machine gun with a "rat-a-tat-tat" flourish. A Chicago outfit called **Untouchable**

Tours stokes the legend with guided visits to such gangland meccas as the site of the 1929 St. Valentine's Day Massacre. *(See "PRACTICAL INFORMATION," page 234.)*

The truth is that the vast majority of Prohibition-era Chicagoans faced no closer brush with mobster violence than the ink stains from their newspaper headlines. In the peak tommy-gun year, 1926, police recorded 75 gangland slayings—less than 10 percent of the annual Chicago murder count in the 1990s, for a city with roughly the same population then as now. A great deal of more consequence was happening in the 1920s to shape the metropolis that is Chicago today. Henry Justin Smith, distinguished editor of the old *Chicago Daily News,* detailed some "symptoms of the renaissance." They included: "development of the lakefront; street, park and boulevard improvements; new bridges; straightening of an eccentric, embarrassing river branch; expansion of transportation service; track elevation program; new university buildings, especially for medical service; and a tremendous array of industrial and commercial structures, hotels, theaters, and so on."

Not that Chicago flourished as a white-gloved model of civic propriety beyond the purview of Capone and his rival gangs. The *WPA Guide to Illinois,* a splendid volume published originally in 1939, recalled the "chauvinistic clowning of Mayor William Hale Thompson," who served three terms between 1915 and 1931, in an era "climaxed by the emergence of the 'wide-open town.' The enormous trade in alcohol and beer, gambling and prostitution, and the various 'rackets' preying on legitimate businesses moved smoothly; the conviction of a gangster was extremely rare."

◆ GANGLAND KILLINGS

Reigning underworld overlord when Prohibition took effect at the start of 1920 was "Big Jim" Colosimo, who operated a notorious cabaret at 2126 South Wabash in the heart of the old Levee. "His massive figure, clad in snow-white linen and a suit of garish checks, blazed with diamonds," wrote Asbury. "He wore a diamond ring on every finger, diamond studs gleamed in his shirt front, a huge diamond horseshoe was pinned to his vest, diamond links joined his cuffs, and his belt and suspender buckles were set with diamonds. He bought diamonds by the hundreds from thieves and needy gamblers, and cherished them as other men cherished books and paintings."

Colosimo was shot to death in the lobby of his club on May 11, 1920, and the man behind the decade's first major Gangland killing was almost certainly his nephew and henchman Johnny Torrio, who took over his lucrative domain and brought Capone to Chicago. Colosimo got the first of the flower-bedecked funerals that became the underworld fashion in the 1920s. His active and honorary pallbearers included three judges, a congressman, a state representative, nine city aldermen, and an assistant state's attorney. That reflected the insidious hold organized crime long maintained over public officials in all branches of government. Several Chicago suburbs in the 1920s became basically Mob fiefdoms, including Capone's base of Cicero. Wags said the way to tell when you'd crossed the Chicago line into that western suburb was simply to sniff: "If you smell gunpowder, you're in Cicero."

◆ AL CAPONE AND HIS GANG

Dion O'Banion, a rival of the Torrio-Capone gang, was shot point-blank in 1924 by three assassins pretending to pick up a funeral arrangement at his Schofield Floral Shop, 738 North State; Hymie Weiss, O'Banion's hot-headed successor, gunned down in 1926 by Capone's men on State Street outside the same flower shop, with some bullets hitting the cornerstone of Holy Name Cathedral across the way; "Machine Gun" Jack McGurn, blasted in the head in a bowling alley at 805 North Milwaukee Avenue on February 14, 1936. Whoever ordered McGurn's murder possessed some sense of history, because this Capone torpedo had been the reputed mastermind of the legendary St. Valentine's Day Massacre exactly seven years earlier. Six members of the Bugs Moran gang and one bystander were lined up against a wall and machine-gunned on February 14, 1929, in the S.M.C. Cartage Co. garage at 2122 North Clark. That sanguinary spot today is occupied by the tranquil side yard of a senior-citizens' home.

Capone's gross income by the late 1920s was estimated at $70 million or more a year. He liked to be called "the Big Fellow," and perhaps he began to take himself too seriously, as longtime *Chicago Daily News* reporter and correspondent Robert J. Casey suggested in a whimsical 1951 *Holiday* magazine article titled "The Bullet Barons." He once flew into a rage because some reporter, implicating him in a murder, misspelled his name as "Caponi." The federal government targeted him as "Public Enemy Number One," putting Eliot Ness on his case, and Capone eventually came to trial in 1931 on charges he had filed no income tax returns for the years 1924 through 1929.

Gangster Al Capone, wearing his trademark hat, dark glasses, and smoking a cigar, listens with amusement as an attorney explains the government's case against him for income tax evasion in 1931. But the IRS had the last laugh when the notorious gangster was sentenced to Alcatraz, where he stayed for eight years. (Underwood Photo Archives, San Francisco)

The world's most famous gangster was "put in his place by the federal income-tax experts," wrote Casey, "and his trial was to show him to be only a false face—a stupid oaf who had seized the hooch-distributing machinery by force and held it by threat." Convicted on five of the 23 tax-evasion counts, he spent nearly eight years in federal prison before being released from Alcatraz in 1939 with physical and mental symptoms of untreated syphilis. There were rumors he would resume command of his ex-empire. "Bunk," said former associate Jake "Greasy Thumb" Guzik. "Al's nuttier than a fruitcake."

After eight years of seclusion on his Palm Island estate off Miami, on January 25, 1947, Capone died at the age of 48, of an apoplectic stroke complicated by pneumonia. His funeral "was extremely modest," wrote Francis X. Busch in his book *The Enemies of the State.* His body "was shipped by rail to Chicago. In a casket that an appraising reporter said 'could not have cost a dime over $2,000,' covered with 'only a sprinkling of gardenias and orchids,' the erstwhile emperor of gangdom was lowered into a grave in the family plot in Mount Olivet cemetery. There were no bands, no crowds, no politicians. Only his closest relatives and a handful of the old gang."

■ DEPRESSION AND WAR

The Great Depression, which began with the Wall Street Crash of 1929 and lingered almost until America's entry into World War II in 1941, brought crushing human misery to Chicago and its Cook County suburbs as elsewhere. The *Chicago Times* of October 3, 1931, described 1,500 huddled men waiting for food on the lower level of Michigan Avenue near Wacker Drive: "Some were young, others old, their clothes were shabby but not tattered. Everywhere the men carried huge rolls of old newspapers or lay covered by the sprawling black and white sheets."

World War II brought prosperity back to Chicago with an unparalleled surge of defense-related employment. As America became "the arsenal of democracy," Chicago rose to be its principal industrial bulwark; the $1.3 billion spent to build war plants in the city was unmatched anywhere else in the country.

■ RICHARD DALEY ERA

Richard J. Daley bestrode Chicago's body politic as the colossal Hizzoner for six mayoral terms from 1955 until his death in 1976. His Chicago was "the city that works," a resuscitated urban bruiser of new expressways, skyscrapers, and other major projects. O'Hare International Airport, which opened in 1955, soon became the world's busiest airport (a title that harried travelers might consider more of a curse than an honor). The forest of fresh skyscrapers would include one of the world's tallest buildings: the Sears Tower at the southwest fringe of downtown. But two unrelated events near the dawn of the Daley era foreshadowed the shift to a post-industrial society: Hugh Hefner published the first issue of *Playboy* from his Chicago apartment in 1953, and Ray Kroc opened the first franchised McDonald's in the suburb of Des Plaines in 1955.

Mayor Richard J. Daley celebrates his 1955 election as mayor of Chicago at home with his family in the Bridgeport neighborhood. Future mayor Richard M. Daley is seated in the middle. (Chicago Sun-Times)

■ HUMAN MOSAIC

Beginning with the arrival of Irish canal workers in the 1830s, Chicago has acted as an economic and social crucible (if not always a melting pot) for immigrants from around the globe. Chicago remains "the most ethnic and culturally diverse of all American cities," according to Richard Lindberg, author of the splendid 1993 *Passport's Guide to Ethnic Chicago*. He locates "the soul of Chicago" not in the bustling Loop or glittering Gold Coast, but in the "ethnic enclaves and side streets seldom previewed by conventioneers and out-of-town guests." The newest waves of immigrants enriching the mosaic include a host of Asians (Koreans, Filipinos, Thais, Vietnamese, Indians, and others); Eastern Europeans and Russians (Jewish as well as non-Jewish); and Hispanics from a dozen Central and South American lands.

Population shifts of recent decades have turned Chicago into a city (like others in America) where the minorities now form the majority, circled by a swelling sprawl of suburbs in which the faces remain overwhelmingly white. Of 2.8 million Chicagoans, African-Americans make up 41.1 percent of the city's population, whites 36.5 percent, while 17.9 percent are Hispanic (the fastest-growing category), and 4.5 percent are Asian or Native American.

By 1990 a single European ethnic group represented an absolute majority of the population in only one of Chicago's 77 officially designated communities (Archer Heights on the Southwest Side, 54.6 percent Polish). By contrast, blacks form a population majority in 31 of those 77 neighborhoods, Mexicans in two others, and Chinese in one. The largest single ethnic group, whether a full majority or not, is African-American in 39 city neighborhoods, Polish in 14, Mexican in nine, German in seven, Irish in three, Puerto Rican in two, and one each of Chinese, Italian, and Russian. Chicago still dyes its river green on St. Patrick's Day, but mostly for the memories. The city's biggest parade, for some years now,

The Chicago River and downtown fountains are dyed green for St. Patrick's Day.

has been the black Bud Billiken Day procession on the South Side. Meanwhile, despite the fact that a good many African-Americans became suburbanites in the 1980s, most suburbs in the Chicago metropolitan area still have a very pale complexion.

To grasp how sharply other facets of Chicago's human mosaic have shifted in the last generation or two, head for the Pilsen neighborhood on the Lower West Side. The name reflects the fact that this was Chicago's Czech heartland for 100 years beginning in the mid-19th century. It was the power base of Anton Cermak, the city's only Czech-American mayor, shot to death in Miami in 1933 while traveling with President-elect Franklin D. Roosevelt. The Czechs migrated west along Cermak Road in the 1950s and '60s to the suburbs of Cicero and Berwyn, as Pilsen evolved into the Mexican-American enclave it is today. Mexicans make up nearly two-thirds of Chicago's burgeoning Hispanic community, which totals one-fourth of the city's population.

(above) Resurrection Plaza lies in the heart of Pilsen, once a Czech neighborhood and today a largely Latino district. (opposite) The kinta cloth worn by this mother and her son are reminders that ethnic pride plays a role in today's Chicago neighborhoods.

■ WHERE IS CHICAGO NOW?

The search for Chicago's soul in the waning years of the 20th century was an elusive matter. As Harold M. Mayer and Richard C. Wade noted, the spot that Burnham's illustrious Chicago Plan of 1909 "had marked for the civic heart of Chicago is now the site of the most elaborate expressway interchange in the city. Just west of the Loop where Burnham had located a domed civic center, the Kennedy, Dan Ryan and Eisenhower come together in a baffling maze of ramps, overpasses, underpasses, entrances and exits." The expressways have cut the heart out of formerly flourishing neighborhoods and provided handy corridors for suburban flight. It is said that many current residents of Du Page and other collar counties rarely if ever come to Chicago; for them, it is an out-of-town destination almost as distant mentally as New York or Los Angeles.

The city reached its peak population of just over 3.6 million in the 1950 census, a figure then 65 percent of the metropolitan area's total. It would increasingly have to learn to coexist with the suburbs; by the most recent census, the city's shrinking population of 2.8 million would represent only 35 percent of the 8.1 million in the greater Chicago area. Residentially, even as African Americans became the city's largest ethnic group by 1990.

After Richard J. Daley's death, Chicago saw its first woman mayor (Jane Byrne) and its first black mayor (Harold Washington, who died in office of heart failure in 1987). Illinois elected its first female black senator in 1992, Carol Moseley-Braun. Meanwhile Chicago in the '90s witnessed a kind of mayoral déjà vu with Richard M. Daley, son of Hizzoner, solidly in office—although the younger Daley did abandon his family roots in the Bridgeport neighborhood for the new Dearborn Park development. The city's economy was shifting its Industrial Age brawn to Computer Age brain more adroitly than many Rust Belt centers, but still facing a dwindling job base. Drugs and street gangs were elevating murder rates to frightening levels, and the school system was failing to educate uncounted thousands of students left adrift by broken homes and aimless parents.

So you may find that today's Chicagoans seem less ebullient than their civic ancestors were when Carl Sandburg cast them as a "bragging and laughing" breed. They may look more bent by the lacerating winter wind, and they may appear less charitably inclined toward the proliferating handout supplicants along the Magnificent Mile and other downtown thoroughfares. They may sound more cynical than ever about the politicians who are forever hiking their taxes and the public payrollers whose loafing skills remain a legend.

But Chicago is still a vital and astonishing place, as much so today as when Mark Twain saw it in 1883: "a city where they are always rubbing the lamp and fetching up the genii, and contriving and achieving new impossibilities. It is hopeless for the occasional visitor to try to keep up with Chicago—she outgrows his prophecies faster than he can make them. She is always a novelty; for she is never the Chicago you saw when you passed through the last time." At a more personal level, on the best days, it is still the place an East Coast visitor in 1873 described as "New York with the heart left in."

■ ABOUT CHICAGO'S NEIGHBORHOODS

To a sociologist or a novelist, Chicago's neighborhoods could merit months of exploration. The residential communities radiating from the city's heart have always been the city's soul. From the earliest days, they defined the ethnic and economic boundaries of an intricate urban mosaic that reflected the successive waves of immigrants from across Europe and elsewhere. Many neighborhoods were self-contained universes, revolving around one's own block of bungalows, where the complexities and frustrations of big-city life could be reduced to a human scale. While these tight-knit communties nurtured, they could also narrow—and the tenacity of Chicago's neighborhood patterns surely bears some relationship to the city's pervasive residential segregation.

There are now fewer Chicago neighborhoods where shared ethnic roots provide the social binding, and the heritage has shifted to non-European in a good many of them. Gentrification has brought changes positive and negative to an increasing number of areas on the central city's fringes, where the rehab challenge (at affordable prices) lures young professionals. Poverty and crime have blighted other parts of the city. But many of the communities, as Dominic A. Pacyga and Ellen Skerrett note in *Chicago: City of Neighborhoods*, are "remarkably resilient, and they continue their day-to-day life rather successfully, even in the face of dramatic economic changes." Not all Chicago neighborhoods and sub-neighborhoods have sharply defined borders, and names even change from time to time. Some of the city's most idyllic neighborhoods are not described in depth here because they remain essentially residential, for example, Sauganash, Edison Park, Chatham, and Beverly. All the areas that are covered can provide eye-opening glimpses of the real Chicago—past and present, warts and all.

ARCHITECTURE

ARCHITECTURE
CORE CURRICULUM

THERE ARE HUNDREDS OF CHICAGO BUILDINGS—as well as some entire neighborhoods such as the 19th-century Pullman model town on the Far South Side—that richly reward the time and curiosity of visitors who possess even a passing interest in architecture. The big leaguers presented here make as good a core curriculum as any for a hurried connoisseur. These selections are by no means etched in stone (or concrete), and a half-dozen other compilers might choose a half-dozen alternatives to the must-see regimen which follows.

For further guidance, the **Chicago Architecture Foundation** operates an extensive syllabus of worthwhile tours from its headquarters at 224 South Michigan Avenue—the recently refurbished Railway Exchange Building, a D.H. Burnham and Company gem from 1904 adorned with gleaming white terracotta. You might also consult the foundation's richly stocked architectural bookstore; *call for hours: 312-922-3432.*

■ WORLD CAPITAL OF MODERN ARCHITECTURE

If one were to designate Chicago the "capital" of anything, then the world of modern architecture would be its domain. The skyscraper—first the swaggering lord of proud cities around the globe and today the sine qua non of any town aspiring to metropolitan status—was born and nurtured a century ago on this swampy Midwest soil. Within the United States, only New York can lay any serious claim to rival Chicago as the prime hothouse for urban life's heavenward thrust—with all its human consequences both happy and hellish—in the handful of generations since the church spire ceased to be the peak on America's skylines. Whatever else you see and do in Chicago, remember that here for the taking is a dazzling crash course in the complex and conflicting architectural currents that have helped shape the 20th century's sinew and soul—from Louis H. Sullivan and Frank Lloyd Wright to Ludwig Mies van der Rohe to latter-day Post-Modern pluralists.

Why Chicago? It was obviously fertile ground after the 1871 fire had razed the heart of town, "and architects, sensing the opportunities that Christopher Wren had had after the Great Fire of London, came seeking work," posited art critic Robert

(opposite) Chicago is famous for its many skyscraper "types:" they vary both in the methods by which they were engineered and the aesthetics by which they were designed.

(previous pages) A view of Chicago's skyline from the Hancock Center.

Hughes in *The Shock of the New*. These architects "found their blank slate, in more than one sense: Chicago had no traditions, no polish, and no interest in either. It was a brawling, hog-gut city, whose one rule of urban development was to grab the block and screw the neighbor." Louis H. Sullivan, the brooding genius of Chicago architecture's richest decades, said that he felt here "an intoxicating rawness, a sense of big things to be done. For 'big' was the word." To him, Chicagoans were "the crudest, rawest, most savagely ambitious dreamers and doers in the world."

■ HEROIC ARCHITECTURE: THE CHICAGO SCHOOL AND THE FIRST SKYSCRAPERS

Boston financier Peter Brooks observed presciently in 1880 that "tall buildings will pay well in Chicago hereafter, and sooner or later a way will be made to erect them." The safety elevator, invented by Elisha Otis in 1857, was undergoing steady refinement as a highrise prerequisite for the non-mountaineering bulk of the population. Fireproofing was making great strides with lessons learned from the 1871 fire. The floating-raft foundation and other anchoring techniques used to distribute load gave taller structures the necessary stability in Chicago's soft and sandy soil. In 1880, the tallest downtown buildings stood five or six stories. By the end of that decade, the future Loop boasted a thicket of structures towering a dozen stories or higher—including a few bold pioneers of what the pre-eminent critic Carl Condit has called "the most radical transformation in the structural art since the development of the Gothic system of construction in the 12th century."

◆ LOUIS SULLIVAN & THE CHICAGO SCHOOL

Louis H. Sullivan was a thinking man's architect who brought philosophy as well as technology into focus. He "taught that the language of modern society is both science and romance, both fact and belief, and that the two must be wedded in one statement," wrote biographer Albert Bush-Brown in 1960. "He broadened the technology of his own day by making it poetic, and he brought it as a symbol to serve the institutions of industrial society; his art arose from his organization of the scientific ideas, technical means, utilitarian demands, and romantic beliefs of his age." Sullivan insisted that architecture embrace what became known as "functionalism." And he understood the characteristic function of the office skyscraper to

The Reliance Building was one of Chicago's first true skyscrapers, depending as it did on its steel frame for support. (Library of Congress)

Chicago's skyline circa 1950 (below) before the predominance of steel and glass skyscrapers (above) that one sees today. (below photo, Underwood Photo Archives, San Francisco)

be its loftiness—"the very organ-tone in its appeal," as he once wrote. "It must be tall, every inch of it tall. The force and power of altitude must be in it, the glory and pride of exaltation must be in it. It must be every inch a proud and soaring thing, rising in sheer exaltation that from bottom to top it is a unit without a single dissenting line."

Sullivan and his Chicago School followers also believed that architecture must be democratic. As the critic Hugh Dalziel Duncan has written, "Sullivan taught that democracy depended on its architects as much as on its statesmen or businessmen." But it is well worth remembering, with Duncan, that these seminal Chicago buildings "were not constructed by the city, by religious organizations, by educational institutions, or by private groups as palatial edifices. They were built by businessmen and they were built for profit. Even the Auditorium, which was the civic and cultural center of Chicago for many years, was built to make money. It was a civic center, a hotel, and an office building. It was financed like any other business venture on the expectation of profit." That bottom-line mindset helps explain the shameful track record of demolitions, verging on corporate vandalism, that cost the city such masterpieces as Sullivan's Garrick Theater Building (leveled in 1961 to erect a parking garage) and Adler and Sullivan's Old Stock Exchange (torn down in 1972 to make way for a nondescript office tower that soon slid into bankruptcy). Only in recent years have preservation laws provided a reasonable guarantee that landmarks highlighted in a book like this will survive to greet 21st-century visitors.

The commercial impetus also accounts for Chicago's boom-and-bust cycles of new architecture. The economic depression of 1893 brought a construction slump after the first flowering of Chicago School structures, as well as a municipal height limit of ten stories for new buildings to counter the over-supply of skyscraper office space. The height limit went up to 260 feet in 1902 and fell back to 200 feet in 1911, in step with changing business fortunes. (There are essentially no limits today, assuming that the proper setbacks and step-backs are factored into a given site.) Another burst of architectural fecundity ensued in the Roaring '20s, styled by Condit a second "heroic age" for the city's skyline.

◆ THE FIRST SKYSCRAPERS

The innovation essential to building skyscrapers was the use of a frame of iron and steel to form a skeleton which would support the structure. This load-bearing grid of muscular metal lifted the burden of carrying a building's weight from the walls, where it had rested since antiquity; for the first time, an exterior wall didn't need to grow thicker as a structure rose higher.

The metamorphosis of the modern building "from a crustacean with its armor of stone to a vertebrate clothed only in a light skin," as Condit aptly visualized it, was manifest in William LeBaron Jenney's design for the nine-story Home Insurance Building. Completed in 1885 at the northeast corner of La Salle and Adams Streets, this was "the major progenitor of the true skyscraper, the first adequate solution to the problem of large-scale urban construction." Don't rush to Chicago's financial canyon to admire it, though; like too many of the city's architectural landmarks, Jenney's transitional keystone fell casualty to the wrecker's ball (in 1931). Still standing at 431 South Dearborn is his 16-story **Manhattan Building**, completed in 1890 as the first skyscraper constructed totally with a weight-carrying iron and steel frame. The possibilities for a building's facade, including walls of glass, would become virtually unlimited. One early hallmark, now known as a "Chicago window," featured a large fixed pane flanked by two smaller sash windows.

■ BUILDINGS OF THE LATE 19TH CENTURY

◆ MODELS OF THE CHICAGO SCHOOL

As skyscraper technology began to reach new heights, so to speak, the masters of the Chicago School of architecture continued to pay homage to traditional building methods in three of the city's most illustrious buildings, which Condit labeled "the final monuments of the art of masonry architecture" in a tradition stretching back past the Gothic cathedrals to the ancient Romans and beyond, Rookery, Auditorium, and Monadock Buildings. They form a pantheon of Chicago School glories that partisans cherish as icons of a heroic age in American architecture. "The high tides of Chicago building rose long ago," Condit wrote wistfully in 1980. His beloved Chicago School is an umbrella term for commercial structures marked by humane functionalism, skillful ornamentation, and vertical power. "A building is an act," Sullivan repeatedly declared—and he meant the act to be moral as well. Still standing after various 20th-century vicissitudes, following are some exemplary Chicago School buildings.

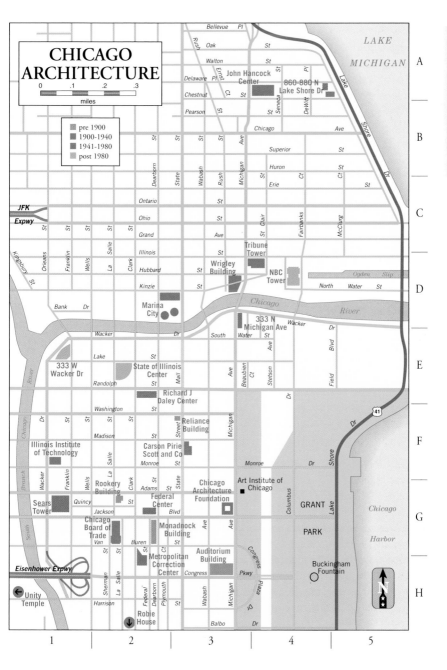

CHICAGO ARCHITECTURE

0   .1   .2   .3
miles

■ pre 1900
■ 1900-1940
■ 1941-1980
■ post 1980

ARCHITECTURE

Auditorium Building   *map page 65, H-3*
  1889, Adler and Sullivan
  Michigan and Congress
Roosevelt University now occupies much of this mixed-use Chicago School landmark, distinguished for its ornamental splendor. It's worth attending any performance in Louis H. Sullivan's Auditorium Theater merely to admire the lavish design details, carefully restored in the 1960s by architect Harry Weese after the derelict stage had been used as a servicemen's bowling alley during World War II.

Rookery Building   *map page 65, G-2*
  1886, Burnham and Root
  209 South LaSalle
The Rookery remains one of the finest examples of what, during its time, was fast becoming an outmoded form of tall-building construction. Named whimsically for the pigeons that inhabited the temporary City Hall built on the site following the Chicago Fire of 1871, the Rookery combines exterior strength and grace.

A wonderful example of overlapping architectural genius, the Rookery also boasts a breathtaking lobby and light court—as done by Frank Lloyd Wright. Before garnering great fame for his stream-lined style, Wright was one of Sullivan's most valued employees, and in 1905, he accepted a commission to remodel the Rookery's lobby and light court (magnificently refurbished in 1991) and did so in an elaborate but disciplined profusion of gold and ivory. Wright's architectural choices show his reverence for simple lines, as well as his respect for the Chicago School and its works.

Monadnock Building
  map page 65, G-2
  1891, Burnham and Root
  53 West Jackson
Load-bearing walls six feet thick at the base support the rhythmically projecting bays of purple-brown brick unadorned by ornamentation. The southern addition of 1893, designed by Holabird and Roche, employs the then-novel skeletal-frame construction.

◆ THE CHICAGO SCHOOL AND THE NEW SKYSCRAPER

Reliance Building
  map page 65, F-3
  1895, D.H. Burnham
  36 North State
In appearance an ornamented precursor of the glass-wall design promulgated by the International Style in the mid-20th century, the Reliance with its slender piers and narrow spandrels ranks as perhaps the most elegant Chicago School skyscraper. Today it houses the stylish Hotel Burnham; *see page 249; call 312-782-1111 or 877-294-9712.*

Carson Pirie Scott & Company Store
  map page 65, F-3
  1899, 1903-04, Louis H. Sullivan
  One South State
This Loop department store, in the judgment of critic Carl Condit, is Sullivan's "unchallenged masterpiece. It is the ultimate achievement of the Chicago School and one of the great works of modern commercial architecture in the world." Sullivan's design focuses the shopper's eye on the merchandise-filled display windows.

The staircase of the Rookery Building demonstrates both the functionalism and grace which are hallmarks of Chicago School architecture.

The ornate Wrigley Building and its "unashamed hedonism" overlooks Michigan Avenue.

Wrigley Building

map page 65, D-3
1921-24, Graham, Anderson,
  Probst & White
400 North Michigan

This confection, sheathed in white terra-cotta, unfurled the Roaring 20s with a beguiling dose of Michigan Avenue whoopee. "The great bravura performance of Chicago architecture," according to Condit, the Wrigley Building should be seen floodlit after dark to fully savor "the unashamed hedonism, sheer visual drama to excite the eye." Exterior details were inspired by the Giralda Tower in Seville, Spain.

Tribune Tower

map page 65, D-4
1925, Hood & Howells
435 North Michigan

The design for this Gothic Revival skyscraper was chosen through a controversial international competition sponsored by longtime *Chicago Tribune* editor and publisher, Robert McCormick in 1922. The landmark edifice soars heavenward like a medieval cathedral complete with flying buttresses near the pinnacle. Embedded in its walls are stones from Westminster Abbey, the Alamo, Hamlet's castle, the Great Pyramid, the Taj Mahal, Fort Sumter, the Arc de Triomphe, and others.

Chicago Board of Trade

map page 65, G-2
1930, Holabird & Root
141 West Jackson

The Art Deco impulse—with its bold silhouettes and streamlined rectilinear forms—gave fresh vitality to other Jazz Age stalwarts such as the Chicago Board of

Art Deco detail on the Board of Trade

Trade, topped with an aluminum statue of Ceres and opened in 1930 as the gloom of the Great Depression descended.

333 North Michigan Avenue

map page 65, D-3
1928, Holabird & Root

The spirits of Robert McCormick, and Eliel Saarinen's second-prize design in the *Tribune's* international competition leaped south across the river to influence the 333 North Michigan Avenue tower, designed by Holabird and Root.

The first of Chicago's distinctive Art Deco skyscrapers, this slab-like 35-story gem, across the river from the Wrigley Building is ornamented in geometric low relief. Scenes from early Chicago history frame the windows of the fifth floor.

Wright considered the Unity Temple (above) in Oak Park to be his "little jewel."
The Robie House (right) is a classic example of Prairie School architecture.

◆ FRANK LLOYD WRIGHT

It is necessary to go a bit farther afield to savor the array of Wright-designed private homes in the Chicago area, most notably Robie House, the quintessential Prairie School residence with its strong horizontal thrust (in Hyde Park, seven miles south of the Loop), and Wright's own house and studio (in the western suburb of Oak Park). "I loved the prairie by instinct, as, itself, a great simplicity," he wrote. Even a cursory Wright circuit provides a refreshing reminder that Chicago's architectural prowess is far from solely based on its penchant for flinging up skyscrapers. In contrast to the vigorous upward thrust of Chicago School skyscrapers, the flowing horizontal planes ingrained in the Prairie School precepts of Wright and his disciples convey a solid peace and calm.

Robie House
map page 65, H-2
1909, Frank Lloyd Wright
5757 South Woodlawn, Hyde Park
The University of Chicago owns this Prairie School landmark. Its broad overhanging roof and long limestone sills forcefully carry Wright's horizontal motif. The very private entrance is at the back of the house.

Unity Temple
map page 65, H-1
1906, Frank Lloyd Wright
875 Lake, Oak Park
One of Wright's most famous buildings, this Unitarian Universalist church and parish home in Oak Park is an early example of reinforced-concrete use. The interior is delicately illuminated by a golden-paned skylight and clerestory windows.

◆ THE INTERNATIONAL STYLE AND ONWARD

After two decades of economic slumber and world war, Chicago architecture awoke to find itself a handmaiden of the sleek and unadorned International Style in the person of Ludwig Mies van der Rohe, who had brought his soaring reputation across the Atlantic in 1938 and designed the new Illinois Institute of Technology campus. The Miesian motto "Less Is More" swept ornament before it, in Chicago as elsewhere. For Mies and his disciples the gospel of naked structuralism amounted to the "telling of truth." Sullivan and his Chicago School peers had also espoused a similar credo of honesty but with quite a different thrust. As part of Sullivan's conception of the skyscraper as a kind of secular humanist temple, decoration was an essential element of his best buildings, while the International Style eschewed it. "No noodles," was Mies's shorthand, and that austere code ruled as skylines soared on six continents starting in the 1950s to emulate Chicago and New York. The city boasts some of his most renowned buildings.

860-880 North Lake Shore Drive
map page 65, A-4/5
1952, Mies van der Rohe
People fated to live in glass houses can count themselves fortunate if they reside in this architecturally refined pair of towers considered exemplars of the unadorned Miesian principles. The nearby glass-walls at 900-910 Lake Shore came later.

IBM Building   *map page 163, B-5*
1971, Mies van der Rohe
333 North Wabash
The architect's last major office design, the IBM exemplifies to a T Mies's less is more aesthetic—but it is also the bane of pedestrians come winter, when the winds whip across its plaza: not quite a hurricane, but enough to topple an unwary wayfarer. On the worst days, management sets up a chain of ropes to aid those battling the headwinds between Wabash and State Streets.

Marina City
map page 65, D-3
1964, '67, Bertrand Goldberg Assoc.,
300 North State
In a total departure from the severe rectilinear patterns of the International Style, Goldberg's organic approach to this much-photographed pair of circular 60-story towers features cantilevered balconies that give (in Condit's words) "the lively appearance of a vertical succession of flower petals."

Federal Center
map page 107, B-2
1964-75, Mies van der Rohe et al.
219 South Dearborn
Alexander Calder's 53-foot-tall red *Flamingo* stabile adds a spark of color to this 4.5-acre Loop plaza complex of two sleekly spare glass-curtain towers rising 30 and 45 stories with a single-story post office at their feet.

The colors of sunset illuminate three well-known examples of skyscraper architecture: The Marina Building (foreground), 35 East Wacker Drive Building built in 1926 (middle), and the Stone Container Building from 1983 (background).

■ POSTMODERNISM AND GIGANTISM

It is tempting to label the reigning motif of Chicago architecture in the 1980s and '90s as "Gigantism"—although Postmodernist pluralism serves as a more definitive net to cast over the astounding variety of designs that have peppered the city's skyline in reaction to the dethroned rigors of the International Style. Detail and ornament are back in good graces, along with richer colors and touches of whimsy in even some of the highest newcomers. By a recent count, Chicago can claim nine of the world's 35 tallest buildings.

John Hancock Center
map page 163, B-3
1969, Skidmore, Owings & Merrill
875 North Michigan

The first Chicago giant to break the 1,000-foot mark, Big John rises in a tapering profile that—according to Ira J. Bach in "Chicago's Famous Buildings"—is "more graceful and soaring than the rectangular and paradoxically also gives the impression of maximum stability."

The building can expect no new rivals soon in their rarefied precincts, given the office-building slow-down here at the turn of the century. Of Chicago's Biggest Three, the Hancock is the favorite among architecture critics. For the Sears and Amoco blockbusters, "More Is Less" sums up the reviews.

Sears Tower
map page 65, G-1
1974, Skidmore, Owings & Merrill
233 South Wacker

Built as a bundle of nine framed tubes, each 75 feet square, the building slims to just two tubes at its 110-story summit.

Critic Richard Solomon salutes it as "an architectural icon marking the apogee of Modernism as a universal architectural style."

Sears management has now deserted the colossal cloud-tickler in favor of a suburban headquarters.

Aon (Amoco Oil) Building
map page 163, C-5/6
1974, Edward Durell Stone & Assoc.
    and Perkens & Will Corp.
200 East Randolph

This 1,136-foot building is Chicago's second highest and the world's 10th highest. It was reclad in speckled granite after its white-marble skin began loosening

Richard J. Daley Center
map page 107, B-1
1965, C. F. Murphy Associates
Dearborn and Clark

Barebones Miesian motifs are boldly executed in this 31-story courthouse swaggerer that boasts a trio of broad bays a startling 87 feet long and 48 feet wide. The russet color of the self-weathering Cor-Ten steel continues to deepen.

The smoothly curved edifice of 333 West Wacker follows the arc of the Chicago River.
Its gigantism is self-evident.

Metropolitan Correctional Center

map page 107, B-2
1975, Harry Weese & Associates
71 West Van Buren

Even a jail can be an architectural show-stopper in Chicago, as witness the knife-edged William J. Campbell U.S. Courthouse Annex (the facility's official name). Its slender triangular design rises 27 stories resembling a gargantuan computer card punched by rows of five-inch-wide windows.

333 West Wacker Drive

map page 65, E-1
1983, Kohn Pederson Fox
333 West Wacker Drive

Among the city's new growth of Postmodernist skyscrapers, this 36-story office tower earns very high marks for the sweeping grace of its 365-foot-long curved wall that matches a bend in the Chicago River, in contrast to its angular other faces looking onto the street.

State of Illinois Center

map page 107, B-1
1985, Murphy/Jahn and,
Randolph & Clark
Clark and Lake Streets

Helmut Jahn's dizzying Postmodern design of dazzling complexity, with its skin of alternating opaque and reflective glass strips, is loved by some and loathed by others (including many of the state employees who spend their days on its 17 atrium-accented floors).

NBC Tower

map page 65, D-4
1989, Skidmore, Owings & Merrill
200 East Illinois

Art Deco returns in style with this 38-story echo of several Chicago masterpieces from the end of the Roaring '20s. It's a testament to the virtues of mining and refining the architectural past—when the result manages to be so creatively deft.

The State of Illinois Center on the Loop dazzles the eye with sunlight and mirror-like reflections.

M U S I C &
T H E   P E R F O R M I N G   A R T S

FROM HIGHBROW TO HIP-HOP, the music of the Second City is far from second-rate. The Chicago Symphony Orchestra ranks among the finest in the world, while Lyric Opera of Chicago boasts a remarkable record of recent critical and financial success. The city's panoply of live theater is often livelier than the best Broadway can muster. Chicago blues, the guitar-driven daddy of rock-and-roll, keeps the musical faith with earthy honesty in scores of clubs around town. Jazz maintains a vital and varied presence.

The arts and entertainment choices run the full gamut from highbrow to no-brow. The free *Reader* newspaper, published each Thursday, features extensive listings of performances and clubs. Thorough listings also appear each Friday in the two metropolitan dailies, the *Sun-Times* and the *Tribune*. There's an array of commercial, dinner, non-profit, and experimental theater beyond the notable companies mentioned here. Theater-goers can save as much as 50 percent on day-of-performance tickets at the several **Hot Tix** locations; *call 312-554-9800 or visit www.hottix.org.*

■ CLASSICAL MUSIC

◆ CHICAGO SYMPHONY ORCHESTRA

The first meeting for the incorporation of the Chicago Orchestral Association was held at the Chicago Club on December 17, 1890, and by 1893, the orchestra was in full force at the World's Columbian Exposition, during which both pianist Ignace Paderewski and composer and conductor Antonín Dvořák appeared. By century's end, the orchestra had presented American premieres of Tchaikovsky's Nutcracker Suite, several Richard Strauss symphonies (including *Don Quixote),* and Camille Saint-Saëns's; they had also embarked on an ambitious tour of the Northeast.

At the dawn of the 20th century, Daniel Burnham was commissioned to design a permanent hall for the Orchestra, a home which would be built and completed during the 37-year tenure of music director Frederick Stock. Newly renamed the Chicago Symphony, the orchestra presented American premieres of seminal works by the age's finest (and most innovative) composers, among them Rachmaninov, Schoenberg, and Mahler. (Mahler's *Eighth Symphony* was presented—

with nearly one thousand performers). During this period Sergei Proko-fiev, Camille Saint-Saëns, Pablo Casals, and Jascha Heifetz made their Chicago debuts with the orchestra.

Frederick Stock's progressive vision included what today might be called "outreach programs." He inaugurated a popular concert series in 1914 to broaden the CSO's appeal; within a few more years, he started a civic youth orchestra and a children's concert series. He even brought classical music—literally—to new audiences by carting musicians to neighborhoods far from downtown; one concert series was held at the Union Stock Yards.

The CSO's musical program continued to be equally forward-thinking. In the 1920s, Igor Stravinsky conducted his own work for the orchestra; a 23-old pianist named Vladimir Horowitz played a Rachmaninov concerto; and Maurice Ravel took up the baton to lead several of his own pieces. More daring for the day was a concert of African-American spirituals presented by Paul Robeson. During the 1920s and '30s, the hall also served as a venue for lectures during the symphony's off-season: in 1924, Harry Houdini delivered a lecture entitled, "Can the Dead Speak to the Living?" Other speakers included Bertrand Russell and Orson Welles as well as maverick pilots Admiral Byrd and Amelia Earhart.

In the 1940s, violinist Isaac Stern, composer-conductor-pianist Béla Bartók, and composer-conductor Leonard Bernstein were among the luminaries who appeared with the Chicago Symphony. Under the batons of Fritz Reiner in the 1950s and '60s and especially of Sir Georg Solti (he was knighted in 1973) from 1969 until '89, the Chicago Symphony Orchestra was heralded as one of the world's finest, winning two dozen Grammys and a bundle of lucrative recording contracts.

The illustrious orchestra entered the 1990s with a hard act to follow—its own. In 1989, 31 years after presenting his first solo piano recital in Orchestra Hall (at the age of 15) Daniel Barenboim began his tenure as music director. Under his leadership, Pierre Boulez was named a principal guest conductor in 1995, and in that same year, ground was broken for the expansion of Orchestra Hall into Symphony Center. In 1999 the CSO opened ECHO, an interactive music and learning center geared to kids but certainly compelling enough for any adult with even a modicum of musical curiosity. At its visitors center (on the first floor of the Education Wing of Symphony Center) visitors can play at video terminals that introduce ECHO, or listen to CSO recordings on a "virtual jukebox." *67 East Adams Street; call 312-294-3435 or visit www.cso.echo.org.*

An evening with the Chicago Symphony remains a glorious experience—whether at Orchestra Hall on Michigan Avenue from September through May, or outdoors in the summer at the Ravinia Festival on the suburban North Shore. The hall stands at *220 S. Michigan Ave.; call 312-294-3000 or visit www.chicagosymphony.org for information.*

◆ LYRIC OPERA OF CHICAGO

West across the Loop in the Civic Opera House, Lyric Opera of Chicago performs the amazing feat of selling more than 100 percent of its tickets year after year—unprecedented in the world of opera. Founded in 1954, the Lyric is recognized internationally as one of the truly great opera companies of our time.

The Civic Opera House itself stands at 20 North Wacker Drive, on the east bank of the Chicago River. In 1929, Samuel Insull (president of the Chicago Civic Opera Association and utility magnate known as the Prince of Electricity) funded the building of a more "democratic" opera house to replace Sullivan's Auditorium Building. The architectural firm chosen, Graham, Anderson, Probst & White (of Wrigley Building and Field Museum fame) hoped their building design would symbolize "the spirit of a community which is still youthful and not much hampered by traditions." The limestone skyscraper is comprised of a 45-story office tower and two 22-story wings with a colonnaded portico running the building's length; its varied decorative motif—a blend of Art Nouveau and Art Deco—was inspired by the Paris Opera House. The house itself seats 3,563, making it the second-largest opera auditorium in North America.

In 1993, after decades of merely renting the Civic Opera Building's stage for performances, Lyric Opera of Chicago purchased all of the theater and backstage space. Today the Lyric receives stellar reviews for an impressive range of works: one recent season included *Queen of Spades,* a rarely performed Tchaikovsky opera; *The Great Gatsby,* an American opera written in the late 1990s; daring productions of *Rigoletto* and *Tosca;* and *Jenufa,* a 1904 Czech opera based on a feminist play. The Lyric's season runs roughly from September through March, but keep in mind that tickets sell out and sell out *fast. For a musical preview of the season call 312-409-3032. The opera's website is more comprehensive; www. lyricopera.org.*

CHICAGO BLUES

—Jeff Johnson, essayist on the blues for the *Chicago Sun-Times*

A music form born on the Mississippi Delta, the blues made its way to Chicago in the 1930s, accompanying the plantation workers as they migrated from Mississippi and Louisiana to Chicago to answer the call for cheap industrial labor. Then in the 1940s—in the words of Joe Seneca's elderly bluesman in *Crossroads*—"Muddy Waters invented electricity." Waters and his fellow Delta-born blues musicians brought their music north from the Mississippi, and soon the music that had been strummed on front porches in the Delta was being played on electrified instruments in the big city. Nightclubs on the city's south and west sides that catered to a largely black and working-class clientele became jumpin' juke joints. Muddy Waters, who generations later would become the most celebrated Chicago bluesman, may have gone to greener pastures a dozen years ago, but the spirit of his "Hoochie Coochie Man" and "Got My Mojo Workin'" crackles through the rhythms and lyrics of his modern-day successors.

Guitarist Buddy Guy, whose South Loop club **Legends** is one of Chicago's finest blues bars *(see below),* recalls the years after his arrival in Chicago in the late 1950s. A South Sider back then could walk up and down both sides of 47th Street for a 10-block stretch and find one club after another with live blues.

A few decades later, the music that had been an entertainment staple for black nightclubs was no longer in fashion. Younger, hipper blacks were dancing to Detroit's Motown sound and to its various counterparts from New York City, Philly, and, of course, Chicago. For this newer generation, the blues represented a lifestyle they'd just as soon forget.

By the '70s, the blues in Chicago was becoming a North Side phenomenon, as interest waned on the South Side except in a few historic clubs within shouting distance of the University of Chicago. With the "houserockin' blues" of Chicago-based Alligator Records paving the way for a new audience of white, upper-middle-class fans, a night on the town meant blues and beers to young college grads who'd been introduced to the music as part of campus life.

◆ BLUES CLUBS

The musical migration to the North Side bars was in a sense just as significant in the evolution of the blues as the movement from the Southern states. Today, many bands are integrated, but most clubs that feature live blues are patronized primarily by young, urban, white audiences.

Make no mistake, though: the blues is not a museum-piece-in-the-making, an artifact to be studied among the archives of early American folk art. It is a living, growing art form, with a legion of devoted fans and new, up-and-coming stars more technically proficient—though less living-and-breathing immersed born and bred within the blues tradition in the about the roots of the music—than their Southern ancestors.

The Chicago club scene is a hit-or miss proposition for the blues. Hit the more trendy bars, and you'll miss the ambiance that should go with the music. The **Kingston Mines**, a club in the chic Lincoln Park neighborhood on the North Side, has a good record for developing local followings for up-and-coming artists. Their schedule is often printed months in advance, though: when it comes to adventuresome bookings, forget it.

B.L.U.E.S. and its younger, bigger brother, **B.L.U.E.S. Etc.**, suffer from the same swinging-singles disease as Kingston Mines and Wise Fools, but their music is up to snuff. The little B.L.U.E.S. club on Halsted is a particularly good place for out-of-towners to get a feel for the music. It was the first North Side blues bar that did not feel compelled to serve a steady diet of bands fronted by a male vocalist-guitarist. And B.L.U.E.S. Etc. is big enough to draw nationally known out-of-town blues artists on the weekends. One place that's guaranteed to put a smile on a visitor's face is **Rosa's,** located off the beaten path in a Latino neighborhood on the West Side. The club, run by an elderly woman from Italy and her son, bills itself as "Chicago's friendliest blues bar." There's no disputing that slogan, just as there's no quarreling with the innovative booking strategy.

Legends may be Chicago's best blues club, rated according to both music and atmosphere. While the scene is hottest when co-owner Buddy Guy is fronting his own band, there are plenty of other reasons to patronize the club. Where else, for example, could you find the city's finest harmonica players spontaneously dueling in a "Harp Attack," or veteran blues artists paying tribute to departed musical greats? The knowledgeable clientele makes it possible for management to book talented but little known out-of-towners who wouldn't draw flies on the North Side. And if arena bands are out slumming after a show in town, Legends is one of their prime hangouts.

Eddie Clearwater is one of Chicago's best known bluesmen.

◆ BLUES CLUBS OF THE SOUTH SIDE

For those who insist on the authenticity of a real South Side blues club the best choice is probably the Checkerboard Lounge. The down-to-earth, comfortable atmosphere inside this club is often compromised by a sense of danger in the streets outside. But management makes a point of ensuring the safety of customers by seeing them safely to their cars and keeping a constant eye out for trouble.

Blue Chicago *Near North*
736 N. Clark St.; 312-642-6261
Good starter spot for folks who've never heard the blues live before.

Blue Chicago on Clark *River North*
536 N. Clark St.; 312-661-0100
Sibling of the State Street joint, and likewise a top choice for blues beginners.

B.L.U.E.S. *Lincoln Park*
2519 N. Halsted St.; 773-528-1012
Cramped room and small stage, but top-flight Chicago performers at what may well be the North Side's best blues club.

Buddy Guy's Legends *South Loop*
754 S. Wabash Ave.; 312-427-1190
Ample elbow room and occasional performances by guitar maestro Guy, a part-owner.

Checkerboard Lounge *Grand Boulevard*
423 E. 43rd St.; 773-624-3240
A living museum of Chicago blues, in a South Side neighborhood that may be intimidating.

Kingston Mines *Lincoln Park*
2548 N. Halsted St.; 773-477-4646
Eclectic mix of local blues stalwarts and newcomers.

Rosa's *Humboldt Park*
3420 W. Armitage Ave.; 773-342-0452
Adventuresome booking, friendly atmosphere in an out-of-the-way location.

◆ CHICAGO BLUES FESTIVAL

Prime time to hear the blues in Chicago is in late May or early June for the Chicago Blues Festival. Each year, the City of Chicago throws this huge weekend-long, free-admission blues bash at its lakefront playground in Grant Park. Committee members work year-round to assemble a collection of talent that is both representative of all sub-genres of the music and conducive to listening by large crowds. The three-day festival might draw up to 400,000 people, who come early to picnic in the park and stay to boogie to the city's homegrown music as the sun sets over a breathtaking view of the skyline.puts dozens of performers on three stages in lakefront Grant Park. The clubs run at top tempo as well that weekend, but there's a

Blues fans flock to Buddy Guy's Legends for its impressive bookings, as well as for charisma of part-owner Buddy Guy. The luckiest patrons are those who get to hear his guitar-playing, too.

daunting array of choices for hearing this juiced-up music live any time of year. No fewer than 141 spots are listed in the 1995 edition of *The Original Chicago Blues Annual* magazine, ranging from the New Checkerboard Lounge and dozens of even grittier settings in black neighborhoods on the South and West sides where white faces may feel very much out of place, to more genteel downtown and North Side stages such as B.L.U.E.S, Blue Chicago, and Kingston Mines.

■ JAZZ

If it can be said that jazz was born in New Orleans, then it certainly went to nursery school in Chicago. Like the blues musicians from the Mississippi Delta who made their way up the river to Chicago, many jazz musicians whose names live on today—Louis Armstrong, Sidney Bechet, King Oliver—were New Orleanians who traveled up the Mississippi a generation before their blues counterparts. And it was the popularity of their music that gave them the opportunity to head north.

Beginning in the late 1910s, the Streckfus brothers' line of pleasure steamboats —"floating ballrooms," of a sort—were plying the Mississippi and drawing huge crowds of dancers at each port from the Big Easy to the Great Lakes. The "colored" (part black) bandleader had a black band, and he led them with an iron baton. One of his players was Louis Armstrong. In 1922, he was hired by his fellow New Orleanian and idol Joe "King" Oliver to play in his Chicago band, and Armstrong joined the Great Migration of 1917, when about a half-million African Americans left the Deep South and went north, most of them to Chicago.

At the same time, jazz was on tap at the Friars' Club, a smoky Near North cabaret where the all-white New Orleans Rhythm Kings delivered the sound of their native city in a smooth, sophisticated way. Regulars at the seedy Friars' Inn included gangsters like Dion O'Banion and Al Capone, as well as 19-year-old prep-school student Leon "Bix" Biederbeck, who'd heard Armstrong and Oliver play when their steamboat docked in his hometown of Davenport, Iowa, a few years earlier. Bix had been hooked. Likewise, the Rhythm Kings were amazed when they heard the King Oliver jazz band at a party on the South Side.

By the time New Orleans pianist Jelly Roll Morton arrived in 1924, Chicago's jazz was firmly established as an African-American music form with its roots deep in New Orleans. The South Side became the center of a thriving scene which drew musicians including Kid Ory and Lil Hardin (later Armstrong's wife). From different parts of the city came an Irish tough named Jimmy McPartland; from Halsted Street came Benny Goodman, whose parents had fled the Russian pogroms.

In the latter half of the 20th century, Chicago's jazz scene became known for the groundbreaking music played by young Chicagoans who'd grown up with their parents' jazz. Among those musicians were Yussef Lateef, Coleman Hawkins, and Sun Ra (born Herman Blount in Mississippi); the ensembles they and their contemporaries formed during this period changed jazz forever. The one-of-a-kind Sun Ra led his Arkestra (sometimes referred to as the *Kosmodrama* Arkestra) in intense modal music that he believed was "intergalactic in its consciousness"— "Space is the Place" was one of his hallmark tunes. In the 1960s, Roscoe Mitchell, Joseph Jarman, Malachi Favors, and a few like-minded others formed perhaps the best known of this period's jazz bands, the Art Ensemble of Chicago, which fused traditional New Orleans–based jazz with the latest of Hard Bop and avant-garde free jazz. They also embraced the politics of the early Black Panthers and sought to reinvigorate African pride. These groups have passed down *their* legacy to a whole new generation of jazz players playing in Chicago's clubs today.

Singing the blues at the Chicago Blues Festival in Grant Park.

■ BEST VENUES: JAZZ, ROCK, AND COMEDY

◆ JAZZ

Andy's *River North/Magnificent Mile*
11 East Hubbard St.; 312-642-6805
Near-Loop mainstay of mainstream
jazz, with sessions at lunch as well as
evenings. Blues on Friday nights.

Gold Star Sardine Bar *Streeterville*
680 North Lake Shore Dr.;
312-664-4215
Potpourri of jazz musicians in a
cramped highrise space with free
admission.

Green Mill *Uptown*
4802 North Broadway; 773-878-5552
First-rate jazz and more, including poetry slams, inside Prohibition-era gangster
hangout.

Hot House *South Loop*
31 East Balbo; 312-362-9707
A great place to hear an eclectic mix of
jazz and world music. Around the corner from Buddy Guy's Legends.

Jazz Showcase *River North*
59 West Grand Ave.; 312-670-2473
Joe Segal's club has stiff cover charges,
but arguably the best jazz in the city.

◆ ROCK/POP

Cubby Bear *Wrigleyville*
1059 West Addison St.; 773-327-1662
No-decor venue for rockers and others
across from Wrigley Field.

Jazz at Andy's, one of Chicago's premier jazz clubs.

Serious fun at Andy's.

Double Door *Wicker Park*
1551 N. Damen Ave.; 773-489-3160
Cutting-edge rock from same management as Wrigleyville's Metro.

Elbo Room *Lincoln Park*
2871 N. Lincoln Ave.; 773-549-5549
High energy subterranean rock club
with easy-on-the-wallet cover charges.

Fitzgerald's *Western Suburbs*
6615 W. Roosevelt Rd., Berwyn;
708-788-2118
Roadhouse flavor in a working-class
suburb.

Metro *Wrigleyville*
3730 N. Clark St.; 773-549-3604
Chicago's premier showcase rock club.

Wild Hare *Lake View*
3530 N. Clark St.; 773-327-4273
Reigning spot for reggae and Afro-
Caribbean acts.

◆ COMEDY

All Jokes Aside *South Loop*
1000 S. Wabash Ave.; 312-922-0577
The city's best African-American comedy club.

Second City *Old Town*
1616 N. Wells St.; 312-337-3992
Mecca of revue and improvisational
comedy still going strong on main stage
with second-banana E.T.C. troupe in
smaller room.

Zanies *Old Town*
1548 N. Wells St.; 312-337-4027
Time-tested 100-seat venue that books
big names and local up-and-comers.

MUSIC & THE
PERFORMING ARTS

■ THEATER

Perhaps the most remarkable development in Chicago's arts scene in recent decades has been the flowering of America's finest regional theater. David Mamet is the best-known playwright to spring from this dramatic renaissance, and Steppenwolf is the most celebrated among the 100-plus professional companies—the bulk of them non-profit either by intent or in practice. Annual theater attendance in the Chicago area totals somewhere around three million, higher than for any of the city's professional sports teams. Other highly regarded companies include the Goodman, Victory Gardens, Next, and Court Theater. Half-price tickets to many shows are available at Hot Tix booths. *Call 312-554-9800 or visit www.hottix.org.*

◆ THEATER VENUES

Court Theater *Hyde Park* 5535 S. Ellis Ave. (UC campus); 773-753-4472 Mainly revivals of classics.

Goodman *Loop* 170 N. Dearborn St.; 312-443-3800, information 312-443-3811 Sturdy perennial with a reputation for polished productions of classical and contemporary works.

Next *North Shore* 927 Noyes Ave., Evanston; 847-475-1875 Challenging scripts that might have a hard time finding a stage elsewhere.

Students rehearse A Midsummer Night's Dream *in the court adjoining the Chicago Art Institute, 1927. (Underwood Photo Archives)*

Swing dancing at Rumors on North Lincoln Avenue.

Second City *Old Town*
1616 N. Wells St.; 312-337-3992
Revue and improv comedy still going
strong on main stage, with second-banana E.T.C. troupe in smaller room.

Chicago Shakespeare Theater *Navy Pier*
800 E. Grand Ave.; 312-595-5600
Lavish productions of the Bard on a reg-
ular basis in a theater on the Navy Pier.

Steppenwolf *Lincoln Park*
1650 N. Halsted; 312-335-1650
Nationally known for the power of its
meaty productions, some of which have
been successfully exported to Broadway.

Victory Gardens *Lincoln Park*
2257 N. Lincoln Ave.; 773-871-3000
Pioneer of Chicago's off-Loop theater

renaissance dating back two decades and
longer, with wide-ranging repertoire.

◆ **DANCE**

Ballet Chicago (No permanent stage)
312-251-8838 Classical ballet troupe,
founded in 1988.

Hubbard Street Dance Chicago
(Various stages) 312-850-9744
Hubbard Street presents work with
high energy and broad appeal.
Athletic, urban, and fun.

Joffrey Ballet of Chicago
(various stages) 312-739-0120
Classical ballet and contemporary
dance company under the leadership of
Gerald Arpino.

CAVALCADE OF CHICAGO MOVIES

Not all movies with a Chicago setting involve gangsters and tommy guns, although Hollywood has made plenty of bullet-ridden epics over the decades. Here's a cavalcade of first-rate films that take place entirely or partly in Chicago; the more recent were shot mostly on location. This two-thumbs-up list is chronological.

The Front Page (1931). Smooth early talkie and the original film version of the Ben Hecht-Charles MacArthur newspaper tale, starring Adolphe Menjou and Pat O'Brien.

Little Caesar (1931). Pioneering gangster film that set the mold, with Edward G. Robinson in the role that forever defined him.

Scarface (1932). Another Chicago mobster vehicle modeled on Al Capone's career, subtitled *The Shame of a Nation* to mollify censors. Paul Muni, Ann Dvorak, George Raft.

His Girl Friday (1940). Faster and funnier remake of *The Front Page,* with the ace Chicago reporter turned into a woman. Rosalind Russell, Cary Grant.

Call Northside 777 (1948). Chicago newspaperman helps a washerwoman prove her son did not kill a policeman. James Stewart and Lee J. Cobb.

Wabash Avenue (1950). Breezy Midwest remake of *Coney Island*, with Betty Grable as a world's-fair shimmy dancer chased by two suitors played by Victor Mature and Phil Harris.

Carrie (1952). Film version of Theodore Dreiser's massive novel about country girl who loses her innocence in Chicago while ruining the wealthy man who loves her. Laurence Olivier, Jennifer Jones.

The Man With the Golden Arm (1956). Frank Sinatra is splendid as a Chicago poker dealer who beats the drug habit in this screen version of the Nelson Algren novel.

Al Capone (1959). Fascinating Rod Steiger portrayal of the Chicago underworld kingpin, with semi-documentary script.

Compulsion (1959). Orson Welles in fine cameo role as lawyer Clarence Darrow for adaptation of Meyer Levin's play about the Leopold-Loeb murder case. Dean Stockwell and Brad Dillman.

A Raisin in the Sun (1961). Film version of Lorraine Hansberry's powerful stage drama about the dreams of a black Chicago family. Sidney Poitier, Ruby Dee, and Claudia McNeil.

Gaily, Gaily (1969). Ben Hecht's farcical and melodramatic memoir of his early career on a Chicago newspaper. Brian Keith, Beau Bridges, and Melina Mercouri.

The Sting (1973). Two con men (Paul Newman, Robert Redford) stage an elaborate revenge on a bigtime gangster in Chicago of the Roaring '20s; the film won an Academy Award for best picture.

A Wedding (1978). Robert Altman mile-a-minute satire filmed at a lakefront mansion in Chicago's North Shore suburbs. Carol Burnett, Paul Dooley, Mia Farrow.

The Blues Brothers (1980). Car chases, anyone? John Belushi and Dan Aykroyd as the manic, music-minded brothers in black.

My Bodyguard (1980). Captivating drama of 15-year-old Chicago boy's hassles at school. Chris Makepeace, Adam Baldwin, Matt Dillon.

Ordinary People (1980). Family agony and tragedy in a well-heeled, tight-strung North Shore home. Best Picture Oscar in 1980. Mary Tyler Moore, Donald Sutherland, Timothy Hutton, Judd Hirsch.

Ferris Bueller's Day Off (1986). North Shore suburbanite (Matthew Broderick) plays hooky for a day's tour of Chicago to cheer up a friend.

About Last Night (1986). Salesman for Chicago grocery wholesaler meets art director for Michigan Avenue ad agency in comic love story. Rob Lowe, Demi Moore, James Belushi.

The Untouchables (1987). Kevin Costner as Eliot Ness and Robert De Niro as Al Capone, with Sean Connery as Ness's Scottish-American sidekick and 1920s' Chicago as the background star. In gangster movies, the more things change, the more they stay the same.

Essanay Studios was founded in Chicago in the early 1900s when movie making was an outdoor art. Not surprisingly, the vagaries of Chicago's climate caused them to relocate to Los Angeles. However, many early motion pictures were made here starring such one-time luminaries as Francis X. Bushman, Beverly Bayne, Wallace Beery, and Ben Turpin. (Chicago Historical Society)

S   P   O   R   T   S

IN 1876, THE SAME YEAR THAT Lt. Col. George A. Custer was shut out at Little Big Horn, the ancestors of today's Chicago Cubs (then called the White Stockings) won the championship in the National League's very first season of baseball. Chicago has carried a passionate torch for its professional sports teams ever since, even though that fledgling flight of high fortune turned out to be prologue to many more seasons dampened by disappointment than garlanded by glory. The decade's prime exception to the heartbreak history is the Chicago Bulls' six National Basketball Association championships in 1991, '92, '93, '96, '97, and '98. Described below are the city's professional baseball, football, basketball, and hockey teams, all followed avidly by modern Chicagoans.

◆ BASEBALL

Chicago Cubs

Wrigley Field, the picture-perfect old-fashioned baseball park of ivy-covered outfield walls and mostly afternoon games, manages to draw more than 2 million fans

In Chicago, sports fans start young.

Game day at Wrigley Field.

each season—a testament to the unquenchable allegiance of Chicagoans in the face of athletic adversity. After its founding in 1876, the club was bought by the Wrigley family who owned it until 1981, when the National League club was bought by the Tribune Company.

In recent years Cubs fans have admired headliners like Sammie Sosa, who hit 66 home runs in 1998, and Ryne Sandberg, who won more Gold Glove awards than any other second baseman before retiring in 1994; outfielder Andre Dawson, who led the team to the National League playoffs in 1989; and first baseman Mark Grace, a paragon of steady hitting. But the team has failed to win a World Series since the Stanley Steamer era in 1908. Its last World Series appearance, in a losing effort, coincided with the end of World War II in 1945.

Nonetheless, even Cubs detractors would agree that Wrigley Field, with its hand-operated scoreboard, gives spectators a taste for baseball's history: the seventh-inning stretch is greeted with "Take Me out to the Ballgame" as sung by a local or visiting celebrity, honoring the legacy and carrying on the tradition of Hall-of-Fame sports announcer Harry Caray. (Appropriately, Pat Pieper, the originator of

SAY IT AIN'T SO, JOE

One potentially great Chicago team which has gone down in infamy in the annals of baseball history was the Chicago White Sox, pennant winners in 1917 and 1919 and World Series winners in 1917:

*T*he White Sox had a fine infield, good catching, pitching as good as Boston's, and in the outfield one of the best hitters who ever lived—Shoeless Joe Jackson. Joseph Jefferson Jackson, of Brandon Mills, South Carolina, couldn't read or write, but he certainly could hit, as attested to by his .356 lifetime batting average —third highest in history, right behind Ty Cobb's .367 and Rogers Hornsby's .358. Jackson hit over .370 four times, once over .400, but never won a batting title because Ty Cobb or George Sisler always ended up just a bit higher.

(continues page 98)

(above) The White Sox team of 1919, the year of the scandal.

(opposite) Shoeless Joe Jackson had the third-highest lifetime batting average in history.

Joe Jackson's illiteracy was widely known and a frequent subject for laughter. People chuckled at various versions of the widely repeated story that in restaurants he would always wait for another ballplayer to order first, since he couldn't read the menu, and then say, "I'll have what he's having."

Shoeless Joe knew people made fun of him, and he didn't like it. Once he hit a long triple and, as he stood on third base, someone in the crowd raised snickers by shouting, "Hey Joe, can you spell 'cat'?" Joseph Jefferson Jackson looked over, squirted a stream of tobacco juice in the heckler's direction, and yelled back, "How about you, big shot—can you spell 'shit'?"

The Chicago White Sox were heavy favorites to win the World Series in 1919, just as they had won it two years earlier. The Cincinnati Reds, National League pennant winners, were a good team, led by center fielder Edd Roush and third baseman Heinie Groh, but on paper the Reds seemed to be no match for the powerful White Sox.

However, in an upset reminiscent of the 1914 Miracle Braves and the 1906 Hitless Wonders, the Reds trounced the White Sox, five games to three. (From 1919 through 1921 the World Series was extended to a five out of nine basis instead of the usual four out of seven.) There were ugly rumors that everything was not as it appeared to be, but such talk was typically dismissed as irresponsible if not downright unpatriotic.

Almost a year later the story broke: eight of the White Sox (thereafter to be known as the Black Sox) had been bribed by gamblers to lose the Series. Those implicated were first baseman Chick Gandil (evidently the ringleader), pitchers Eddie Cicotte and Lefty Williams, outfielder Happy Felsch, shortstop Swede Risberg, utility infielder Fred McMullin, and third baseman Buck Weaver, who knew about the fix but may or may not have participated in it.

And, yes, Shoeless Joe Jackson. As Shoeless Joe was leaving the courthouse in Chicago after confessing his involvement, a small boy, tears in his eyes, is reported to have tugged at his sleeve. "Say it ain't so, Joe," he pleaded.

Apocryphal or not, it was an entire nation that was praying it wasn't so. When it turned out to be all too true, the shock rocked the country. All those involved were banished from baseball for life. But a disillusioned public wondered about the extent of the corruption: if a World Series could be fixed, how many other games were being thrown? With confidence in the integrity of the game shattered, baseball itself was on trial.

—Lawrence S. Ritter and Donald Honig,
The Image of Their Greatness, 1992

the "Play ball!" order, was another Wrigley Field announcer.) In spite of giving in to pressure from the broadcast media to play night games (the Cubs were the last team to introduce floodlights and play night games, in 1988) a majority of the Cubs' home games are still played in daylight hours.

Home:	Wrigley Field, 1060 West Addison Street
Information:	773-404-2827 for schedule
	312-831-CUBS for tickets in Illinois
	800-347-CUBS for tickets outside Illinois
Season:	April through September

Chicago White Sox

Although a mutual animus has always divided South Side fans of the White Sox from the Cubs' North Side partisans, the city's two baseball teams are yoked in a tradition of championship futility. Founded in 1901 by Charles Comiskey, the White Sox last won the World Series in 1917, back when the first doughboys were sailing to France to make the world safe for democracy. The "Black Sox" betting scandal disgraced the 1919 World Series losers, and the Sox have appeared in the post-season classic just once since then: yes, a defeat by the Dodgers in 1959.

The American League's White Sox play in a newer stadium which was built to save the team from being kidnapped to Florida in the late '80s. The new park has all the conveniences of a modern stadium—unobstructed views, monitors throughout the walkways so that not a moment of the game will be missed —but home-team home runs are still applauded with fireworks launched from behind the scoreboard.

Home:	Comiskey Park, 333 West 35th Street
Information:	312-674-1000 for general information
	312-831-1769 for tickets
Season:	April through September

Transportation to the Parks

Both teams are best reached by public transportation. Wrigley Field is reached by the Howard Street L line to Addison Street. Comiskey Park can be reached on a Dan Ryan L train to 35th Street.

◆ FOOTBALL

Like their baseball counterparts, the **Chicago Bears** have a long history in the sport. George Halas, organizer of the American Professional Football Association (later to become the NFL) founded the Bears and coached the redoubtable "Monsters of the Midway" in the 1930s and '40s. Also like their baseball brethren in disappointing seasons, "da Bears" have reached the Super Bowl only once since its inception in 1967. That glorious 46-10 triumph in January 1986, when William "Refrigerator" Perry became a household name and coach Mike Ditka was certified a genius, led not to another pigskin dynasty but only to disappointment. The increasingly erratic and irascible Ditka lost his job after the 1992 season. New head coach Dave Wannstedt arrived from Dallas bearing a winning tradition and a fresh infusion of hope, which was heightened when the Bears made it to the second round of the 1994 NFL playoffs before fading. Dick Jauron now heads the team.

Hope, indeed, is the fuel that keeps Chicago fans clicking through the turnstiles season after roller-coaster season.

"Red" Grange (second from left), one of many Chicago sports legends, at a Chicago Bears game after signing on with the team in 1925. (Underwood Photo Archives)

Home: Soldier Field, 425 East McFetridge Drive
Information: 847-615-2327 for tickets and information. Subscriptions account for most tickets; however, they can sometimes be obtained from subscribers at the stadium before games.
Season: August (pre-season) through December (January if in playoffs)
Transport: Take the Jeffery Express (Number 6) bus to Roosevelt Road and Lake Shore Drive. The stadium is just south of the Field Museum of Natural History.

◆ BASKETBALL

After drafting Michael Jordan in 1984, the **Chicago Bulls** had a star to lead an otherwise merely mortal crew of players. In spite of Jordan's talents, the Bulls continued to come up short. The disparity between Jordan's abilities and those of his supporting cast was perhaps never more clear than in the 1986 double-overtime playoff with the Boston Celtics, in which Jordan scored 63 points and the Bulls still lost.

The advent of a new decade, however, ushered in a new spirit and a new coach, Phil Jackson. Under Jackson's leadership, Jordan led the team to three consecutive NBA championships in 1991, '92, and '93, before retiring temporarily from basketball in the wake of his father's murder. After devoting a year to a controversial effort to stake out a career in professional baseball, Jordan returned to the Bulls in the middle of the 1994–95 season. His presence sparked the team, but not enough to carry the Bulls through the championship playoffs. He went on, however, to lead the Bulls to three more championships—in '96, '97 and '98.

Blessed with the unparalleled talents of Jordan, the world's most famous athlete in the '90s, the Bulls became the toughest sports ticket in Chicago—as well as the most expensive. Their move from the cavernous old Chicago Stadium to the spanking new United Center on the West Side provided a state-of-the-arena setting for Jordan and his supporting cast. Unfortunately, Jordan retired for good in 1999 and the Bulls fell into a slump.

Home: United Center, 1901 West Madison Street
Information: 312-455-4000 for game times (usually 7:30 P.M.)
 312-559-1212 for tickets
Broadcast: WMAQ, AM 670.
Season: November to May

◆ HOCKEY

No Chicagoans are more rabidly devoted to their team than the hockey-loving followers of the **Chicago Blackhawks,** who share United Center with the Bulls. The prospect of their first Stanley Cup title in three decades was dangled and then snatched away in 1992 when the Pittsburgh Penguins swept four straight games in the final series. As it is, three National Hockey League championship trophies repose in the Blackhawks' case—for the 1934, 1938, and 1961 seasons.

The team enjoyed its heyday in the '60s, when the Ross Trophy (for leading scorer in the NHL) was won by Blackhawk Bobby Hull in '60, '62, and '66, and Stan Mikita in '64, '65, '67, and '68. The Blackhawks may well see another successful era. And Chicago fans are hopeful.

Home:	United Center, 1901 West Madison Street
Information:	312-455-7000 (games usually start at 7:30 P.M.)
Season:	October through April
Information:	312-455-7000 (games usually start at 7:30 P.M.)

The Blackhawks Hockey team (above) draws enthusiastic crowds to their United Center venue. The Chicago Bulls also play at the United Center but no longer with Michael Jordan (left) photographed here collecting one of the many trophies earned during his illustrious career with the team.

THE LOOP AND
SOUTH OF THE LOOP

■ HIGHLIGHTS *page*

THE LOOP & SOUTH OF THE LOOP

■ OVERVIEW

Getting about: Strictly speaking, the Loop's boundaries are defined by the girdle of elevated train tracks shadowing Wabash, Van Buren, Wells, and Lake Streets—the nexus of the century-old "L" rapid-transit system that novelist Nelson Algren called Chicago's "rusty iron heart." Stand beneath the lattice of steel at one of the 90-degree "L" curves while a couple of Chicago Transit Authority trains make the turn, and you'll be assaulted by a mega-decibel screech hardly less deafening than a heavy-metal concert or planes taking off on an O'Hare runway. In practice, today's Loop extends beyond the tracks to the Chicago River on the north, a bit across the river on the west, Congress Parkway on the south, and beyond Michigan Avenue to Grant Park and the lakefront on the east. Covering not much more than a square mile, it's easily explored on foot, while a car in the Loop is a millstone that should be quickly dumped in a parking garage.

For lodging and restaurants see pages 238 through 272.

THE LOOP &
SOUTH OF THE LOOP

■ "THE LOOP" STORY

In Chicago all roads have always led to the Loop—even before there came to be an actual Loop created when the cable-car lines spun their web around downtown in the 1880s, indeed even before the city was chartered in 1837. Today's visitors, once whisked into town from O'Hare International Airport, can feast on the city's smorgasbord without ever taking more than a brisk walk—two miles maximum— from the traditional civic hub at State and Madison Streets.

Not that the Loop itself has escaped the changes that have transformed this metropolis, where the central city lies beyond the mental horizon of many suburbanites (who now outnumber city dwellers almost two to one). Development has stretched the city-core boundaries in all directions—even creating a New East Side to defy the hoary local joke that "East Side" lies somewhere below Lake Michigan's waters.

Along State Street, there aren't enough major stores left to shop till you drop— or even till you stagger. But in daytime hours, at least, the Loop's pulse still races with activity, a bustling and diverting place that also happens to be a nonpareil outdoor museum of modern architecture. If you wander through the Loop you'll see buildings of great architectural merit, walking through canyons with your chin tilted toward the sky. *(See "ARCHITECTURE," pages 58-77 for details)*. Nearby is a wealth of shops, restaurants, nightspots, museums, galleries, and other attractions in such areas as South Loop, New East Side, River North, and Streeterville.

North Michigan Avenue has seized State Street's retailing banner and flies it skyscraper-high. These and other close-in quarters—some now populated by honest-to-god residents—are the expanded heart of Chicago, where the judgment made seven decades ago by a visitor named D. H. Lawrence still holds: "It seemed to me more alive and more real than New York." And Lawrence was here in fog and rain, when "muddy-flowing people oozed thick in the canyon-beds of the streets." Imagine it on a sunny day.

The Loop, to borrow a phrase once tagged to the Broadway theater scene, is a fabulous invalid. It's still alive and kicking, energized by the hives of corporate and government offices that occupy the thickets of skyscrapers. The hulking new **Harold Washington Library Center** anchors the Loop's south end looking ever so much like a fortress of knowledge.

■ THE LOOP TODAY

◆ STATE STREET AT MADISON   *map page 107, B/C-1*

One logical place to begin exploring the Loop is ground zero—State and Madison, starting point for the city's street addresses. State Street, that onetime Great Street lined for decades with the densest concentration of department stores anywhere, is down to a few major retailers. This part of the Loop is pretty quiet most nights with a handful of old-line restaurants hanging on and an occasional live performance in State Street's gloriously restored **Chicago Theater**. A block away stands the old Oriental Theater, refurbished and renamed the **Ford Center for the Performing Arts**. It now houses the **Goodman Theatre**, Chicago's oldest and largest resident theater *(www.goodman-theatre.org; 312-443-3800)*. Other Loop theaters include the **Shubert** *(22 West Monroe; 312-977-1710)*, the **Auditorium Theatre** *(50 East Congress Pkwy.; 312-922-2110)*, and the recently renovated **Cadillac Palace** *(151 West Randolph St.; 312-782-1600)*—opened in 1926 as the flagship for vaudeville's Orpheum Circuit.

◆ LOOP LANDMARKS

Carson Pirie Scott Building
map page 107 C-1

While window-shopping at Carson Pirie Scott, savor the intricately ornamented cast-iron panels that frame the glass. Their spidery leaf and floral designs are the creation of Chicago School stalwart Louis Sullivan for what is considered one of his most masterful buildings.

"This rich but delicate pattern gives an unusually luxurious effect to an entrance already distinguished by its semicircular shape and its location at the corner of the building," observe Ira J. Bach and Susan Wolfson in Chicago on Foot. *Southeast corner of State and Madison*

Marshall Field's
map page 107, C-1

Magnificently restored Marshall Field's, just to the north between Washington and Randolph streets, now boasts an 11-story atrium flanked by glass elevators and anchored by a cast-iron water fountain that was in

One of the Loop's most famous landmarks is the Marshall Field's clock, at State and Randolph.

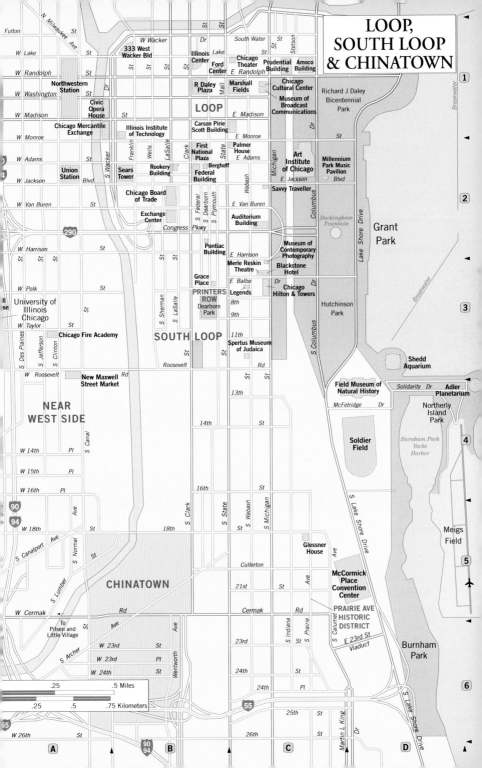

the original floor plans but not included when the building went up around 1900. Field's has a cherished spot in the memories of countless Chicagoans for its lavish Christmas displays and its adherence to the first Marshall Field's famous credo, "Give the lady what she wants." *111 North State St.; 312-781-1000.*

Palmer House Hilton
map page 107, C-2

The Palmer House is grande dame among Loop hotels. The first Palmer House opened just 13 days before the Chicago Fire of 1871 burned it to the ground. The second, torn down in 1925 to make way for the present 23-story structure, is said to have been the first hotel with elevators, telephones, and electric lights. In the Loop's heyday, the Empire Room of the Palmer House was a legendary big-band nightspot; now it's a setting for private parties. *17 East Monroe St. between Wabash and State; 312-726-7500.*

Berghoff
map page 107, B-2

West of State Street another block south at 17 West Adams stands the Berghoff, a don't-miss dining spot if you relish a pinch of history and a dash of beer-hall jollity with your sauerbraten or wienerschnitzel. Launched as a beer garden at Chicago's 1893 world's fair, the Berghoff ranks as the city's oldest functioning restaurant. Expect lines for lunch and early dinner, along with high noise levels, hard-boiled service, and respectable Teutonic fare. An ideal solvent is Berghoff's own draft beer, light or dark.

Federal Center Plaza
map page 107, B-2

Some of those legal heavyweights ply their profession in the two Federal Center high-rises that flank Dearborn between Adams and Jackson as testament to the mature majesty of Ludwig Mies van der Rohe's late work. Completed in 1975, these steel-and-glass swaggerers overlook a sizable plaza embellished with **Alexander Calder's red "Flamingo" stabile.** It is the southernmost of three plazas fronting on the west side of Dearborn that give this architecturally premier Loop thoroughfare a more open and airy feeling than is afforded by most skyscraper canyons.

First National Plaza and Chagall's Mosaic
map page 107, B-2

First National Plaza, completed in 1972, covers an entire city block at the center of the Loop. The bank's corporate headquarters, this sloping **A**-shaped skyscraper rises 60 stories and is graced by *The Four Seasons* —a brilliantly colored mosaic mural created by Marc Chagall late in life as a gift to the city of Chicago.

Chicago's Picasso in Daley Plaza
map page 107, B-1

Richard J. Daley Plaza, home of Chicago's **Picasso** (now a beloved civic treasure, whether it be woman, bird, or beast) is a likely place to witness the urban theater of a protest rally, as well as the setting on a dozen summer and fall weekdays for a farmers' market. How do you like those apples?

Like the Eiffel Tower in Paris a century ago, the Chicago Picasso took some getting used to—an adjustment that began with

Berghoff, on West Adams in the Loop, is Chicago's oldest running restaurant.

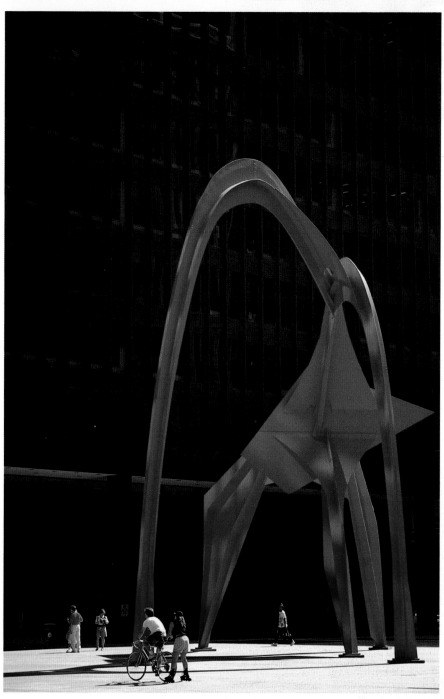

Alexander Calder's "Flamingo", posing in the Federal Center Plaza.

The Picasso sculpture in Daley Plaza. At its dedication Mayor Richard J. Daley said , "...what is strange to us today will be familiar tomorrow."

the 1967 unveiling by Mayor Daley. There were gasps from the crowd when the mayor pulled the streamer that dropped the statue's blue fabric covering. Then Daley began clapping and said to the audience of 50,000: "We dedicate this celebrated work this morning with the belief that what is strange to us today will be familiar tomorrow." In one of her later poems, Gwendolyn Brooks spoke to Picasso's mission: "Art hurts. Art urges voyages—and it is easier to stay at home, the nice beer ready."

◆ DEARBORN AVENUE BUILDINGS   *map page 107, B-2*

Lining Dearborn at the southern extremity of the Loop are four century-old gems of the Chicago School: the **Monadnock Building** (Burnham and Root, 1891, for the original southern half) the **Fisher Building** (D. H. Burnham, 1896); the **Old Colony Building** (Holabird and Roche, 1893), and the **Manhattan Building** (Jenney and Mundie, 1889-91). Now an apartment complex, the 16-story Manhattan was briefly the world's tallest commercial building when it went up as one of the first complete steel-and-iron frame structures. The rounded corner bays of the Old Colony were a device of the time used by architects to create highly desirable corner offices.

◆ LA SALLE STREET FINANCIAL CANYON   *map page 107, B-2*

If you're old enough to remember ticker tape, La Salle Street (the Loop's western spine, two blocks beyond Dearborn) may have a familiar look. This is where Chicago staged its triumphal parades to salute military heroes, astronauts, the very occasional championship sports team, and other luminaries back when the magnitude of such processions could be measured in the tons of confetti left behind. Today, the **La Salle Street** financial canyon is more than ever the Wall Street of the Midwest.

Chicago Board of Trade

Buttressing the south end of the financial canyon is the Board of Trade Building, completed in 1929 just in time for the Great Depression, with a gilded aluminum statue of the Greek grain goddess Ceres perched at the 45-story summit. The Art Deco interior by Gilbert Hall deserves a leisurely look, and the visitors' gallery is open each weekday for a view down on the apparent bedlam of the futures markets. *141 West Jackson Blvd.*

Exchange Center

Running south behind the Board of Trade is the three-building **Exchange Center** (Chicago Board Options Exchange, One Financial Place, Midwest Stock Exchange), built in 1983-84 as testimony to that decade's speculative boom and clad in polished red granite. A landscaped plaza softens the setting to the west, and the complex houses **Everest restaurant,** where both the 40th-story view and Alsatian chef Jean Joho's cooking rank with the finest in town.

Rookery Building and Frank Lloyd Wright

Even more exquisite than the Board of Trade lobby, Frank Lloyd Wright's gold-and-ivory ornamentation of the light court inside this building fully reflects its original 1905 glory after a recent restoration (see "ARCHITECTURE" *page 66). 206 South La Salle.*

The iconoclastic Wright, incidentally, had his own contrarian view of the Loop and its heavy traffic. "The automobile is going to ruin this city," he told a newspaper reporter in the 1920s. "This is a dreadful way to live. You'll be strangled by traffic." Asked by the reporter what should be done, Wright replied, "Take a gigantic knife and sweep it over the Loop, cutting off every building at the seventh floor. If you cut down those horrible buildings, you'll have no traffic jams. You'll have trees again. You'll have some joy in the life of this city. After all, that is the job of the architect—to give the world a little joy."

Parking in downtown Chicago has long been a nightmare. This novel "elevator parking facility" of 1941 proved to be too slow in operation. (Chicago Historical Society)

PEERING INTO THE FUTURES (MARKET)

One of Chicago's most animated shows can be watched free of charge each weekday from 8 A.M. to 2 P.M. It's not a theatrical performance as such, although the actors are colorfully costumed and wildly expressive. Nor is this a sporting event, despite the fact that it features high-stakes winning and losing. The players sometimes seem frantic past the point of bedlam, and the rules appear more arcane than cricket to uninitiated spectators peering down from the visitor galleries. But what you're watching is actually a time-tested bastion of free enterprise that was formed by 82 merchants in 1848 to stabilize grain prices. This is the world's oldest and largest futures market, the Chicago Board of Trade—"The Pit" of Frank Norris's 1903 muck-raking novel and the stuff of headlines on today's financial pages.

Occupying a 45-story Art Deco skyscraper at the foot of LaSalle Street's financial canyon, the Chicago Board of Trade now has two trading floors. Both are outfitted with the tiered octagonal wooden pits that look a bit like risers for a church choir or senior-class photo, and computerized quotation-board displays whose ribbons of lighted figures could be mistaken for the giant sports-book scoreboards at Las Vegas casinos. The original Agricultural Commodities floor deals in orders for wheat, corn, soybeans, cotton, beef, and a variety of other farm products (including those ever-popular pork bellies). The newer Financial Futures floor does business in U.S. Treasury bonds and notes, stock indexes, municipal-bond indexes, and other instruments.

Only the 1,400 Board of Trade members have the right to trade on the exchange floor, which is why a full seat was selling for about $360,000 in 1992 (and as much as $550,000 in 1987). Each pit deals in a specific commodity, whether wheat or Treasury bonds, and where the traders are standing indicates the future delivery month in which they are dealing. The rules require traders to use "open outcry" in making their buy or sell offers—thus the waves of shouting (actually a very controlled form of chaos). Sellers call out quantity first, then price; buyers do the reverse. The animated hand gestures help to clarify the bids in the din of voices; the palm of the hand facing out indicates a trader is selling, while an inward palm is an offer to buy. Other finger and hand signals indicate the price being bid and the number of futures contracts involved. Traders wear badges color-coded to denote their floor privileges and bearing an acronym of no more than three letters by which their trades are recorded. Exchange rules require jackets and ties on the floor; but the lightweight, loose-fitting trading jackets (in the distinctive colors of the various brokerage firms) look more like tear-away football jerseys than formal business attire.

The main function of the futures markets, as the presentation in the visitor galleries takes pains to assert, is first to determine the value of the myriad commodities and instruments traded, and then to transfer the risk of price fluctuations over the months ahead. Those seeking protection from unwanted price changes are known as hedgers, while the risk-takers who fuel the markets are the speculators. From the days of "The Pit" to the present, those who speculate have been the high-rolling stars—and the market-cornering scoundrels—in the Board of Trade's storied history. Like the wheeler-dealer Curtis Jadwin in the Norris novel, the speculator is "a sort of creature of legends, mythical, heroic, transfigured in the glory of his millions."

If you become an instant fan of the trading tumult, there are also viewing galleries that overlook the floors of the Chicago Board Options Exchange, 400 South La Salle Street (linked to the Chicago Board of Trade by a pedestrian bridge, and dealing in stock options); the Midwest Stock Exchange, 440 South La Salle Street (the world's fifth largest stock exchange); and the Chicago Mercantile Exchange, 30 South Wacker Drive (known as "The Merc" and even more boisterous than the Board of Trade).

An active day on the floor of the Chicago Board of Trade.

◆ OTHER NOTABLE LOOP SIGHTS

Sears Tower   *map page 107, B-2*
Rising in stark counterpoint three blocks west of the Rookery's dulcet delicacy is the unadorned muscle of the **Sears Tower**—a 110-story behemoth. Wait if possible for a clear day, then ride the hyper-speed elevator to the 103rd-floor skydeck (or a newer 100th-floor observatory annex used on busy days) for world-class panoramas. Sears Tower's souvenir shops stock every conceivable Chicago-branded souvenir—a surfeit of park-it-in-the-closet-back-home items.

Civic Opera House   *map page 163, A-6*
North up Wacker Drive, the sleek twin towers of the Chicago Mercantile Exchange (with yet another visitors' gallery to marvel at the trading frenzy) look north across Madison Street to the Civic Opera House, built by the speculative shark Samuel Insull in 1929 just before his financial house of cards toppled. It has been home since the 1950s to the phenomenally successful Lyric Opera of Chicago. (*For more on the Lyric Opera see page 47.*) *20 N. Wacker; 312-332-2244, www.lyricopera.org.*

Riverside Plaza Building
West across the Chicago River stands another fine 1920 Art Deco skyscraper, the Riverside Plaza Building. Worth seeing is the wonderful ceiling mural by John Warner Norton in the lobby concourse leading to the Northwestern rail station. An echo

In this 1820 view of Chicago, the earliest known to exist, Fort Dearborn can be seen to the left of the river. The source of the "Loop" nickname can be seen. (Chicago Historical Society)

Dearborn and Randolph circa 1900.

of the building's original ownership by the old *Chicago Daily News,* it depicts with figurative license the process of putting the newspaper to press.

333 West Wacker Drive Building

map page 107, B-1

North of Lake Street, which preceded State as Chicago's prime commercial boulevard in the mid-19th century, Wacker Drive turns east to follow the river; there the facade of the 36-story 333 West Wacker Building, one of city's finest skyscrapers of the 1980s, echoes the river's curvature. *(Also see pages 75 and 77.)*

Other Large Buildings in the Loop

map page 107, B&C-1

Located at Lake Street and Clark is the **State of Illinois Center**, a mixed-use complex built over disused railyards. Continuing east, past three large hotels (the **Hyatt Regency Chicago**, the **Fairmont** and the **Swissotel**); and the Lakeshore **Athletic Club Illinois Center** (a workout wonder with a 100-foot high indoor climbing wall), one comes to the 1,136-foot **Aon Building**—still often called the Amoco Building. This is Chicago's second tallest structure and the world's 10th tallest. It was reclad in granite after its original white marble panels began loosening like bad teeth. The 42-story **Prudential Building** (officially One Prudential Plaza) now looks like a relative pygmy, among the giants, but it was the city's tallest building for a decade after it went up in 1955.

Site of Fort Dearborn of 1803-12

map page 107, C-1

At Michigan and Wacker, pavement markers outline the first Fort Dearborn (1803-12), ground zero for Euro-American settlement in Chicago. The fort was built on the natural shoreline of Lake Michigan shoreline; the New East Side developments (east of Michigan Avenue) were built on landfill deposited in the early 20th century.

Michigan Avenue Historic Architecture
The **Chicago Cultural Center,** at 78 East Washington, was formerly the main public library. Here you will find the lively **Museum of Broadcast Communications,** only one of several notable attractions in the center; *312-744-6630.*

The **Railway Exchange Building,** on the northwest corner of Michigan and Jackson, is a white terra-cotta beauty designed by D.H. Burnham and Co. in 1903. It houses the **Chicago Architecture Foundation,** an essential resource for books and guided tours. Just across the street, at 301 South Michigan, is the **Savvy Traveller,** the city's prime lure for globetrotting browsers looking for travel books and paraphernalia.

Adler and Sullivan's 1889 **Auditorium Building,** at 430 South Michigan, was rescued from a generation of decay after World War II.

■ GRANT PARK   *map page 107, C-2*

Grant Park, the greensward buffer between Loop and lake, presents a grab bag of pleasures. Near Michigan Avenue and Randolph Street, at the northwest end of the park, the new **Millennium Park Music Pavilion** was designed by architect

A Sunday stroller (above) and a bespangled young gourmet at the annual Taste of Chicago Festival (opposite) take in the pleasures of summer in Grant Park.

Frank J. Gehry; if you've seen his work for the Guggenheim Museum in Bilbao, you won't be surprised to see the gleaming strips of steel curving around the stage. The new pavilion is now the site for outdoor concerts including the symphony's summer performances and Chicago's annual blues, gospel, and jazz festivals.

Two rose gardens and a spread of prairie wildflowers add color to **Richard Daley Bicentennial Plaza** (between Jackson and Randolph) where you can ice skate in the winter, and roller skate or play tennis in warmer seasons. **Taste of Chicago,** the 10-day, start-of-summer, food and music mega-festival, takes place here in late June and early July. Farther south, flanking Congress Drive at the park's western edge, stand two of the city's most vigorous sculptures, *The Bowman* and *The Spearman*—depictions on Native Americans on horseback by the Yugoslav master Ivan Mestrovic. Directly east is the beloved **Buckingham Fountain,** a Beaux-Arts confection of pink Georgia marble. On summer evenings the fountain becomes the stage for a computer-coordinated symphony of water and colored lights.

■ ART INSTITUTE OF CHICAGO   *map page 107, C-2*

Save time for the city's most venerable cultural landmark, the Art Institute of Chicago, founded in 1879 and moved into its present Michigan Avenue building. Guarded by a beloved pair of bronze lions to herald the 1893 World's Columbian Exposition, the building was designed by Shepley, Rutan, and Coolidge. Some of its wealthy patrons in the Robber Baron era, including Mrs. Potter Palmer and

(above) Art Institute of Chicago patrons admire Gustave Caillebotte's "Paris Street on a Rainy Day," while (opposite) another patron goes in for a close-up of Chuck Close's "Portrait of John."

*A detail of a stained-glass window designed by Marc Chagall
for the Art Institute of Chicago.*

Martin A. Ryerson, were willing to take a flyer on certain upstart radical French artists, even if collectors in New York disdained them. The controversial new school of French painting suited these Chicagoans just fine—and thanks to them the Art Institute possesses an Impressionist collection as fine as any on either side of the Atlantic. Georges Seurat's beguiling *Sunday Afternoon on the Island of La Grande Jatte* is the institute's signature work, worth a visit all on its own. The museum houses Toulouse-Lautrec's *At the Moulin Rouge,* as well as priceless Cezannes, Renoirs, Monets, Gauguins, and Van Goghs; treasure troves in many other fields of fine and decorative arts, from Old Masters to Chinese bronzes; and the exquisite trading room of the Old Stock Exchange. The Art Institute of Chicago merits as much time as you can manage until feet and eyes beg for mercy—it's too rich a feast for a single meal. Every Tuesday free admission. *111 South Michigan Ave.; 312-443-3600, www.artic.edu.*

■ SOUTH OF THE LOOP:
PRINTER'S ROW, DEARBORN PARK, AND RIVER CITY

Some of Chicago's richest—and raunchiest—heritage lies immediately south of the Loop in a mile-and-a-half of much-redeveloped territory stretching from Congress Parkway to the Prairie Avenue Historic District and McCormick Place-on-the-Lake convention center.

Residential and mixed-use developments in this Burnham Park/South Loop community include Printer's Row, Dearborn Park, and River City. The urban pioneers—yuppies and other neighborhood frontiersmen—who've moved into these lofts, apartments, condominiums, and townhouses enjoy a short commute to Loop offices along with the extracurricular allures of the central city, including handy access to Chicago Bears' football at lakefront Soldier Field just south of the Field Museum. Whether they've yet created a genuine neighborhood is a debatable point on which a strolling visitor may begin to form an opinion.

◆ PRINTER'S ROW

map page 107, B-3

One axis of the district is the two blocks of Dearborn Street running from Congress south to the old Dearborn Station at Polk Street. In the late 19th and early 20th centuries, this was the locale of a vigorous Chicago printing industry that rivaled New York's. The print shops eventually went broke or went elsewhere, but the rugged brick loft buildings with their fine detailing remained, ready to take on new lives through the recent conversions.

Printer's Row today is full of beautifully renovated restaurants, shops, and lofts.

◆ CHICAGO HILTON AND TOWERS   *map page 107, C-3*

One South Loop hotel worth an admiring look even if you're not a guest is the Chicago Hilton and Towers, overlooking Grant Park on Michigan Avenue between Balbo Avenue and Eighth Street. First called the Stevens and then the Conrad Hilton, this was once the world's largest hotel with nearly 3,000 rooms and an 18-hole miniature golf course on the roof. The Hilton positively gleams and a reduced the room count is to 1,620.

Near the Balbo corner, the plate-glass windows that were cracked in 1968 on a legendary Democratic convention night perfumed by tear gas. As Nora Sayre reported in Britain's *New Statesman,* "Outside the Hilton, a nice little old lady and I were suddenly hurled against the wall when 100 policemen seized their blue wooden barricades to ram the crowd (mainly onlookers and the press) against the building with such force that many next to me, including the old lady, were thrust through plate-glass windows. People sobbed with pain as their ribs snapped from being crushed against each other." *720 South Michigan at Balboa; 312-922-4400.*

◆ SMALL MUSEUMS   *map page 107, C-3*

The **Spertus Museum of Judaica** spans 3,500 years of Jewish history. The joys and sorrows of the Jewish experience are expressed in galleries ranging from rich displays of ceremonial treasures to tragic pieces in the Zell Holocaust Memorial. The Rosenbaum Artifact Center hosts workshops and tours oriented to spark children's curiosity about history. One popular attraction is a "dig site" where kids can hunt for archaeological objects. *618 South Michigan Ave.; 312-922-9012.*

Part of Columbia College, the **Museum of Contemporary Photography** was founded in 1967 as an offshoot of the college's highly regarded photography curriculum. The museum showcases photography as both an art and a documentary form. *600 South Michigan Ave.; 312-663-5554.*

◆ BURNHAM PARK MUSEUMS   *map page 107, C&D-2&3*

Along the lakefront, where Grant Park melds into Burnham Park, lies the new museum campus for the Field Museum of Natural History, the Shedd Aquarium, and the Adler Planetarium.

Christmastime at Marshall Field's, in the heart of the Loop.

The Field Museum of Natural History features, among other exhibits, the famous Tyrannosaurus Rex named Sue as well as this outdoor model of an Apatosaurus skeleton.

Field Museum of Natural History

map page 107, D-4

Marshall Field, founding father of the department store and of the famous publishing family, endowed the present Field Museum of Natural History, which is said to be the largest Georgia marble building in the world—yet another among the myriad "biggest" brags mustered by the Windy City. The museum moved north in 1920 from its original Jackson Park location in the Fine Arts Building constructed for the 1893 World's Columbian Exposition and now occupied by the Museum of Science and Industry. From the spectacular Hall of Dinosaurs with countless skeletons—including **Sue**, the world's largest and most complete T. Rex—and stuffed elephants to a pharaoh's tomb and a premier collection of art by Pacific Ocean peoples, and a universe of other exhibits. The natural and civilized worlds are unveiled here. The McDonald's on the ground floor is not an ethnographic exhibit; those are real Big Macs, a museum fast-food concession to popular taste. *1400 South Lake Shore Dr. at Roosevelt Rd.; 312-922-9410.*

Adler Planetarium

map page 107, D-4

The short walk east along Solidarity Drive (bespeaking the clout of Chicago's large Polish-American community) to Adler Planetarium provides spectacular views of the Loop skyline. The intriguing sculpture directly in front of the planetarium is Henry Moore's 1980 bronze, "Sundial." Sears, Roebuck & Co. executive Max Adler funded the star-gazing mecca, which presents sky shows daily in its domed Zeiss projection theater and displays a superb collection of antique astronomical instruments. By far the best place in Chicago to see the stars, given the city's glaringly bright streetlights. *1300 South Lake Shore Dr.; 312-322-0300, www.adlerplanetarium.org.*

Shedd Aquarium

map page 107, D-4

John G. Shedd, a Marshall Field & Co. board chairman, gave the money to build Shedd Aquarium—yes, the world's largest indoor aquarium. Shedd's headline attraction, the enormous Oceanarium for marine mammals, has drawn huge crowds since its 1991 opening while grappling with controversy over its capture of beluga whales—two of whom died here in 1992 after receiving anti-parasite medication.

The aquarium's Coral Reef tank is a 90,000-gallon kaleidoscopic marvel of tropical fish, coral, and other sea creatures. *1200 South Lake Shore Dr.; 312-939-2438, www.sheddnet.org.*

At the Shedd Aquarium.

A new development rises near the Prairie Avenue Historic District in the South Loop.

■ PRAIRIE AVENUE HISTORIC DISTRICT   *map page 107, C-5*

About two miles south of the Loop and just west of the McCormick Plaza Convention Center is the Prairie Avenue Historic District.

The first Chicago suburbanite, hardware dealer Henry B. Clarke, built a Greek Revival home here in 1836 that still stands as the city's oldest building. Merchant princes erected a string of mansions that made Prairie Avenue the poshest Chicago address in the two decades following the Great Fire of 1871.

It's best to drive or take a taxi to Prairie Avenue Historic District, where a few mansions survive to evoke the halcyon days when Field, George Pullman, Philip Armour, Potter Palmer, and their entrepreneurial peers made this Chicago's neighborhood of choice.

◆ GLESSNER HOUSE   *map page 107, C-5*

The estimable Chicago Architecture Foundation maintains this 35-room bastion of rough-hewn granite, the only remaining building in the city designed by the

Romanesque Revival master Henry Hobson Richardson. Built in 1886, it has been lovingly restored inside in the English Arts and Crafts style favored by the Glessners with some of their original furnishings.

One negative review did come from Montgomery Schuyler, a 19th-century architecture critic who wrote, "The whole aspect of the exterior is so gloomy and forbidding and unhomelike that but for its neighborhood, one would infer its purpose to be not domestic but penal." *1800 S. Prairie Ave.; 312-326-1480, www.glessnerhouse.org.*

■ CHINATOWN, PILSEN, AND LITTLE VILLAGE *map page 9, B&C-4*

Chinatown's retail strip lies along Wentworth Avenue less than a mile west of the vast McCormick Place convention center. The ongoing vitality of this Chinese-American enclave is symbolized by the colorful **Chinatown Gate** designed by Peter Fung in 1975 to arch across Wentworth just south of Cermak Road. Now counting around 10,000 residents, the densely packed and expanding little neighborhood began shifting here from the south edge of the Loop just before World War I. The imposing building bedecked with red-and-green pagoda towers at 2216 South Wentworth was built in the 1920s by the On Leong Merchants Association, the community's principal tong society. Most of Chinatown's numerous restaurants remain bastions of Cantonese cuisine; steamed-dumpling devotees swear by the dim sum at Hong Min and Three Happiness *(221 and 209 West Cermak Rd., respectively).* The strip is further enlivened by Chinese bakeries, groceries, tea and herbal shops, and arts and souvenir emporiums.

It's three miles straight west from Chinatown to the heart of the city's largest Mexican community in the adjoining **Pilsen** and **Little Village** neighborhoods between 18th and 26th Streets. The nation's biggest Bohemian-American settlement in the years before World War II, this area was the political bailiwick of Chicago's only Czech mayor, Anton Cermak, who was fatally shot in Miami while appearing with President-elect Franklin D. Roosevelt in 1933. Now 26th Street also goes by **"Avenida Mexicana,"** and Benito Juarez High School is a pride of the community. Hand-painted wall murals focusing on Mexican history, culture, politics, and religion are a Pilsen trademark along 18th Street and elsewhere.

(following pages) The curved pagoda-like rooftops of Chinatown make a pleasant contrast to the square values of modern highrise architecture.

SOUTHWARD TO
HYDE PARK & KENWOOD

■ HIGHLIGHTS

SOUTH TO HYDE PARK

■ OVERVIEW

Just south of Chinatown and the McCormick Convention Center is the neighborhood of Bridgeport. Bridgeport was the neighborhood home to Mayor Richard J. Daley who lived walking distance to Comiskey Park, home to the Chicago White Sox baseball team. Well further to the south of the city center is Hyde Park, home to the University of Chicago, one of America's foremost educational institutions. Also in this neighborhood is the Museum of Science and Technology, billed as Chicago's number one tourist attraction. Kenwood was once one of the city's most exclusive neighborhoods and still boasts some impressive mansions.

For lodging and restaurants see pages 238-272.

■ BRIDGEPORT AND COMISKEY PARK

◆ BRIDGEPORT   *map page 9, C-4*

South of Chinatown and the Pilsen neighborhood one comes to the neighborhood known as Bridgeport. Mayor Richard J. Daley, the most famous lifelong White Sox fan, lived within walking distance of old Comiskey in the Bridgeport neighborhood immediately west, in a brick bungalow in the 3500 block of Lowe Avenue. One of Chicago's earliest neighborhoods, Bridgeport started out as Hardscrabble, a shantytown settlement of Irish laborers who began arriving before 1840 to dig the Illinois & Michigan Canal. Six Chicago mayors—including Hizzoner's son, Richard M. Daley—have hailed from Bridgeport, which has an ethnically diverse population these days. Its Irish taverns were immortalized a century ago by Finley Peter Dunne's "Mr. Dooley" columns in the old *Chicago Daily News,* and Schaller's Pump at 37th and Halsted streets boasts a storied reputation as the city's heavyweight political bar.

A prime Bridgeport employer for more than a century was the **Union Stock Yards**, which finally closed in 1971. Warehouses and light industry have filled some of the vacated slaughterhouse space west of Halsted between 39th and 47th Streets, where everything was extracted from the pig "but the squeal," and Upton Sinclair found his shocking raw material for *The Jungle.*

Standing as a lonely sentinel at Exchange and Peoria is the triple-arched **Old Stone Gate**, erected in 1879 at the original entrance to the stockyards; the design is attributed to John W. Root of Burnham and Root. **The Back of the Yards** neighborhood to the southwest was the first venue for Saul Alinsky's innovative community-organizing efforts just before World War II.

◆ COMISKEY PARK   *map page 9, C-4*

The massive structure on the west side of the Dan Ryan at 35th Street is Comiskey Park, which opened in 1991 as the new and improved home of the baseball White Sox. Erected with state financing to save the franchise from a threatened move to St. Petersburg, the stadium lacks the gritty South Side feel of its demolished 1910 predecessor. At least the field is real grass, and the sightlines are unimpeded by the forest of pillars that infested the old park. Even North Side Cubs fans are likely to concede the superiority of new Comiskey's ballpark food, a legacy of former White Sox owner Bill Veeck.

◆ ILLINOIS INSTITUTE OF TECHNOLOGY   *map page 9, C-4*

Head east from Bridgeport for a crash course in the Modernist precepts of Ludwig Mies van der Rohe on the Illinois Institute of Technology campus, just east of the Dan Ryan Expressway between 31st and 35th streets. Having left Nazi Germany for America, Mies became chairman of the Armour Institute of Technology architecture department in 1938. When Armour and another school merged in 1940 to form Illinois Institute of Technology, Mies embarked on a visually unified design of the new South Side campus. His work on the series of overlapping courts and quadrangles went on until he retired from the IIT faculty in 1958.

■ KENWOOD   *map page 9, D-5*

Continuing south from the Institute you come to Hyde Park and the Kenwood neighborhood just to its north. Kenwood prospered in the last two decades of the 19th century as one of Chicago's most desirable addresses, and that era's surviving mansions are a principal pride of the community's integrated beachhead south of 47th Street. The private **Madison Park** stretch of closely set residences, running for three blocks from Woodlawn to Dorchester avenues between 50th Street and Hyde Park Boulevard, is a racially diverse enclave with an almost rural air. On a grander scale, the 42-room mansion at 4901 South Ellis Avenue was built in 1903 for Sears, Roebuck executive Julius Rosenwald, a renowned philanthropist who contributed $3 million to the founding of the Museum of Science and Industry. Kenwood Park, a square-block oasis of green, is still known in the neighborhood as Farmer's Field. It is said that a cow grazed its grass as recently as the 1920s, when life in Hyde Park and Kenwood was obviously more rustic than it is today

■ HYDE PARK   *map page 9, C&D-5*

The brooding Henry Moore bronze could be a human skull or a mushroom cloud. Twelve feet high and perched on a base of black polished granite, it occupies the site on the **University of Chicago** campus where one of mankind's most fateful accomplishments took place on December 2, 1942. Beneath since-demolished football bleachers along Ellis Avenue, a team of physicists led by

CHICAGO FACES

"Chicago forever keeps two faces, one for winners and one for losers; one for hustlers and one for squares…One face for Go-Getters and one for Go-Get-It-Yourselfers. One for poets and one for promoters…One for early risers, one for evening hiders…

—Nelson Algren

Jane Addams

This rogues' gallery contains Chicagoans of large but diverse stature: from hero to villain, intellectual to athlete.

In 1889, Jane Addams founded Hull House to serve the many poor immigrants streaming into her city. After advocating social reform for 46 years, she won a Nobel Peace Prize in 1931.

During the same years, legendary gangster Al Capone was busy filling the role of Public Enemy Number 1."

Al Capone

Beyond the fame of these good and evil faces, Chicago can claim impressive celebrity in the worlds of both academia and sport. The University of Chicago claims more Nobel laureates than any other university in the nation: Enrico Fermi, shown here, won the 1938 Nobel Prize for physics.

Enrico Fermi

In addition to leading the Bulls to several championships, Michael Jordan holds countless NBA scoring records and is today Chicago's biggest celebrity.

Michael Jordan

Enrico Fermi achieved the first self-sustaining chain reaction and so gave birth to the nuclear age. That it happened here reflects the scientific and intellectual muscle of this century-old university, the institution which has been the magnet holding together the surrounding Hyde Park neighborhood as a bastion of brainpower—and one of Chicago's most extraordinary neighborhoods.

Hyde Park stands out as an island of surprisingly stable racial integration. According to the most recent census, the African-American percentage of the population here has held steady at 38 percent since a decade earlier, with the small decrease in white residents to 53 percent accounted for by the near-doubling of Asians to eight percent. Along with the similarly mixed southern section of the Kenwood neighborhood immediately north, this balanced integration is holding steady amid the virtually all-black canvas of Chicago's expanding South Side ghetto.

Hyde Park was open countryside a distant half-dozen miles from downtown Chicago in 1853 when developer Paul Cornell bought 300 acres of lakefront land between 51st and 55th Streets. There he created a sylvan community that had some of the flavor of a small New England town. It was not until 1889 that Hyde Park would be annexed to Chicago. The founding of the University of Chicago by John D. Rockefeller in 1892 marked the neighborhood's prime watershed, but the next year's staging of the World's Columbian Exposition on the South Side lakefront also had a major impact on development.

■ UNIVERSITY OF CHICAGO   *map page 9, D-5*

◆ HISTORY

The University of Chicago, as the WPA Guide to Illinois put it a half-century ago, "sprang fully fledged into the world as a large and splendidly equipped university, its entry smoothed by the oil millions of the Rockefellers." An early student ditty went: "John D. Rockefeller, wonderful man is he,/Gives all his spare change to the U. of C." The "spare change" eventually mounted to $35 million, and grants from Rockefeller foundations over the decades have multiplied that sum many times. The university's first president, Hebraic scholar William Rainey Harper, was only 35 when the campus opened in 1892; he focused on recruiting a first-rank faculty, which has continued to be the institution's pride.

A pickup game of football on the University of Chicago campus.

Its most remarkable president, Robert Maynard Hutchins, had just turned 30 when he assumed the post in 1929. A dynamic and controversial administrator during his 22-year tenure, Hutchins revolutionized the undergraduate curriculum with his Chicago Plan, which concentrated on general liberal studies for freshmen and sophomores. He introduced study of the Great Books, reorganized the graduate school, and abandoned intercollegiate football as part of his campaign against non-academic pursuits. Later in life, Hutchins founded the Center for the Study of Democratic Institutions within the Fund for the Republic as a "community of scholars."

In the Eisenhower era, the University of Chicago had something of a reputation locally as a hotbed of radicalism, perhaps a legacy of the impressions left by Hutchins' sweeping reforms of the 1930s. It has always boasted a superb academic record in many fields of research, with the largest number of faculty Nobel laureates of any American university. Because the campus is shadowed by high-crime neighborhoods to the west and south, visitors may detect a fortress mentality on the part of some students. As in the past, the aggregate campus tone is more earnest than exuberant: this is definitely not a party school.

◆ UNIVERSITY OF CHICAGO CAMPUS   *map page 9, D-5*

The mixed bag of buildings on the 175-acre U.C. campus reflects a century's worth of commissions involving more than 70 architects, a good many of world stature.

School of Social Services Administration Building: Ludwig Mies van der Rohe's pavilion-like School of Social Services Administration Building, a 1965 design in black steel and glass, stands at 969 East 60th Street on the south side of the Midway. A block to the east, Laird Bell Law Quadrangle is a splendid 1960 ensemble by Eero Saarinen, also the architect for Woodward Court residence hall at 5825 South Woodlawn. But the heart of the campus continues to be the staunchly late English Gothic original University of Chicago Quadrangle, laid out in 1892 by Henry Ives Cobb in emulation of Oxford and Cambridge. During a 1960 campus visit, Saarinen praised the "beautiful, harmonious visual picture" created by the Indiana-limestone complex. "Wandering in the University of Chicago today," he said, "one is amazed at the beauty achieved by spaces surrounded by buildings all in one discipline and made out of a uniform material; where each building—through its common material—is aging in the same way."

Rockefeller Memorial Chapel

The most imposing Gothic Revival structure on campus, Rockefeller Memorial Chapel, was built in 1928 with a bequest from the university's founder and renamed in his honor after his death a decade later. The walls of Bertram G. Goodhue's masonry design rise from a base eight feet thick. Steel is used only in the roof beams, which support an exquisite vaulted tile ceiling. The 72 bells in the 207-foot carillon tower are the finest in the city. One of the world's choicest ancient Near Eastern collections, including such impressive artifacts as a huge Assyrian winged bull, is displayed in the museum of the university's Oriental Institute. *1156 East 59th St., between Woodlawn and University. www.Rockefeller.uchicago.com.*

Smart Museum of Art

Another notable U.C. cultural facility, the Smart Museum of Art, boasts a rich collection spanning several millenia in such varied fields as ancient Greek ceramics, sculpture by Auguste Rodin and other modern masters, and furniture by Frank Lloyd Wright (including the superb dining-room set from the Robie House). The university's highly regarded Court Theater Company occupies a handsomely functional 1981 building by Harry Weese. *5550 South Greenwood Ave.; 773-702-0200.*

Frank Lloyd Wright's Robie House

(See photo page 71)

The Hyde Park mecca for Prairie School pilgrims is Frank Lloyd Wright's Robie House, described with no false modesty on the Chicago Landmarks Commission plaque outside as "his boldest example of a Prairie House design and one of the most significant buildings in the history of architecture." Now owned by the university and used by its alumni association, the house was designed by Wright in 1909 for a manufacturer of bicycle and auto parts. The citation from the city's earlier Architectural Landmarks Commission sums up Wright's achievement at 5757 South Woodlawn: "A home organized around a great hearth where interior space, under wide sweeping roofs, opens to the outdoors. The bold interplay of horizontal planes about the chimney mass, and the structurally expressive piers and windows, established a new form of domestic design."

The Robie House has been recently renovated. Free tours take place at noon Monday through Saturday. *5757 South Woodlawn; 708-848-1976.*

Oriental Institute Museum

Also worth visiting on campus is the Oriental Institute Museum with its marvelous Middle Eastern artifacts reflecting 75 years of archeology by this University of Chicago school. *1155 East 58th St.; 773-702-9520.*

■ HYDE PARK SIGHTS   *map page 9, D-5*

Museum of Science and Industry

Today's most visible legacy of the 1893 Chicago World's Fair is the massive Museum of Science and Industry, which occupies the Palace of Fine Arts built for the exposition in lakefront Jackson Park. Billed as Chicago's No. 1 tourist attraction, with yearly attendance around 4.5 million, this is the place to descend into a full-scale replica of an Illinois coal mine or a captured World War II German U-boat—two banner headliners among more than 2,000 exhibits. The museum entered the space age in 1986 by opening its Henry Crown Space Center and Omnimax Theater, where a 3-D film simulates lift-off and flight in a full-size Space Shuttle mockup. A Mercury space capsule and Aurora 7 are also on display. There's now a museum admission charge, but Thursday remains a free day. *South 57th St. at Lake Shore; 773-684-1414, www.msichicago.org.*

Chicago's 1893 World's Columbian Exposition featured re-creations of classic architectural forms. It was built in Jackson Park near where the Museum of Science and Industry now stand. (Library of Congress)

"Me and Me" by Chicago artist Ed Paschke, 1992, oil on linen.
The Hyde Park Art Center helped boost the reputation of Mr. Paschke and many other talented young artists known as the "Hairy Who" school. (courtesy Phyllis Kind Gallery)

Hyde Park Art Center

Located in the old Del Prado Hotel, the museum carries on as a neighborhood fixture with a reputation for giving boosts to the careers of talented young artists; Ed Paschke and his Hairy Who colleagues are among the most notable alumni. *5307 South Hyde Park Blvd.; 773-325-5520, www.hydeparkart.org.*

The opening of the World's Columbian Exposition in Jackson Park during 1893 boosted the morale of Americans during a deep economic depression. (Underwood Photo Archives, San Francisco)

Midway Plaisance

Stretching west from Jackson Park at the southern edge of the U.C. campus is Midway Plaisance, a block-wide parkway running a mile in length, where the Bazaar of Nations provided the 1893 World's Fair's liveliest entertainment. A 250-foot-high Ferris wheel revolved above the Midway, and one of the exposition's biggest hits was Little Egypt, a belly dancer who titillated and scandalized Victorian-era tourists in the Streets of Cairo pavilion. The Midway today serves as a year-round student and neighborhood playground—with ice skating and occasional cross-country skiing in winter. Lorado Taft's somber "Fountain of Time" sculpture, in which a hooded figure gazes over a pool at a procession of human figures moving through life, dominates the Midway's western end at the entrance to Washington Park. Midway Studios, where the illustrious sculptor did much of his work, functions today as the university's art center. *6016 South Ingleside Avenue.*

Du Sable Museum of African American History

The expanding museum brings to life black history and culture on the eastern perimeter of Washington Park. *740 East 56th Pl.; 773-947-0600, www.dusablemuseum.org.*

Watering Holes

One vanished Hyde Park institution of note, the **Compass Bar,** occupied the site where a fire station now stands at 55th Street and University Avenue. Its Compass Players, who included Mike Nichols and Elaine May, evolved into the famed Second City satirical troupe.

Another local landmark, the **Woodlawn Tap,** soldiers on as a perennial campus hangout at Woodlawn and 55th Street. If you're asking directions, call it Jimmy's.

Other Wright Houses in Hyde Park

A Wright commission from 12 years earlier, **Heller House** at 5132 South Woodlawn (privately owned, please do not disturb occupants) gives hints of the coming Prairie School movement in its widely projecting eaves, and in the open feeling of the third story with its molded plaster frieze by sculptor Richard Bock. But the bottom two stories present a closed face to the outside world. North across Hyde Park Boulevard in the landmark Kenwood District, two Wright houses from the start of the 1890s were done by the young architect on a moonlighting (or "bootleg") basis under the name of a friend while he was still employed as chief draftsman by the Adler and Sullivan firm. Wright designed the frame dwelling with deep eaves at 4858 South Kenwood Avenue for insurance broker George Blossom, while its brick-and-stucco neighbor (No. 4848) was commissioned by Warren McArthur.

N E A R   W E S T
&   R I V E R   N O R T H

RIVER NORTH &
NEAR WEST

■ OVERVIEW

Home to the University of Illinois-Chicago campus the Near West Side is located just across the South Branch of the Chicago River from the Loop. It has traditionally been the heart of Little Italy and Greektown. Just across the Chicago River north of the Loop is the River North area. Dominating this neighborhood is the gigantic Merchandise Mart. Many restaurants, nightclubs, and galleries also make the Near North their home. The majority of galleries in River North are along Superior and Huron Streets in the so-called "Su-Hu" district. In the Near West area most restaurants are set along Randolph Street. Many galleries operate out of lofts on streets emanating from Randolph as well.

For lodging and restaurant information see pages 238-272.

■ NEAR WEST SIDE

The parvenu here is the University of Illinois at Chicago, whose moonscape campus landed on the Near West Side's Harrison-Halsted neighborhood in the 1960s and wiped out a sizable chunk of a close-knit Italian community that fought hard but failed to keep urban renewal at bay. Two-story Hull House, known as the first settlement house for the poor in America, looks like a red-brick interloper, wedged along Halsted Street against the gray concrete masses that form the university.

◆ HULL HOUSE   *map page 107, A-3*

The wrecker's ball leveled most of the 13 buildings in the Hull House complex, where Jane Addams did her remarkable settlement work beginning in 1889 to give so many immigrants a better shot at the American dream. But the original Hull House, was preserved by the University of Illinois Chicago and restored as a museum in the mid 1960s, where visitors are reminded that this center-city area a bit west of the Chicago River was long one of the city's most vibrant and varied melting pots. Located on the UIC campus, *800 S. Halsted Street; 312-413-5353.*

Addams herself described the ethnic richness at the turn of the 19th century: "Between Halsted Street and the river live about 10,000 Italians. In the south on 12th Street are many Germans, and side streets are given over to Polish and Russian Jews. Still farther south, thin Jewish colonies merge into a huge Bohemian colony, so vast that Chicago ranks as the third Bohemian city in the world." Northwest were French Canadians, with Irish to the north and beyond that a few "well-to-do English speaking families" along with one man "still living in his own farmhouse."

Addams spent the last 46 years of her life at Hull House, which she called "my place of work and residence." The Nobel Peace Prize she won in 1931 honored her decades of effort for international amity, women's suffrage, child-labor laws, better schools, improved public sanitation, and a host of other worthy causes. A shrewd businesswoman, Addams was also an impulsively generous soul with an assortment of eccentricities: she couldn't pass a hanging picture without straightening it. And a friend who traveled regularly with her reported that Addams always dressed completely in the hotel room closet, even arranging her hair perfectly in the semi-darkness. Of her Hull House, a prosperous Greek-American merchant remembered from his boyhood visits that "we walked into it as though we walked into our own house, and in that nurturing warmth that animated everything and all, there sounded in our ears the soft words and sentences of the young women of the house, the only soft and kind words we immigrant boys heard in those days."

NEAR WEST & RIVER NORTH

◆ UNIVERSITY OF ILLINOIS AT CHICAGO *map page 107, A-3*

But the campus, along with the large medical complex west of Ashland, has undeniably brought growth and stability to the area. Intrepid homeowners have restored fine old houses in the **Jackson Boulevard District** and elsewhere, while new townhome developments have sprung up as well. Slicing through the area are intersecting expressways, which meet in a spaghetti-bowl tangle of ramps and overpasses just northeast of the university. You may still hear it called Circle Campus, an earlier name the administration has banished; it's now the University of Illinois at Chicago.

Campus

It's worth taking at least a brief stroll among the stark ensemble of university buildings designed by Walter A. Netsch Jr., a Skidmore, Owings and Merrill partner whose previous credits included the Air Force Academy in Colorado Springs. Netsch's UIC design motif was communications, focused on an open amphitheater descending from the center of a concrete Great Court, which forms the roof of six lecture halls. Chicago weather has conspired to dampen Netsch's hope that the amphitheater would serve as an outdoor forum for debate, drama, discussions, and political rallies. Its extent of use by UIC's 25,000 mostly commuter students varies widely with the season. The 28-story University Hall, housing administration and faculty offices, spreads as it rises so that it is 20 feet wider at the top than the base. Enter the west side of campus on Taylor Street or Wood Street; enter the east side on Halsted. *www.uic.edu*

Student Center

Best place to get a feel for campus life, if you can find your way among the labyrinth of pillars and walkways, is the teeming Student Center. Many undergrads are the first generation in their family to attend college, and they have the same things on their minds as students elsewhere—including where to find real-world work. *Chicago Illini Union on the west campus, 828 S. Wolcott Ave., 312-413-5200; Chicago Circle Center on the east campus, 750 S. Halsted; 312-413-5112*

Maxwell Street Market

Now swallowed up by the University of Illinois at Chicago, one of Chicago's trademark attractions in the first half of this century was the raucous Maxwell Street open-air bazaar, where Jewish merchants sold goods of all kinds from stalls and pushcarts in a tumult reminiscent of New York's Lower East Side. Among the distinguished alumni of the Maxwell Street neighborhood were Supreme Court Justice Arthur Goldberg, "King of Swing" Benny Goodman, and actor Paul Muni. "In its heyday, the street represented the trappings of free enterprise," writes Richard Lindberg in the new Passport's Guide to Ethnic Chicago. He adds that "the liveliest debate in town was not in Bughouse Square, where orange-crate orators espoused social-

Buying potatoes on Maxwell Street during the depression. (Chicago Sun-Times)

ism, but between buyer and seller haggling over the price of a pair of knickers on Sunday morning at Maxwell and Halsted." The famous flea market hung on as a scruffy shadow of its heyday self until the site was leveled in 1994 for uic expansion. The **New Maxwell Street Market,** a sanitized successor, operates to the south each Sunday along Canal Street between Roosevelt Road and 15th Place *(map page 107, A-3).*

◆ LITTLE ITALY   *map page 9, B-3*

Little Italy's remnant west of the university is the only real ethnic community left in this once-variegated territory running west to Ashland Avenue from roughly Roosevelt Road in the south to Fulton Street in the north.

The tastes of Little Italy, to the southwest of the campus, include sit-down pasta and other robust fare in bursting-at-the-seams places like Tuscany, Rosebud Cafe, and Vernon Park Tap; stand-and-stuff-your-face sandwiches at Al's No. 1 Italian Beef; and the warm-weather treat of flavored syrup on shaved ice from the sidewalk stand of Mario's Italian Lemonade. For a casual visitor, the food spots and the green street-lamp banners proclaiming "A Touch of Italy" are the only obvious clues to the enclave's Mediterranean roots. You'd probably need to move in for a while to penetrate the ethnicity that remains, and you'd discover that many former Little Italy residents come back each Columbus Day to celebrate mass at **Our Lady of Pompeii Church**, on the corner of Lexington and Lytle Streets.

◆ GREEKTOWN   *map page 107, A-1*

Immediately north of the university, the dozen and more Greek restaurants packed along Halsted between Adams and Van Buren are virtually all that's left of a **Hellenic community** so sizable a century ago that the area was known as the Delta (after the triangular letter in the Greek alphabet).

Each restaurant has its partisans, and you'll hear in all of them the cry of "Opaa!" as waiters brandish the *saganaki,* a flaming cheese appetizer created not in Athens but here in Chicago. Tucked among the cheerfully noisy restaurants are a few shops like the Athenian Candle Company, which also purveys incense; the Pan Hellenic Bakery, for baklava or spinach pie to go; and the Athens Grocery, stocked with feta cheese and vats of plump Greek olives. You can taste the commercial flavor of Greece along Halsted, but the residential community has dispersed throughout the Chicago area.

◆ BATCOLUMN   *map page 107, A-1*

Visitors heading west from the Loop to Greektown on Madison Street get a visual wallop from an astonishing public sculpture. It's Claes Oldenburg's "**Batcolumn**," at 600 Madison, a latticework baseball bat that stands 100 feet tall outside the Social Security Administration Center across the street from the Presidential Towers apartment complex along the former Skid Row.

Of interest several blocks west from the Bat Column is the **Museum of Holography** billed as the world's most complete center for the three-dimensional projection of images. *1134 West Washington Blvd. at May St.; 312-226-1007 .*

◆ WHOLESALE MARKETS

The wholesale meat and produce warehouses along Randolph Street at Desplaines occupy the site of the 1886 Haymarket Affair, when eight policemen and two bystanders were killed by a bomb thrown during an outdoor rally called to protest brutality against workers at the strikebound McCormick Harvester Works. Eight anarchists were convicted of murder, despite a lack of evidence they'd had any part

Claes Oldenburg's "Batcolumn" at 600 Madison.

in the bombing; four were hanged and a fifth committed suicide by exploding a dynamite cap with his teeth. A policeman's statue honoring the dead officers stood until 1970 at the bombing location. After it was twice toppled (with the radical Weathermen claiming credit the second time), the sculpture spent four years at Police Headquarters before finding its current home in the atrium of the Police Training Academy at 1300 West Jackson Boulevard.

And if you think fire departments lack a sense of irony, head for block-long DeKoven Street, east across the Dan Ryan Expressway from the university. The red-brick **Chicago Fire Academy,** where fledgling firefighters get their training, was built in 1960 at 558 West DeKoven, on the very site of the O'Leary family house and barn where the Great Fire of 1871 started. **"Pillar of Fire,"** an elegant bronze sculpture by Egon Weiner, marks the location of the barn where the fire apparently began—but most probably without any cow kicking over a lantern. Patrick and Catherine O'Leary's humble frame house survived the conflagration, which raged northward on strong winds. A prosperous Bohemian later built a two-story brick residence with a white marble front where the O'Learys had lived. Now it must be one of the safest places in the city for a fire to break out.

For many immigrants Union Station (left) was the first stop in Chicago. It remains the rail hub of the nation today as well as serving suburban commuter trains (above). (photo left courtesy of the Chicago Sun-Times).

THE BALLET OF BRIDGES

One of the most impressive ballets a visitor is likely to view in Chicago can also be one of the most aggravating for drivers and pedestrians who happen to be in a hurry. This outdoor spectacle is the synchronized raising and lowering of Chicago River bridges to allow the passage of pleasure boats from spring through fall. Twenty of these spans cross the river in an arc running from Lake Shore Drive to the Eisenhower Expressway, and the city boasts 52 movable bridges in all. The local bridge count hardly ranks in the same big leagues with such canal-laced cities as Venice and Amsterdam, but the up-and-down performances that Chicago's bridges present when the yachts come through is like nothing you'll see in Italy or Holland.

Virtually all Chicago's movable bridges are trunnion bascules, a design so identified with the city that it is known internationally as the "Chicago style." Bascule is derived from the French word for "seesaw," and that's roughly how the bridges work, pivoting on a horizontal shaft (the trunnion). When not in action, they look like stubby workaday spans, but their profiles are endowed with touches of class. *Chicago Tribune* architecture critic Blair Kamin has written of "bridge-tender houses that seem transplanted from the boulevards of Paris; handsome ornamental railings; majestic pylons; leaded mansard roofs; delightful relief sculpture."

You'll have a few minutes to admire these details while waiting to cross when the bridges go up. Particularly notable is the **Michigan Avenue bridge,** now an official city landmark, built in 1920 as the first of its kind to carry two levels of traffic. Its neighbor to the east, the 269-foot **Columbus Drive bridge,** ranks as the world's second-longest trunnion bascule design (exceeded only by a 295-foot span over Spain's Bay of Cadiz).

The less conspicuous **Kinzie bridge,** spanning the north branch of the Chicago River, played a supporting role in the most invisible major disaster in the city's history. Pilings sunk into the river bed to protect the span from being hit by boats punctured one of the abandoned and little-known (at the time) tunnels that had carried freight around downtown Chicago earlier this century. The puncture ruptured in April of 1992, unleashing the great subterranean flood that brought the Loop to its knees. But that's another story, best saved for a rainy day.

(opposite) The Kinzie Bridge is one of 52 movable bridges crossing the Chicago River.

■ RIVER NORTH

Cradled in two arms of the Chicago River, the near-Loop enclave now called River North was settled first by Irish laborers in the 1840s. It had hummed in the half-century after the Chicago Fire of 1871 as a hive of factories built mostly of sturdy red brick, with a patina of mansions dressing up its eastern fringe. Then the industrial enterprises began giving way to warehouses between the world wars, and the handsome dwellings found themselves slumming as rooming houses. In the 1960s, the Cabrini-Green highrise public housing just to the northwest cast a shadow of poverty and crime, as most of the remaining warehouse and factory operations pulled up stakes.

Left intact were the solid shells of all those derelict lofts, which turned out to be an irresistible lure for artists and other creative spirits in search of cheaper quarters with ample elbow room. The artful arrivals soon reached critical mass to generate River North, Chicago's answer to New York's raffish SoHo quarter. Some called it SuHu, playing off the concentration of galleries on Superior and Huron Streets—while one wag suggested WeeWee (west of Wells Street). The district became a hothouse of studios, galleries, restaurants, and clubs, so fashionable by the start of the 1990s that restless artists were staking out more pristine (and less pricey) neighborhoods to the west. Meanwhile, the retailing triumph of North Michigan

Dining at Reza's Persian restaurant, one of many great dining spots in the River North area.

Merchandise Mart, a wholesale outlet for furnishing and design products, was built in 1930. It still ranks second only to the Pentagon as America's largest building.

Avenue was giving a trickle-down boost to development along Wabash, State, Ontario, and other stretches on River North's eastern edge.

River North's boundaries extend roughly to Chicago Avenue on the north and Rush Street on the east, a territory of not much more than a square mile best explored on foot. Although no longer an urban frontier, it still sees frequent comings and goings of businesses and attractions. Try **Reza's Persian** restaurant for delicious Middle Eastern food; *436 West Ontario.* The stimulating **Peace Museum** is a block south from Erie Street; *350 West Ontario; 773-638-6450.*

◆ MERCHANDISE MART   *map page 163, A-5*

The Merchandise Mart, which has been anchored since 1930 on the river's north bank between Wells and Orleans. This 25-story blockbuster—call it Art Deco on steroids—began life as the world's largest building (superseded a decade later by the Pentagon). It still ranks as the biggest commercial structure anywhere, with 4.2 million square feet of floor space devoted to home and office furnishings as well as other design products.

Department store magnate Marshall Field III erected the mammoth mart as a national center of wholesale showrooms and offices, but the Great Depression was already entrenched by the time the facility opened in 1931, and Joseph P. Kennedy picked it up at a bargain price in 1945.

The general public is barred from wandering around the showrooms in the mart or the mid-'70s **Chicago Apparel Center** just to the west, but guided visits are available through the Tours at the Mart program.

Tourists are also welcome to admire the south lobby's **Jules Guerin murals** depicting the history of trade around the globe. And they're more than welcome to spend time and money in the mart's new two-level shopping mall and international food court. One of the Apparel Center's two towers is topped by the Holiday Inn Mart Plaza, notable for the splendid skyline panoramas from its 525 guest rooms. *200 World Trade Center Chicago; 312-527-7600 or 800-677-6278.*

◆ NOTABLE BUILDINGS IN NEAR NORTH

Marina City   *map page 163, B-5*
East along the river past the sleek Westin River North, the circular twin towers of Marina City are a fixture among Chicago's postcard images three decades after Bertrand Goldberg designed the distinctive mixed-use complex with its flower-petal balconies. At the outset of the '90s, the commercial space that Goldberg hoped would make Marina City virtually a self-contained community had deteriorated into a ghost town. That was a source of rising anxiety for condominium owners in the 60-story towers, where apartments shaped like a blunt wedge of pie have always presented a decorating challenge.

IBM Building   *map page 163, B-5*
Ludwig Mies van der Rohe's final office design, the 52-story IBM Building, presents the instructive contrast of a firmly rectilinear profile just to the east of all-curves Marina City. Miesian pilgrims can revere a bust of the master Modernist in the lobby of the IBM, which has garnered deserved

praise from architecture critics for the superb proportions of its precisely detailed curtain wall of dark aluminum and bronze-tinted glass (see page 72 for more).

North of the IBM Building
A hike north up State behind the IBM Building passes one of Chicago's best wurst joints, teeming Gold Coast Dogs, on its way to River North's sleekest piece of new architecture. The 515 North State Street building, headquarters of the American Medical Association, went up in 1990 as the first major commercial design in this country by Japan's Kenzo Tange. The glass-and-aluminum curtain walls of the 30-floor tower are pierced near the top by a four-story, see-through cutout. Lunchtime picnickers can find a congenial venue on the building's landscaped plaza—not a bad place to munch a Gold Coast hot dog.

Jazz Record Mart   *map page 163, B-4*
Just behind the plaza, the Jazz Record Mart claims the largest stock anywhere of jazz and blues titles; *444 North Wabash.*

NEAR WEST & RIVER NORTH

◆ TREE STUDIOS   *map page 163, B-4*

The art milieu of an earlier era is manifest along State between Ohio and Ontario in the yellow-brick **Tree Studios Building,** constructed in 1894 by Judge Lambert Tree to provide 17 artists with working space arranged around an interior court-yard that remains a small oasis of urban calm for anyone who ventures through its Ohio Street entrance. Some artists still reside at Tree Studios, now owned by the Medinah Temple Association, whose Medinah Temple fronting on Wabash Avenue to the east represents the Shriners' notion (circa 1912) of a Moorish mosque, com-plete with onion domes, crescents, and Islamic motifs in the grillwork and stone trim. The circus is a yearly crowd-pleaser in the temple's 2,000-seat auditorium. *613 North State St.; 312-337-7541.*

◆ FOOD AND ENTERTAINMENT

Food as entertainment forms one motif of a stroll west on Ontario from Rush to Wells. Ghosts of marionettes whis-per inside the former McCormick Mansion, now the setting for **Lawry's The Prime Rib,** where today's showbiz features a spinning salad bowl, and beef trolleys almost as formi-dable as an armored personnel carrier. Chicagoans of a certain age recall fondly the puppet theater that enlivened the mansion during its Swedish incarna-tion as the Kungsholm.

Excalibur, the Romanesque Revival fortress on the northwest corner of Ohio and Dearborn is a nightclub with a checkered past. Built in 1892, it housed the Chicago Historical So-ciety until 1931, did Depression-era

Tree Studios, built by the Shriners in 1912, was modeled after their notion of an Islamic mosque.

time as a Moose lodge, and was briefly home of the famed Bauhaus School of Design in the 1940s. In the last few decades, it has watched several nightclubs arrive and depart; as of this writing, the entertainment complex styles itself Excalibur.

South across Dearborn, that Neo-Georgian Revival structure is a Commonwealth Edison substation, a 1989 design by Tigerman McCurry to echo the 1929 power facility it replaced. The design was also devised to be compatible with the neighboring **Hard Rock Cafe**, a 1985 Tigerman McCurry commission. The world may not have needed another Hard Rock Cafe, but this one continues to pack in suburbanites and tourists as well as the occasional wayward Chicagoan. For a double dip of rock nostalgia, step west to the next-door **Rock-N-Roll McDonald's**, so called because its memorabilia-crammed interior takes customers on a nostalgia bender back to the rock heyday of the 1950s and '60s. The Big Macs are merely a side dish here to the flashing pinball machines, red '63 Corvette, and life-size white sculptures of the four Beatles on parade. For slightly more serious dining in the '50s time warp, it's two more blocks west on Ontario to Ed Debevic's, a whimsical and very popular reincarnation of an Eisenhower-era diner where you needn't be ashamed of ordering meatloaf.

◆ GALLERY QUARTER

West and north of all this pop culture lies the heart of River North's gallery quarter along Erie, Huron, and Superior as well as north-south Franklin and Orleans Streets. Many of the 50-plus galleries here schedule openings of new shows for Friday evenings, a prime time to stroll and browse while sipping the jug wine that's often part of the program. Widely available in the neighborhood is Chicago Gallery News, which lists exhibits, hours, and other useful details for SuHu hopping. Reliable Italian and Mexican fare with a Chicago twist is dished up respectively at Scoozi! and Nacional 27, two noisy Huron Street outposts of the Lettuce Entertain You empire. A place with a more venerable pedigree is the Green Door Tavern, 678 North Orleans, a bastion of burgers, chili, and other stick-to-the-ribs fare since 1921, in a building that went up a year after the 1871 Chicago Fire.

◆ CATHEDRALS

Holy Name Cathedral *map page 163, B-3*
Back east on Superior at State Street, the hats of five former cardinals hang from the ceiling of Holy Name Cathedral, which has served the Roman Catholic Archdiocese of Chicago since it was erected in 1874 to replace a smaller late-Victorian

church destroyed in the Chicago Fire of 1871. The archdiocese, which serves 2.5 million Roman Catholics, remains one of the most influential powers in the Chicago area, although shifts in population have necessitated the closing of several inner-city churches it governs.

The parking lot opposite the cathedral on the west side of State was occupied in the 1920s by a row of shops, including Schofield florists, where mob chieftains Dion O'Banion and Hymie Weiss were gunned down by Al Capone's hitmen during the Prohibition wars.

Episcopal Cathedral of St. James   *map page 163, B-4*
Another post-fire church, the Episcopal Cathedral of St. James, at Wabash and Huron, has a typical English Gothic exterior of the 1870s. But the interior, carefully restored in 1985, is a revelation for its wealth of Arts and Crafts Movement stencil work, executed in 1888 in 26 colors focused on stylized plant motifs. This treasure is an example of the mixed bag of surprises in the ever evolving River North.

Our Lady of the New Millennium travels around Chicago visiting the city's various parishes. Here she rests in a church parking lot near Midway Airport.

MAGNIFICENT MILE
& GOLD COAST

■ HIGHLIGHTS   *page*

GOLD COAST &
MAGNIFICENT MILE

■ OVERVIEW

The Magnificent Mile refers to the mile long stretch of Michigan Avenue from the Chicago River to Lake Shore Drive. This broad avenue is the greatest shopping street in the city with a concentration of hotels within several blocks to the east and west. Streeterville is a narrow strip of land just off the eastern and southern end of Michigan Avenue that runs to the waterfront culminating in Navy Pier— a sort of Chicago Disneyland and summer playground for locals and tourists alike.

The Gold Coast refers to the exclusive residential neighborhood just north of the end of Michigan Avenue and bordering South Lake Shore Drive up to North Avenue. The fabled mansions of Chicago's elite rest here.

For lodging and restaurants, see pages 238-272.

MAGNIFICENT MILE
& GOLD COAST

■ MAGNIFICENT MILE   *map page 163, B-3,4&5*

Amid the North Michigan Avenue building boom of the last two decades, the Old Chicago Water Tower has stood its ground as the civic talisman that miraculously survived the Great Fire of 1871. But the circling skyscrapers have contrived to shrink this mock-Gothic good-luck charm once vilified by Oscar Wilde as "a castellated monstrosity with pepper boxes stuck all over it," so that the cream-yellow **Water Tower** at first glance now resembles a runty mascot best suited to adorn souvenir postcards and coffee mugs. Hard to believe, but the 154-foot-high tower was the tallest Michigan Avenue structure north of the Chicago River as recently as 1920. That was the year when widening of the thoroughfare and the opening of its double-deck bridge gave birth to "the Magnificent Mile," which eventually dethroned downtown State Street as Chicago's premier shopping district in the 1970s and fueled the recent lakeward development in Streeterville to the east.

This is the patch of 1990s' Chicago where it's easiest to slip into the tourist groove, as you meld into the throngs of giggling suburban teen-agers, badge-marked conventioneers, and other promenaders. You can hop a horse-drawn carriage, ride a London-style red double-decker bus, cough up some coins for sidewalk musicians, play miniature golf indoors, tuck into a trademark deep-dish pizza, and round up a wad of brochures complete with discount coupons. The Magnificent Mile does lack the spacious grandeur of the Champs-Elysées, and the Water Tower hardly manages the gravity of the Arc de Triomphe, but Chicago's avenue far surpasses its legendary Paris counterpart in the serious matter of shopping.

◆ THINGS TO DO

For gleam-in-the-eye shoppers, the Magnificent Mile is the place in Chicago that really matters: Bloomingdale's, Saks Fifth Avenue, Neiman Marcus, Lord & Taylor, Marshall Field's, and a host of designer-label specialty shops from Burberry's to Tiffany's including a traffic-stopping F.A.O. Schwarz toyland that opened in 1992 just north of the Water Tower. Never mind that 15 mph is a rush-hour fantasy as Michigan Avenue traffic jams grow more intractable by the year. When the myriad tiny white lights twinkle on the avenue's procession of trees in the Christmas season, there is still enough magnificence to go around. Towering above all along the avenue is the **John Hancock Building** with its top floor observatory affording one of the finest views in the city and a good place to get yourself oriented for exploring this district. *(see "ARCHITECTURE," page 74).*

Aiming to recapture some of the avenue's old magic from the Grinch of commercialism, the local merchants' association has created a holiday tree-lighting ceremony. Slated for the Saturday before Thanksgiving each year, it features a procession of horse-drawn carriages, double-decker buses, costumed Christmas characters, and musicians parading south down Michigan from Oak Street to the Wrigley Building as the twinkling Italian lights are turned on block by block. Carolers and mayoral remarks cap the event, intended to put some human spirit back into the concrete canyon.

■ STREETERVILLE   *map page 163, C-4&5*

Streeterville is the neighborhood resting between the Chicago River to the south, Chicago Avenue to the north and east to Lake Michigan from North Michigan Avenue. The area began as a shantytown perched on landfill a century ago. Now it is one of the cities priciest chunks of real estate hosting office buildings, residential towers, and medical facilities. Of interest to the tourist are Navy Pier, Olive Park, the Museum of Contemporary Art, and the North Pier Terminal, a former commercial pier now given over to the tourist trade as a festival marketplace with a nice mixture of diversions including a plethora of food stands.

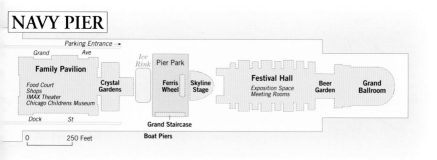

◆ NAVY PIER ENTERTAINMENT CENTER

Anchoring the lower reaches of Streeterville and just east of the three-lobed Lake Point Tower apartments is the Navy Pier, built in 1916 as a shipping and recreational complex. During both world wars it served as a Navy training facility and was home to the Chicago branch of the University of Illinois 1946-1965.

MAGNIFICENT MILE
AND GOLD COAST

OLD TOWN

A · ▼ · B · Lincoln Park · ▼ · C · ▼ · D · ▼

Eugenie St
Second City
Twin chors
North St
Old Town Ale House
N Orleans
N North Park
N Wieland

Lincoln Statue
N Clark
N LaSalle Dr
Chicago Historical Society
Home of Roman Catholic Archbishop of Chicago
Ave
Burton St

Chess Pavilion
International Museum of Surgical Science

1

0 · .25 · .5 Miles
0 · .25 · .5 · .75 Kilometers

W Schiller St
GOLD COAST
Evergreen St
Goethe St
N Astor St
Schiller St
Banks
James Charnley House
E Goethe St

Lake

2

Scott St
House of Glunz
vision
N Wells St
N LaSalle St
N Clark St
N Dearborn St
N State St
E Scott St
W Elm St
E Elm St

Michigan

Hill St
W Maple St
E Cedar St
E Belevue St
E Oak St
Oak Street Beach
Breakwater

3

Walton St
Locust St
Chestnut
Chicago Ave
W Superior St
W Huron St
W Erie St
N Franklin St
N LaSalle St
N Clark St
N Dearborn St
N State St
N Wabash St
N Rush St

E Walton St
E Delaware Pl
E Chestnut St
E Pearson St
E Chicago Ave
E Superior St
E Huron St
E Erie St
E Ontario St

The Drake
Playboy Building
John Hancock Center
Museum of Contemporary Art
Lake Shore Park
41
N Fairbanks Ct
N McClurg Ct

Washington Square
Connors Park
Fourth Presbyterian Church
Water Tower
Holy Name Cathedral
Episcopal Cathedral of St James
Terra Museum of American Art
Medinah Temple

MAGNIFICENT MILE

Ohio Street Beach
Milton Lee Olive Park

4

Ohio St
W Grand Ave
W Illinois St
W Hubbard St
W Kinzie St

RIVER NORTH
N Michigan Ave
E Grand Ave
Jazz Record Mart
Tribune Tower
Wrigley Building
N Water St

STREETERVILLE
Illinois St
Lake Point Towers
North Pier Terminal
Sheraton Hotel and Towers
Ogden Slip
Gateway Park

Navy Pier
Streeter

5

Merchandise Mart
N Wells St
IBM Building
Marina City
333 West Wacker Bld
W Wacker Dr
South Water St
Stetson St
Field Blvd

Chicago River
E Wacker Dr
Lower Wacker Dr

Locks

Illinois Center
E Randolph St
R Daley Plaza
Mall
Prudential Building
Amoco Building
LOOP
E Madison St
Palmer House
Civic Opera House
Wells
Chicago Mercantile Exchange
Clark
Dearborn
State
Wabash
Michigan
Columbus

Chicago Cultural Center
Museum of Broadcast Communications
Richard J Daley Bicentennial Park
Lake Shore Drive

6

Illinois Institute of Technology
E Monroe St
E Adams St
Art Institute of Chicago
Grant Park

Practically unused during the 1970s and 1980s, the 3,000-foot-long pier is now a major entertainment center. Attractions include a 1500-seat outdoor musical stage, 71 palm trees, a jetting fountain, a carousel, the Grand Ballroom with an 80-foot domed ceiling, and a 150-foot high Ferris wheel modeled after the first one built in 1893 for the World Columbian Exposition.

Chicago Children's Museum
Stimulating hands-on exhibits. Originally founded in 1982 as a response to dwindling arts programs in the Chicago public schools, in 1995 the Children's Museum's three locations were united on the Pier. *312-527-1000, www.childrensmuseum.org.*

Chicago Shakespeare Theater
In 1999 this theater (formed in 1986) moved into its new seven-story facility on the Pier. *312-595-5600.*

Smith Museum of Stained Glass Windows
A showcase of windows made from 1870 to the present. *312-595-7437.*

Navy Pier has become one of Chicago's premier attractions for locals and visitors alike. The pier is still used as a dock for Lake Michigan excursion boats (above) while the pier itself has myriad attractions, including a Ferris wheel (right).

◆ OLIVE PARK   *map page 163, D-4*

The formidable municipal water-filtration plant to the north of Navy Pier is fringed by Olive Park, a landscaped grace note that affords superlative views of the lakeshore skyline. Immediately to its west nestles one of Chicago's smallest public beaches, Ohio Street Beach, where sunbathers face a northern exposure that will quickly remind them it's a long way to the nearest tropical strand.

CAPTAIN STREETER'S DOMAIN

Chicago's gallery of rogues, which would need a couple of Art Institutes to hang its innumerable portraits, contains few characters more engaging or determined than George Wellington (Cap) Streeter. This rascally showman, who'd gone bust as a circus and theater owner, defied law and order as well as his high and mighty neighbors for more than three decades from a lakefront shantytown that he styled "the District of Lake Michigan" and claimed allegiance only to the federal government. Cap eventually lost his turn-of-the-century domain, but lived to be 84, and even Mayor William Hale Thompson turned out for his funeral. East of Michigan Avenue, some of the city's priciest real estate bears his name today as the Streeterville neighborhood.

The Streeter saga began here in 1886 when Cap and his wife, Maria (Ma), got their broken-down steamboat stuck on a sandbar several hundred feet from that era's shoreline, roughly due east of where the John Hancock Center towers today. As Lois Wille tells the tale with gusto in *Forever Open, Clear and Free: The Struggle for Chicago's Lakefront*, Streeter filled in and staked out 186 acres of sand and debris around the derelict vessel, which he dismantled in 1889 to build a shack he christened "The Castle." One day, according to Wille's account, a wealthy Lake Shore Drive property owner told Streeter, "You've got to get out of here. This is my land. I've got riparian rights." The leathery Cap barked back, "I've got squatter's rights and the right to eminent domain. Now git." He squirted tobacco juice at the businessman's feet, while Ma waved her ax and a pistol.

Declaring himself governor of "the District of Lake Michigan," Cap sold beer on dry Sundays and performed marriages. There were pitched battles over the years with police and a number of deaths, but he held out until 1918 and weathered into a local celebrity. "He clung on through hard times and good, growing constantly in pride, aware that the newspapers had made him a public figure," wrote Henry Justin Smith and Lloyd Lewis in *Chicago: The History of Its Reputation*. They found him "always glad to be interviewed, but holding a long Springfield rifle, with a bayonet, on his arm as a threat to the constables." He was a Chicago original.

Shopping along the Magnificent Mile of North Michigan Avenue.

◆ MUSEUM OF CONTEMPORARY ART   *map page 163, C-3*

A few blocks north of Ontario is the Museum of Contemporary Art which opened its striking new galleries and sculpture garden in 1996. The MCA's former location, 237 East Ontario, was the first U.S. building wrapped by Christo. There'll be a challenge to your perceptions in whatever special exhibition the museum happens to be hosting, and its permanent collection ranges from Surrealism to Pop Art with an emphasis on Chicago artists. There are fine examples of antic canvases from the local "Hairy Who" school by Ed Paschke, Jim Nutt, Roger Brown, and others. *220 East Chicago Ave. next to Lakeshore Park; 312-280-2660.*

■ NORTH MICHIGAN AVENUE:
  "ONE MAGNIFICENT MILE"

The city's prime shopping district begins here on North Michigan Avenue at the Chicago River. *(See essay on pages 173-175.)*

Chicago Architecture Foundation

A pier at the southwest corner of the Michigan Avenue Bridge is the departure point for the ultra-informative river cruises offered by the Chicago Architecture Foundation *312-922-3432, www.architecture.org; Ticketmaster: 312-902-1500.*

Sheraton Chicago Hotel and Towers

map page 163, C-5

The terrace cafe, here, is perfect for watching pleasure boats plying the river on a sunny day. It's also a cozy rest-and-recovery spot after tackling the varied enticements of North Pier.

Wrigley Building

map page 163, B-5

Overlooking the Chicago River on Michigan Avenue's west side, somewhere near the homestead site of pioneer settler Jean Baptiste Point du Sable, the Wrigley Building may bring to mind a wedding cake with its swirls and squiggles of terra-cotta decoration. Nonetheless, this is one of the city's most beloved icons, a romance more plausible once you've seen its shimmering white transformation when the floodlights go on after dark.

Hotel Inter-Continental Chicago

Just north of the Wrigley Building, the 41-story Hotel Inter-Continental Chicago sports a prominent mosque-like dome bespeaking its earlier life as the Medinah Athletic Club. *See pages 238-272 for more on lodging in Chicago.*

Billy Goat Tavern

Off the lower level of Michigan Avenue between the Wrigley Building and Tribune Tower, Billy Goat Tavern claims fame as the greasy inspiration for John Belushi's "cheesebugga, cheesebugga" sketches on "Saturday Night Live." Stick to the beer.

Tribune Tower

map page 163, B-5

Across the avenue to the north, the Tribune Tower provides more exterior entertainment and edification than a score of less flamboyant buildings: a facade imbedded with chunks of stone from the Alamo, the Taj Mahal, and a host of other landmarks around the globe; oversized reproductions of famous *Chicago Tribune* front pages etched in copper; a glass-fronted studio for the Tribune Company's WGN radio station; and a cap of full-fledged flying buttresses that recall the great Gothic cathedrals.

The Gothic Revival design by Hood and Howells was chosen in an international competition in the early 1920s—although the great architect Louis Sullivan was not impressed. "It is an imaginary structure—not imaginative," said Sullivan in the last year of his life. Of the Tribune building's flying buttresses, he complained that the designers had crowned the tower with a monstrous spider.

West Side of Michigan Avenue

If the skyscraper life is beginning to pall, the west side of Michigan Avenue's two blocks from Erie to Ohio brings low-rise

The Water Tower on the Magnificent Mile is one of the city's most famous landmarks.

relief and a nice mix of allures: **Stuart Brent Books,** a Chicago literary fixture with a proprietor of vigorous opinions; next-door **Garrett Popcorn Shop** (but buy your fresh-popped bag after leafing through the bookstore). Other places to stop include **Crate & Barrel,** the five-story headquarters store of this housewares heaven; **Hammacher Schlemmer,** the guru of gadgets; and a number of galleries, including the long-esteemed Richard Gray. Deep-dish stalwarts Pizzeria Uno and Pizzeria Due lie in wait a block or two inland. *Uno: 29 East Ohio St.; 312-321-1000. Due: 619 North Wabash Ave.; 312-943-2400.*

Terra Museum of American Art
map page 163, B-4

Basically, one wealthy man's inspired vision of American art from the mid-19th to early 20th centuries with a trove of American Impressionist works. *666 North Michigan Ave.; 312-664-3939.*

Swanky Shops along North Michigan

Mall-aise can easily set in along North Michigan Avenue if you have an allergy to recreational shopping. One antidote is the perspective a newspaper writer brought in 1927 to its first generation of swanky shops: "Scattered up and down Michigan Avenue are many exclusive shops furnished in the latest Louis XV, Spanish, and Italian styles. Unlike most museums, these have no admission fee; but a cover charge is added to the price of each purchase."

Approach the vertical malls as though they were well-stocked interactive exhibits in the art of conspicuous consumption.

Water Tower Place Department Stores
map page 163, B-3

Take a suburban mega-mall, stand it on end, add a sleek hotel plus pricey condominiums, and you have Water Tower Place, the marble-clad fortress that is Hancock's next-door neighbor to the south. This was a mid-1970s prototype for the vertical shopping mall, replete with atrium and other mesmerizing accouterments that make visitors from the outlands feel as though they'd brought suburbia with them. You could spend the better part of a day—and a lot of people do—filtering through Water Tower Place's two department stores (Lord & Taylor and Marshall Field's) and seven levels of specialty shops (including stylish **Rizzoli International Bookstore** and Gallery). Through a separate entrance on Pearson Street, elevators whisk guests to the 12th-floor lobby of the Ritz-Carlton Hotel, which vies with the Four Seasons for top ranking locally.

Water Tower Visitor Information
map page 163, B-3

The Water Tower has been reopened to the public as a visitor information center for the Chicago Office of Tourism. The stock of brochures is exhaustive, and the staff knowledgeable and helpful.

The tower disguises a 138-foot high standpipe built to equalize the pressure of water pumped through the station from a new Lake Michigan tunnel and intake unit (a forerunner of the circular cribs that hover on today's offshore horizon).

West of the Water Tower, where the Magnificent Mile's prosperity now oozes, blossomed Chicago's equivalent of Greenwich Village in this century's early decades. Before World War I, it was home to writers the likes of Sherwood Anderson, Ben Hecht, Ernest Hemingway, Carl Sandburg, Edgar Lee Masters, and Alfred Kreymborg. Towertown has vanished from the local gazetteer today, but a few ghosts linger on some of the blocks heading west to the current River North galleries quarter.

Fourth Presbyterian Church
map page 163, B-3
North of the Water Tower and F.A.O. Schwarz, on the west side of Michigan at Chestnut, is the Gothic Revival–style Fourth Presbyterian Church, built in 1914 for a blue-blooded congregation whose spiritual descendants attend today. At lunchtime or on Sunday afternoon, you may be fortunate enough to find a concert in progress.

Malls and Hotels
God keeps a foothold at the Presbyterian Church, but Mammon is firmly entrenched in the final two blocks before Michigan fades into Lake Shore Drive at Oak Street: Bloomingdale's anchors the upscale shopping in the 66-story 900 North Michigan Avenue tower, which also contains the highly rated Four Seasons Hotel; and One Magnificent Mile rises 58 stories at 940-980 North Michigan with Polo Ralph Lauren, Chanel, Giacomo, and their kin on three levels at the base. Around the corner, the block of Oak stretching west to Rush Street is a wall-to-wall browser bonanza of boutiques, galleries, and salons.

The Drake Hotel
map page 163, B-3
The Drake is a low-rise these days at 13 stories, but once, it was a grande dame among the city's luxury hotels.

919 North Michigan Avenue
The Drake's splendid Art Deco neighbor to the south across Walton Street is 919 North Michigan Avenue, a Holabird & Root skyscraper formerly known as the Playboy Building and before that as the Palmolive Building. It went up in 1930 just as the Great Depression brought a hiatus of almost two decades in major Chicago commercial construction.

The mast atop the building supported an aerial navigation beacon, which was a landmark of the night sky for decades but went dark in the 1970s—when twice-as-tall neighbors began to dwarf it. Condo cliff-dwellers in the upper stories of the Hancock Center the next block south complained that the powerful beam cast a blinding light into their apartments. It's bad enough waking up above the clouds, as Hancock inhabitants occasionally find themselves doing on low-ceiling mornings, without having your private life in the spotlight. On a clear day, the views from the center's 94th-floor observatory are, if anything, better than from the higher Sears Tower aerie a mile-and-a-half to the southwest.

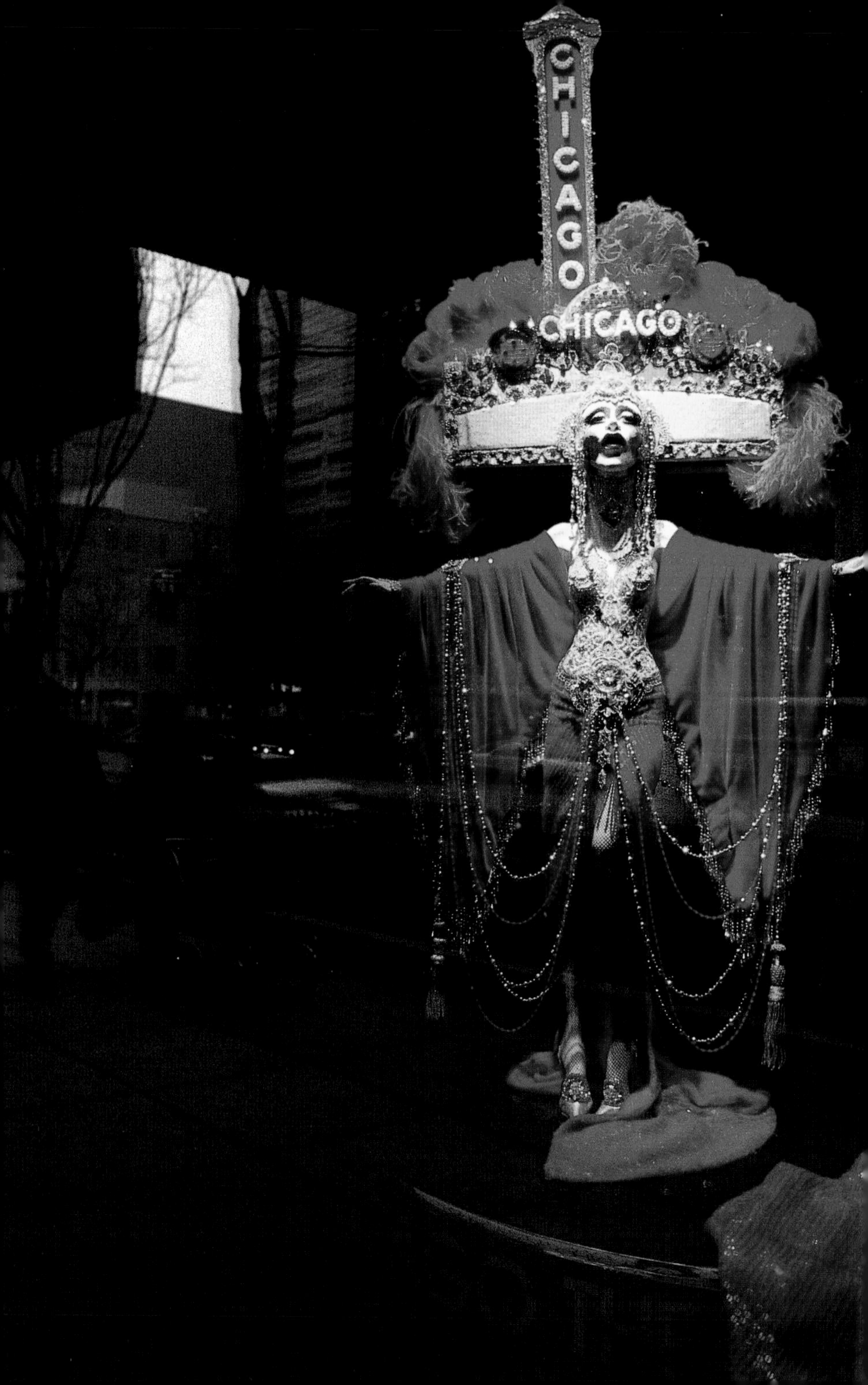
CHICAGO
CHICAGO

Interesting Shops Along (or Just Off) North Michigan Avenue

—by Michael Austin

State Street has the old department stores, the traditional architecture and the downtown feel of the Loop with screechy L cars circling above and subway cars rumbling below, but Michigan Avenue is the place to shop in Chicago. And while Grant Park and the lakefront is a beautiful sight along one stretch of Michigan Avenue, make sure you tell your cab driver that it's *North* Michigan Avenue you want — the Magnificent Mile of shops between the Chicago River and Oak Street Beach. High rents in this part of town keep clothing boutiques out (See Lincoln Park shopping), but if it's clothes you seek, almost every department store you can think of is here—From Marshall Field's to Bloomingdale's, Neiman Marcus to Nordstrom. Oak Street, which runs perpendicular to Michigan Avenue at its north end, is home to dozens of clothing boutiques but most of these stores adhere to the old chestnut: "If you have to ask how much it is you can't afford it." The rest of us mere mortals shop the boulevard — Michigan Avenue — which is splattered with stand-alone mega stores and vertical malls. Here follows a largely subjective selection of interesting retailers that are either unique to Chicago or of special interest to a Michigan Avenue area shopper. The following list begins with shops at the south end of the avenue, just past the river, and continues northward.

Hammacher Schlemmer
445 North Michigan Ave., 312-527-9100, M-Sa 10am-6pm, Su noon-5pm.
The reason this store is worth mentioning is because the New York-based catalogue dealer has only one other store in the country. These are not your average goods. How about a one-person electric car, a chair that looks like a giant baseball glove or a portable backyard ice rink? They also sell more practical items, such as fog-free shower mirrors, wind-defying umbrellas and wall-mounted clothes steamers.

Femme de Carriere
520 North Michigan Ave., 312-222-1008, M-Sa 10am-8pm, Su 11am-6pm.
This Canadian retailer, literally "Career Woman," has only two other stores on the East Coast and features what it calls "career wear with an edge." Mostly patronized by professional women looking for clothes that are stylish yet businessy, Carriere stocks only its own line of moderately priced clothes and occupies space in Michigan Avenue's newest "tall mall," The Shops at North Bridge, anchored by a Nordstrom department store.

Window displays along Michigan Avenue's Magnificent Mile, Chicago's premier shopping district.

Shabby Chic
46 East Superior St., 312-649-0080, M-Sa 10am-6pm, Su noon-5pm.
This is Rachel Ashwell's only store outside of California. Housed in an old walk-up that supposedly survived the Great Chicago Fire, the store is awash in white and gentle shades of pink and tan and features Ashwell's own line of custom slip covers for new and vintage furniture. There's also fabric by the yard in several plain, striped and floral patterns, vintage tabletop items, and gargantuan framed mirrors fit for Victorian mansions.

Joy of Ireland
700 North Michigan Ave., 312-664-7290, M-F 10am-7pm, Sa 10am-6pm,
Su 10:30am-5pm (Tea Room hours: M-Sa 11:30am-5pm.)
A gift store and tea room, with imported goods from Ireland, Scotland and Wales (but mostly Ireland), this boutique features authentic Irish caps and sweaters, Waterford crystal, Beleek, and Royal Tara china. There are also CDs, books, Irish newspapers and snacks, jewelry, pewter, hand-made pottery, and traditional tea service, with crustless sandwiches and pastries, in front of huge windows overlooking Michigan Avenue from the third floor.

Chiaroscuro
700 North Michigan Ave., 312-988-9253, M-F 10am-7pm, Sa 10am-6pm,
Su noon-5pm.
This store on the fourth floor of Chicago Place Mall is worth walking into just for the visual explosion of color you'll see in the tables, chairs, chessboards, cookie jars, hand-painted shower curtains, glassware, mirrors, clocks, and dozens of other items created by more than 200 artisans from around the country. Owner Ronna Isaacs has two rules when she buys new pieces: "Is it an interesting piece and is it price accessible?" she says. "That's it."

Museum of Contemporary Art Store
220 East Chicago Ave., 312-397-4000, T 10am-8pm, W-F 10am-6pm,
Sa-Su 10am-6pm. Closed Mondays.
The real draw here (but not the only one) is the collection of art books upstairs. The store stocks 3,500 titles on several art periods and genres all dating from 1945 to the present and claims to have the largest art book collection in the city. On street level, the store offers unique gift items such as Robert Indiana's iconic "Love" doormats, vases made from Slinky toys, Chilewich baskets and trays, mobiles, and jewelry.

Chicago Architecture Foundation Store

875 North Michigan Ave. (John Hancock Center), 312-751-1380,
M-Sa 10am-7pm, Su 10am-6pm.

Located in the sunken plaza of the black John Hancock skyscraper, this store has fewer books than does its sister store on South Michigan Avenue in the Santa Fe Building. However, it *does* have a fine selection of uniquely Chicago gifts, such as Frank Lloyd Wright–inspired Tiffany lamps, skyline photographs, and hand-made note cards. There are also bas relief architectural tiles, neckties, and jewelry. And should you need tickets for a walking or bus tour, you can purchase them here.

Children in Paradise Bookstore

909 North Rush St., 312-951-KIDS (5437), M-Th 10am-7pm,
F-Sa 10am-8pm, Su noon-5pm.

From board books for infants to classic nursery rhymes to timeless novels for adolescents and adults alike—such as *Jane Eyre* and *The Adventures of Tom Sawyer*—this store could keep your kids reading until they head off to college. There are also books for expecting mothers, as well as hand puppets, videos, and audio cassettes to entertain wee children. On Tuesday and Wednesday mornings at 10:30, the store hosts a story hour in the couch area.

Hear Music

932 North Rush St., 312-951-0242, Daily 10am-10pm.

The concept is simple: listen before you buy. It sounds implausible, but you can un-wrap any of the 10,000 new CDs in this store and listen to it for as long as you like. "It's like a music library," says manager Stephen Pearlman. "We want to introduce you to a lot of different styles of music. We carry everything." Prices are maybe a dollar higher than you would pay at a national record store chain, but peace of mind has got to be worth it.

Tender Buttons

946 North Rush St., 312-337-7033, M-F 10am-6pm, Sa 10am-5:30pm.
Closed Sundays.

This tiny boutique stocks thousands of new and antique buttons ranging in price from 75 cents to $225 each; almost all are imported from Europe. The store also sells antique carpenter's levels, silver spoons, Scottish agate brooches, and vintage belt buckles. The store's collections of buttons for blazers and of those made of mother-of-pearl are particularly large.

■ GOLD COAST   *map page 163, A/B-1&2*

Neighboring blocks are sometimes worlds apart in Chicago, and visitors can get a choice example of how swiftly the landscape shifts by making the brisk four-minute walk from Astor and Goethe (GO-THEE) to State and Division. Astor Street is elegant and architecturally distinctive enough to be the heart of a namesake historic district. One of the city's creme de la creme addresses since the 1880s, it is lined with mansions built by several generations of Chicago's major movers and shakers. Astor speaks in a cultivated and well-heeled whisper, modulated by the discreet crinkle of old money.

The language is loud, lubricious, and boozy on the action-packed block of Division Street from State west to Dearborn. For the last three decades, this has been Chicago's prime nocturnal meat market, a vortex of elbow-to-elbow singles bars where the pickup lines vary from year to year but the point of the boy-meets-girl exercise remains the same. If the history of such social traditions interests you, you'll need to stop for a kamikaze at Butch McGuire's, which opened in 1961 as the city's first full-fledged singles bar. This raucous block is at its best—or worst—during Chicago's annual St. Patrick's Day binge, when it helps if you can stomach green beer and battalions of drunks.

◆ ASTOR STREET   *map page 163, B-1&2*

Astor runs a half-mile down the Gold Coast from North Boulevard to East Division Street, where an invasion of nouveau-riche–looking apartment skyscrapers built since the 1970s has somewhat sapped the sylvan atmosphere along the shaded streets. A stroll up Astor makes for a soothing change of pace for shoppers who have overheated their charge cards in Michigan Avenue's highrise malls to the south. As for those singles bars, which hover near the Gold Coast's southern extremity, they can be approached in the spirit of the anthropologist. An urban archeologist might be better equipped to pick through the decline and fall of Rush Street, the once naughty, then dispirited, now revitalized nightlife strip that runs diagonally into State Street just south of the Gold Coast proper.

An evening view of Lake Shore Drive and the Gold Coast as seen from the Hancock Building. Oak Street Beach is visible in the foreground.

In addition to becoming a great patron of the French Impressionist painters, Mrs Bertha (Potter) Palmer also launched a cooking school for debutantes in her mansion, as she believed girls needed practical knowledge to properly manage a staff, or fill in should the cook quit. (Chicago Sun-Times)

Surviving Mansions

A rich chunk of Chicago heritage was lost when the old Palmer Castle (see essay, next page) fell to the wrecker's ball in 1951 to make way for a 22-story apartment tower. The neighborhood's surviving Gilded Age mansions include the three-story Venetian Gothic townhouse designed by Holabird and Roche at 1258 North Lake Shore; a Georgian Revival design by that firm at 1260 North Lake Shore; the vine-covered townhouse row built by Potter Palmer at 36-48 East Schiller; Burnham and Root's trio of sandstone and red-brick rowhouses at 1308-1312 North Astor; and the Romanesque Revival residence at 1443 North Astor.

James Charnley House
map page 163, B-2

Even more notable, though hardly typical of the era, is the James Charnley House (1365 North Astor), officially the work of Adler and Sullivan but almost certainly an 1892 creation of the young Frank Lloyd Wright, then a draftsman for that famous firm. There's hardly a hint of Wright's later Prairie School revolution in the blocky three-story townhome built around a skylighted central stairwell and garnished with a second-floor balcony.

THE POTTER PALMERS AND THEIR CASTLE

Real-estate and department-store magnate Potter Palmer and his wife, Bertha, began the Gold Coast land rush in 1882 by deserting the South Side to build their $1 million castellated residence at 1350 North Lake Shore Drive on the eastern outskirts of a neighborhood settled by German immigrants in the 1840s and Swedes in the 1860s. The Palmer castle, described by an architecture critic as "a mansion to end all mansions," spurred a quintupling of land values over the next decade on the Gold Coast (roughly bounded by the lake, North Avenue, La Salle Street, and Oak Street).

The Palmers' entryway set a tone of conspicuous opulence with its soaring octagonal space three stories high, hung with Gobelin tapestries, strewn with tiger skins and Oriental rugs, and set off with a massive fireplace. The mansion's most peculiar feature was an absence of outside doorknobs or keyholes on any of the doors, which had to be opened from the inside by a servant. Bertha Palmer became the undisputed queen of Chicago society, as well as a prime patron of the new-fangled and controversial French Impressionist art. She entertained labor leaders and social reformers along with industrialists and socialites. And, as Finis Farr recounted in his 1973 *Chicago* history, "in the cavernous kitchens of the mansion, Mrs. Palmer conducted a cooking school for society girls. Why should a rich girl learn to cook? There were several reasons, according to Bertha Palmer: For one thing, a young woman needed practical knowledge to direct a husband's household property.... But suppose the young couple should be so pushed for money they could afford only one servant. Then it would be a good thing if the bride could prepare meals, on that servant's twice-monthly day off."

A rich chunk of Chicago heritage was lost when the old Palmer place fell to the wrecker's ball in 1951 to make way for a 22-story apartment tower—but at least curious Chicagoans were allowed a chance to tour the erstwhile castle for 50 cents.

North State Parkway Luminaries

map page 163, B-1

The most luxurious Gold Coast apartment building of its day, and still a handsome structure, **1550 North State Parkway** originally boasted a single 15-room apartment on each of its 12 floors renting for $8,400 a year—in rock-solid 1912 dollars. Designed with a Beaux Arts facade by the distinguished Benjamin Marshall, it had five servant's chambers per apartment, as well as a grand salon and petit salon, an orangerie, two dressing rooms in the main bedroom "so that a valet can enter the gentleman's dressing room without passing through the bedchamber," and a range with three broilers "so that steaks and fish need never be prepared on the same broiler." Today's apartments at 1550 are smaller, and the three-broiler ranges have gone the way of the valet.

In a league of its own is the rambling residence of the **Roman Catholic Archbishop of Chicago,** just south of Lincoln Park at **1555 North State Parkway.** No fewer than 19 chimneys sprout from this Queen Anne pile set on spacious grounds; it is the oldest surviving structure in the Astor Street District, dating to 1880.

The sacred dwelling had a profane neighbor of some notoriety in the 1960s when Hugh Hefner and his nubile bunnies cavorted in the **Playboy Mansion, 1340 North State.** After Hefner took his Playboy philosophy to California, the School of the Art Institute bunked its students in the 1899-vintage Georgian residence for a number of years before it went back on the market.

At **1209 North State,** Art Moderne has its moment at the **Frank Fisher Apartments,** a brick design of 1936 by Andrew Rebori with terra-cotta detailing by artist Edgar Miller.

Oak Street Beach

map page 163, B/C-2

East beyond the eight lanes of Lake Shore Drive (the Outer Drive, in local parlance) stretches a thin strip of sand that is Chicago's most fashionable beach. On a sunny summer afternoon, Oak Street Beach resembles a giant casting call for one of those beer commercials where every body is lithe and youthful, beautifully bronzed, and perfectly proportioned. Volleyball, Frisbee-flipping, and other landlubber diversions are more popular than swimming and wading, because Lake Michigan water can be chilly even in August.

International Museum of Surgical Science

map page 163, B-1

Not for the extremely squeamish is the International Museum of Surgical Science, a 32-room survey course in medical history inside the headquarters mansion of the International College of Surgeons at 1524 North Lake Shore. From trepanning and blood-letting to kidney-stone crushing and pre-anesthesia amputations, the detailed exhibits serve as a graphic reminder of how physically painful life could be prior to the

James Charnley House on North Astor.

medical revolution of the past century. Museum artifacts include one of Florence Nightingale's white-lace nursing caps, the first stethoscope, an early iron lung, and a cast of the Emperor Napoleon's death mask. The equally handsome neighboring stone mansion to the north houses the consulate of Poland—an incongruously aristocratic setting for a former people's republic. *International Museum of Surgical Sciences, 1524 N. Lake Shore Dr.; 312-642-6502.*

Chess Pavilion
map page 163, B-1

A more cerebral shoreline alternative is the Chess Pavilion, just south of North Avenue, where the boards are set in concrete and you bring your own chess pieces. In January or February, when storm-driven waves have sculpted fantastic ice forms at water's edge, the beach provides a bracing outdoor art show for well-bundled walkers.

(above) Chess game at the Chess Pavilion on North Avenue Beach.

(opposite) The good times roll on a summer day at one of the Gold Coast's lakefront parks.

LINCOLN PARK
& NEAR NORTHWEST

■ HIGHLIGHTS

OLD TOWN &
LINCOLN PARK

■ OVERVIEW

The Lincoln Park district, Old Town, and the Near Northwest encompass the collection of neighborhoods north of North Avenue where German, Polish, and Ukrainian immigrants originally settled. The area includes the neighborhood along Lincoln Avenue, one of the best "new" (gentrifying since the 1970s) neighborhoods in the city. Chicagoans most popular playground is lakefront Lincoln Park, also in this area. Wells Street is dotted with cute shops and good restaurants north and south of North Avenue in Old Town. There is also great nightlife near Halsted, Lincoln, and Fullerton near De Paul University's urban campus. Another good shopping area may be found near the corner of Armitage and Sheffield in west Lincoln Park. Just north of Lincoln Park is Lakeview, home to the Chicago Cubs Wrigley Field. Further afield to the northwest are Chicago's extensive Polish and Ukranian neighborhoods along Milwaukee Avenue.

For lodging and restaurant listings see pages 238-272.

LINCOLN PARK &
NEAR NORTHWEST

■ OLD TOWN   *map page 187, B-5*

Although not the oldest, Old Town is indeed one of Chicago's most venerable communities. It was first settled around 1850 by German immigrants, many of whom became farmers who grew potatoes and cabbage in the fields north of North Avenue. A newspaper account of a parade down Sedgwick Street in 1879 reported festivities that included a costumed "Duke Ulrich" who reviewed the marchers while suspended from a clothes basket and was "kept alive by large potations of lager-beer which he drew up in a dinner pail with a string."

The neighborhood—originally called North Town—remained strongly German into the first decade of this century, when North Avenue was known as "the German Broadway." Then it saw an influx of Hungarians and Russian Jews in the World War I era, followed by other ethnic groups that eventually erased all but the patina of Germanic character, which can be savored today only in rare throwbacks like the Golden Ox restaurant (just west of Old Town proper at North and Clybourn). Gone from the neighborhood is the tradition of saloonkeeper aldermen, last and most famously exemplified by Mathias "Paddy" Bauler, who ran the 43rd Ward's Democratic affairs for close to a half-century until the 1970s from his saloon at North Avenue and Sedgwick Street. "Chicago ain't ready for reform," was Bauler's most famous observation, and he also liked to tell reporters, "I'll talk about anything, as long as the statute of limitations has run out."

The vicissitudes of the Great Depression left many of Old Town's 19th-century wooden houses showing serious wear and tear by 1948. In that year a civic-spirited group of residents formed the Old Town Triangle Association, which ever since has played a key role in reinvigorating the community. During City Council hearings that led to the Old Town Triangle area's designation as a landmark district in 1976, the pastor of St. Michael's parish testified that "the real strength of Chicago lies not in the Sears Towers, or the Hancock Centers, but in the neighborhoods such as this one. Chicago, to be humanly alive, must sustain little homes inhabited by the common man." In fact, Old Town property values have skyrocketed, driving out most low- and middle-income families.

◆ OLD TOWN TRIANGLE DISTRICT SIGHTS

The Old Town Triangle refers to a loosely defined area running between North Lincoln Avenue and North Clark Street as the triangle's hypotenuse to the east, running into N. Larrabee Street on the west of the triangle and with North Avenue on the south forming the base of the triangle. Some streets in the Old Town Triangle District run for only a block or two, cut off to discourage through traffic, but almost all deserve at least a bit of meandering preferably on foot. Also be aware that various published maps refer to North Lincoln Park West Street as *North* North Park Avenue or Lincoln Park West Street.

St. Michael's Church
map page 187, B-6

As rich in history as any Chicago church, St. Michael's has been the heart and soul of the neighborhood since German Catholics built their first house of worship at North and Hudson in 1852 for a mere $730. The second St. Michael's, completed in 1869 in red brick with a 200-foot tower, was gutted by the Chicago Fire. But its double brick walls formed the core of the grander present church, which boasts a monumental altar of carved wood capped by a figure of the patron saint with sword and jeweled crown. It is said that you are within the boundaries of Old Town if you can hear the pealing of St. Michael's' five bells.

Midwest Buddhist Temple
map page 187, B-5

The church's nearest religious neighbor, within eye-shot a block to the north, is the Midwest Buddhist Temple. A testament to Old Town's ethnic diversity, the temple was built in 1972 with a shingled gable roof that echoes traditional Japanese designs; the centerpiece of its shrine is a small, standing gold Buddha.

The temple devotes one weekend each summer to a lively Ginza Festival open to the public. It's the only vestige of Old Town's former Little Tokyo, which was dispersed (mainly to the suburbs) in the 1960s and '70s by the construction of the Sandburg Village residential complex to the south of North Avenue.

Meyer Farmhouse
map page 187, B-5

Two blocks west of the Japanese temple stands the 1874 Meyer farmhouse, on a block of Lincoln Park West that is a virtual museum of vintage residences erected when the neighborhood rebuilt itself in the 1870s and '80s. Henry Meyer is long gone, along with the cows and chickens he kept. But the frame farmhouse he built in 1874 on what was then a meadow still stands as a private residence at 1802 North Lincoln Park West, not much more than two miles north of the Loop. Enlivened by the artfully carved wooden trim that typifies the neighborhood's stock of homes built immediately after the Chicago Fire of 1871, this is one among myriad surprises to reward the visitor who pokes up and down the shaded streets and cul de sacs of Old Town. *1802 North Lincoln Park West.*

LINCOLN PARK
AND OLD TOWN

A · B · C · D

1 2 3 4 5 6

Roscoe St — Roscoe St
Buckingham Pl
Aldine Ave
Melrose St
Belmont Ave
Briar Pl — Briar Pl
LAKEVIEW
Barry Ave — Barry Ave
W Wellington — Wellington Ave
Oakdale — Oakdale Ave
George — Surf St
Wolfram
W Diversey Ave

Belmont Harbor

Lake Shore Drive West

Lincoln Park

41

W Lill Ave — Schubert Ave
Wrightwood Ave
LINCOLN PARK
Freemont — Wrightwood Ave — Deming Pl — Deming
W Lill — Lill St — Deming Pl — St James
Altgeld St — W Roslyn
Biograph Theater
W Fullerton — Arlington Pl
W Belden — 440 W Belden

Frances J Dewes House
Wrigley Mansion
2400 N Lakeview Ave

North Pond

Diversey Harbor

John Cannon Dr

Stockton Dr

Peggy Notebaert Nature Museum

Lincoln Park Conservatory

Lincoln Park Zoo

Lake Shore Drive

South Lagoon

To DePaul University
W Webster
Oz Park
W Dickens
W Armitage

Chicago Academy of Sciences
South Pond

W Wisconsin
OLD TOWN TRIANGLE
W Menomonee — 1838 1826 1802 St
Midwest Buddhist Temple
W Eugenie — Willow St
Steppenwolf Theater
St Michaels Church
Twin Anchors — Second City
Lincoln Statue

Lincoln Park

North Ave Beach

Chicago Historical Society
Home of Roman Catholic Archbishop of Chicago

N LaSalle Dr

W North
64
W Blackhawk
Old Town Ale House
E North
Ave
Burton

Chess Pavilion
International Museum of Surgical Science

GOLD COAST
41
Schiller St
James Charnley House
Banks St

North Branch Canal
N Clybourn

W Schiller St

L a k e   M i c h i g a n

1826-1834 North Lincoln Park West

map page 187, B-5

The most distinguished provenance belongs to the five two-story brick rowhouses at 1826-1834 North Lincoln Park West, designed in a simplified Queen Anne motif in 1884-85 by the great architect Louis Sullivan. Few such examples of the Chicago School master's early work survive anywhere, and these townhouses bear the imprint of his hand in their intricate terracotta ornamentation.

1838 North Lincoln Park West

map page 187, B-5

Brewer Frederick Wacker, a leader of the German community, employed a Swiss architect in 1874 for the brick-and-clapboard home with the faintly Alpine air at 1838 North Lincoln Park West. Its carved gingerbread trim is a premier Old Town Triangle example of that art form. The smaller neighbor at 1836 North Lincoln Park West was originally the Wacker coach house at the back of the lot. In the 1880s it was moved forward and remodeled as a mother-in-law house (a small semi-detached cottage) by Charles Wacker, later the first chairman of the Chicago Plan Commission.

Crilly Court

map page 187, C-5

Leafy St. Paul Street stretches for a single block, as does Concord Place, while Fern Court manages about a block and a half. Intersecting St. Paul at mid-block is one of the city's most distinctive enclaves, Crilly Court, which could pass for a tranquil side street in London's West End. It was developed in 1885 by contractor Daniel F. Crilly

with two-story rowhouses on the west side of the court and a four-story apartment building on the east. The names carved above the entrances to the apartments are those of Crilly's children: Edgar, Erminnie, Oliver, and Isabelle. One early tenant was Eugene Field, a children's poet and pioneering newspaper columnist. Crilly Court and its immediate neighbors were early beneficiaries of the post-World War II rehabilitation drive that helped make Old Town Triangle a coveted address. These buildings are now condominiums.

Sedgwick Street Spots

map page 187, B-5/6

Sustenance for weary walkers is available at two time-tested Sedgwick Street spots that well predate Old Town's gentrification.

Marge's, at the corner of Sedgwick and Menomonee, traces its roots to a saloon opened more than a century ago. It prospers today as an admirably old-fashioned tavern, even if the neighborhood yuppies are sometimes a bit thick on the ground. A block south at Sedgwick and Eugenie, **Twin Anchors** has drawn a steady stream of customers since 1932 for its barbecued baby back ribs; Frank Sinatra was a finger-licking fan. Another congenial place that defies trends and fashion is the no-frills **Old Town Ale House**. *219 West North Ave.*

Second City

map page 187, C-6

The ale house's famous neighbor is that fountainhead of contemporary comedy, Second City. Ever since Mike Nichols and others set up satirical shop in 1959, Second City's distinctive brand of ensemble and

Armitage Street near Halsted in Old Town.

improvisational humor has thoroughly re-shaped American notions of what's worth a laugh. Its famous alumni include Alan Arkin, John Belushi, Bill Murray, John Candy, Mike Myers, Christopher Guest, and Joan Rivers. Even after four-plus decades, Second City revues manage to be fresh more often than stale, and weekend shows in the 290-seat main room can be a tough ticket. A reverent nod is appropriate as you enter the Second City building at 1616 North Wells: the richly detailed orna-ment on its facade is an architectural trea-sure rescued from the much-mourned Garrick Theater when that Adler and Sulli-van landmark was demolished in 1961 to make way for a Loop parking garage.

Wells Street   *map page 187, C-6*

This area went through a meteoric flame-out in the 1960s and early 1970s as a counter-culture ghetto synonymous with "Old Town." The two blocks from North Avenue south to Schiller Street blossomed into a smaller, tamer version of San Fran-cisco's Haight-Ashbury. Wells today is just another commercial strip of shops, restau-rants, and a couple of music clubs. Its longest-lived retailer, House of Glunz, has been selling fine wines for more than a cen-tury at Wells and Division. The aura of the neighborhood's German heyday lingers here amid the stained-glass windows, an-tique bottles, and murals depicting wine-making. A visit makes an evocative final stop to cap an Old Town exploration.

■ LINCOLN PARK   *map page 187, C/D - 1-6*

Lincoln Park's wealth of recreational allures provides for millions of Chicagoans and out-of-towners each year. Its beaches, harbors, ponds, picnic groves, bike paths, and sports fields are scattered along the full five-and-a-half-mile length of the city's largest park, while its southern expanse is home to the perennially popular Lincoln Park Zoo, as well as

Lincoln Park's North Avenue Beach is one of Chicago's many waterfront parks where the city's residents can find relief from the pressures of urban life. Daniel Burnham, who first proposed the Chicago Plan of 1909 to preserve the lakeshore line for the public, wrote: "The lakefront by right belongs to the people. It is a living thing, delighting man's eye and refreshing his spirit."

Lincoln Park Conservatory and the museums of the Chicago Historical Society and Chicago Academy of Sciences. A favorite spring-to-fall pastime on Lincoln Park's grassy diamonds is 16-inch softball, a sport virtually unique to Chicago that is played barehanded with a great deal of gusto.

The park itself forms the eastern edge of the lively Lincoln Park neighborhood, where an evening parking spot can be as precious as a cool drink in the desert. Restaurants, theaters, music clubs, and shops abound along the bustling corridors of Lincoln Avenue, Halsted Street, and other thoroughfares between the community's north and south boundaries around Diversey Parkway and North Avenue. Amid the clamor, gracious blocks of older homes supply welcome oases of tranquility, while the DePaul University campus adds a reflective air. Like its Old Town neighbor to the south, Lincoln Park is an expensive address these days after three decades of urban renewal and gentrification.

(opposite) Simone de Beauvoir, upon seeing the manicured parks of Chicago's waterfront on a warm summer day once declared, "It was the luxury of the Côte d'Azur." (University of Chicago Archives)

◆ SEEING LINCOLN PARK

Lincoln Park Zoo

map page 187, C-4

Some things in life remain free even in this pricey part of Chicago—including the family-thronged North Avenue beach and Lincoln Park Zoo, one of the few major zoos anywhere that charge no admission fee. A gift of two swans from New York's Central Park in 1868 started the zoo's collection, which now totals around 2,000 beasts and birds arrayed on a compact 35-acre site that reflects the state of the zoo-keeping art. A particular pride is the Great Ape House, where visitors can go nose-to-nose (through thick plate glass) with playful gorilla youngsters from the world's finest captive ensemble of that endangered distant genetic cousin to the human race. Less exotic creatures from the barnyard are a revelation to big-city kids at the Farm-in-the- Zoo south of the main facility.

Birdwatchers can tune up their water-fowl skills at the zoo's recently refurbished **Rookery,** where ducks, geese, and other species come and go freely amid the rock garden.

South Pond

map page 187, C-4&5

Renting a paddleboat on the South Pond adjoining the farm makes for a pleasant sunny-day putter. Northwest of the pond is the replica of a 10th-century Viking long-boat that was sailed from Norway for the 1893 World's Columbian Exposition.

Paddleboats and kayaks can often be seen skimming across the Lincoln Park Lagoon.

Lincoln Park Conservatory is best visited during February and March for its azaleas, April for its lilies, November for its chrysanthemums, and December for its poinsettias.

On the pond's western shore, the landmark architecture is much more appealing than the forgettable fast food at Cafe Brauer, a 1908 Prairie School gem designed by Dwight Perkins that sat idle and rotting for a half-century until a concerted civic effort restored it to beauty and service a few years ago. The Great Hall upstairs is magnificently adorned with tile murals, stained glass, and bronze chandeliers.

Lincoln Park Conservatory
map page 187, C-4
Nearby, Lincoln Park Conservatory is at its most inviting during four annual shows: azaleas in February and March, lilies and other spring plants in April, chrysanthemums in November, and poinsettias over the Christmas holidays.

Chicago Historical Society Museum
map page 187, C-6
Dating back to the 1850s, this once rather musty museum has shaken off its torpor and put a lively step in many of its exhibits. It houses an extensive collection of Lincoln memorabilia and artifacts. The former President was an honorary member of the society. *1601 North Clark St. at North Ave.; 312-642-4600.*

Peggy Notebaert Nature Museum
map page 187, C-5
The Chicago Academy of Sciences opened this nature museum in 1999. Designed to embrace the natural landscape of Lincoln Park, the open, airy space includes a Butterfly Haven and seven acres of outdoor exhibits. *435 East Illinois St.; 773-775-5100.*

LINCOLN PARK &
NEAR NORTHWEST

Statue of Ulysses S. Grant

The equestrian statue along the park's Cannon Drive might feel more at home if it could gallop the three miles south to Grant Park, which surprisingly lacks a sculpture of the Civil War commander and U.S. President whose name it bears.

Statue of Abraham Lincoln

map page 187, C-5

A splendid bronze by Augustus St. Gaudens, it stands on the east side of the Chicago Historical Society.

Last Resting Places

Ira Couch: Yes, that *is* a mausoleum at the south end of Lincoln Park, tucked in a grove of trees behind the Chicago Historical Society not far from the splendid bronze statue of Abraham Lincoln by Augustus St. Gaudens. The solitary tomb, near the southwest corner of the city's largest park, shelters the remains of pioneer Chicago hotelkeeper Ira Couch. His determined family went to court to keep the gravesite undisturbed when the rest of the sprawling municipal cemetery was cleared in the years after 1868 to make way for this major link in a proposed urban greenbelt of parks and boulevards.

David Kennison: Only one other burial is known to remain in Lincoln Park. Its site farther north near the Farm-in-the-Zoo is marked with a boulder to commemorate the remarkable life of David Kennison. The last living participant in the Boston Tea Party, Kennison died in 1852—at age 115, by his sometimes disputed account. All the other loved ones resting here suffered the fate described by traveler Sara Jane Lippincott, who praised the park in 1873 as "already very beautiful, with a variety of surface and ornamentation most wonderful," but noted that its entrance "is a little depressing, being through a cemetery, for those old settlers are fast being resettled and reestablished elsewhere. Even the dead must 'move on' in Chicago."

◆ RESIDENTIAL LINCOLN PARK

The western fringes of the park are the venue for beguiling residential blocks lined with homes that date back as far as the 19th century's Gilded Age.

2121 North Hudson

One of the oldest, this charming frame cottage has decorative shingles and raised basement. "This is Policeman Bellinger's Cottage, saved by heroic efforts from the Chicago Fire of October 1871," announces a plaque on the building—which was designed by W. W. Boyington, also the architect for the most famous survivor of that conflagration—the Old Chicago Water Tower.

SPECIALTY SHOPS IN THE LINCOLN PARK AREA

—by Michael Austin

The best shopping in Lincoln Park is centered around the intersection of Armitage and Sheffield, which also has an L stop on the Ravenswood Brown Line and is a short cab ride from almost any downtown hotel. Because it is a fashionable neighborhood, it has plenty of upscale boutiques, catering mostly to women. It is also home to DePaul University but the majority of its students can't afford to live there unless they're in campus housing. Still, it is a bargain compared to Michigan Avenue or (gasp!) Oak Street.

Jane Hamill
1115 West Armitage Ave. (a block west of Armitage/Sheffield intersection); 773-665-1102, M-F 11am-7pm, Th 11am-8pm, Sa 10:30am-6pm, Su noon-5pm.

Chicago designer Jane Hamill offers her own contemporary styles (with a hint of retro thrown into the mix) in bright colors and a variety of fabrics. And she stocks a wide range of sizes — not just racks upon racks of sixes. Hamill also finds hanger space in her boutique for a few other like-minded designers' lines, and sells vintage-looking jewelry.

Expressly Wood
825 West Armitage Ave.; 773-477-7050, M-Th 11am-7pm, F 11am-6pm, Sa 10am-6pm, Su noon-5pm.

This bright, airy corner store boasts one of the largest selections of jewelry boxes in the city, drawing from more than 200 artists and ranging from traditional to whimsical. The niche store also offers a large selection of wooden frames, clocks, and desk accessories, plus a kids section with wooden trains, bookends, puzzles, and games.

Lori's
824 West Armitage Ave.; 773-281-5655, M-Th 11am-7pm, F 11am-6pm, Sa 10am-6pm, Su noon-5pm.

This is ground zero for women's shoe buying in Chicago. The place that is short on atmosphere and long on inventory offers discounted designer shoes ($40–150) from Franco Sarto, Fruit, Kenneth Cole, janet & janet, Charles David and several others makers. "Ask any woman in the city about Lori's and they know what you're talking about," says saleswoman Lorraine Van Houten.

Cynthia Rowley

808 West Armitage Ave.; 773-528-6160, M-F 11am-7pm, Sa 10am-6pm, Su noon-5pm.

Maybe it's because Cynthia Rowley grew up in the Chicago area, but this store is the New York designers largest. Rowley's upscale yet playful designs display nicely in this funky boutique, which also sells Rowley-designed dinnerware and has a short rack of men's fashions. Clothing starts at around $150, but can soar, in at least one case, up to $1,000 for a leather dress.

Art Effect

651 West Armitage Ave.; 312-664-0997, M-Th 11am-7pm, F 11am-6pm, Sa 10am-6pm, Su noon-5pm.

This store is noteworthy for its eclectic mix of housewares, gifts, clothing, accessories, cosmetics, and fragrances. Here, you can find martini shakers, coffee table books, silver candelabra, leather wallets, aromatic candles, globes, wall clocks, picture frames and of course, miniature plastic reproductions of sushi pieces.

Gepperth's Meat Market

1964 North Halsted St.; 773-549-3883, M-F 9:30am-6pm, Sa 8:30am-4:30pm. Closed Sundays.

A traditional meat market that is as clean as a hospital operating room, this family-owned spot has a take-out freezer containing prepared foods such as German saurbraten and brazed lamb shanks. They also sell dried venison snack meats (think: jerky) and packaged goods, including jarred shallots and ginger, sun-dried tomato mustard, white truffle oil and Danish chocolates.

B. Leader & Sons

2042 North Halsted St.; 773-549-2224, T-F 10am-5:30pm, Sa 10am-5pm. Closed Mondays.

This family-owned jewelry manufacturer and retail store was established in 1909 and still uses some of the original jewelry-making equipment. More noteworthy, though, is the store's extensive inventory of watches, including Hermes, Maurice Lacroix, Festina, Swiss Army and Tissot. "Jewelry can be very intimidating," says third-generation owner Michael Leader, whose son also works in the store. "This is not a fancy joint."

Bennett Wines
2050 North Halsted St.; 773-404-4944, T-F 3-8pm, Sa noon-7pm, Su 1-6pm.
Closed Mondays.
Proprietor Liesel Bennett tastes every wine before it goes on display in her tidy wine boutique, which offers a limited selection (30-50 labels) of quality European bottlings at discount prices ($6-$20). "I don't carry any junk of any kind," she says. "I buy well. I buy early and I buy a lot at a time. I've never in 15 years had one person complain about a wine I've sold them."

NOTE: Although Bennett Wines *(above)* and Aroma Workshop *(below)* share the same street address, they have separate street entrances on Halsted.

Aroma Workshop
2050 North Halsted St.; 773-871-1985, M-Th noon-8pm, F 11am-7pm,
Sa 10am-6pm, Su 11am-5pm.
You go to this place for several reasons, but most of them have to do with either your nose or your state of mind. This tiny shop deals in essential, aromatherapy, and perfume oils, which are the basis for all scentible bodycare, "wellness" and fragrance products. There is a New Age feel to the store, but it can also be a place where you help create your own personal perfume or cologne and then bottle it or get it infused into soap, candles, lotions, or massage oils. And they'll keep your recipe in their Rolodex for your next visit.

Saturday's Child
2146 North Halsted St.; 773-525-TOYS (8697), M-Sa 10am-6pm
(Th until 7pm), Su 11am-5pm.
This is an old-time toy store with a creaky wooden floor and a high pressed tin ceiling. The store is known for its children's book selection and infant toys. All the classics are here: dolls, wooden toys, butterfly nets, puzzles, models, masks, dress-up clothes, hand puppets—anything that promotes creativity in kids. The sales clerks will also gladly gift wrap your purchases.

Cleveland Avenue Townhouses
The three blocks of Cleveland Avenue from Dickens north to Fullerton boast an eclectic mix of handsomely restored townhouses, ranging from an Art Deco facade with a two-story leaded-glass window (No. 2150) and an 1874 Italianate duplex with white Corinthian entrance columns (No. 2234-36), to a Gothic brick jumble with a Georgian Revival porch (No. 2314) and an 1880 dowager with a square bay window and roof turret (No. 2325).

440 West Belden   *map page 187, B-4*
Just east of Cleveland, this decorative Queen Anne design reflects the formative period of Louis Sullivan, who was 27 in 1883 when he executed this first known residential commission for the firm that would become Adler and Sullivan.

2400 North Lakeview   *map page 187, B-3*
The sleek glass-and-aluminum highrise a block north and east overlooking the park, stands as a counterpoint to the earlier designs of the neighborhood. It is the last apartment building designed in Chicago by Modernist Ludwig Mies van der Rohe.

(above) Sailing on Lake Michigan.

*(opposite) The exquisitely embossed door of
The John Barleycorn Memorial Pub at 658 West Belden Avenue.*

◆ ARLINGTON AND ROSLYN PARK DISTRICT

Two shaded blocks of late-19th-century townhouses form the tiny Arlington and Roslyn Park District as designated by the Chicago Landmarks Commission.

The Wrigley Mansion *map page 187, B-3*
The mansion is richly ornamented with terra-cotta, copper, and iron trim. Designed in 1897 by Richard E. Schmidt, it was bought in 1911 by chewing-gum maestro William Wrigley. *Corner of Arlington Place and Lakeview.*

466-468 Deming Place *map page 187, B-3*
Another tree-lined refuge from the clamor of Clark Street shopping. These twin townhouses offer visual enticements with their huge bay windows and intriguing brickwork patterns.

Francis J. Dewes House
map page 187, B-3
One of the most astounding facades in the city fronts the Francis J. Dewes House, erected in 1896 for a German brewer. The Baroque Revival mansion's entrance is flanked by a pair of huge Greek caryatids (actually, one is male) who support a wrought-iron balcony with classical columns and an elaborately decorated frame. *503 West Wrightwood.*

◆ LINCOLN AVENUE *map page 187, A-C – 3-5*

Lincoln Avenue, which darts diagonally northwest through the neighborhood along an 18th-century Native American trail, provides a time-tested mix of culture and entertainment.

The Biograph Theater
map page 187, A-3
Famed as the spot where the FBI and Chicago police gunned down the bank robber John Dillinger when he came out of a movie on July 22, 1934, now regrettably carved into a multiplex like so many vintage cinemas. *2433 Lincoln Ave.*

John Barleycorn Memorial Pub
This pub disdains the giant-screen TVs of sports bars in favor of projecting slides that show masterpieces of painting and sculpture. *Lincoln Ave. and Belden.*

Victory Gardens
A pioneer in the city's off-Loop theater renaissance with a 195-seat main stage and a 60-seat studio. *2257 North Lincoln Ave.*

Red Lion
The long-established Red Lion recreates the warm, welcoming atmosphere of a British pub (yes, you can get chips with vinegar). *2446 Lincoln Ave.*

Uncle Dan's
A treasure trove of army-navy surplus gear. Tempting seasonal sales. *2440 Lincoln Ave.*

LINCOLN PARK &
NEAR NORTHWEST

Famed bank robber John Dillinger was gunned down by law enforcement officials as he exited the Biograph Theater in July 1934.

◆ HALSTED STREET   *map page 187, A – 1-6*

This street, which intersects Lincoln at Fullerton, is a dining and entertainment stalwart that blossomed in a 1980s burst of development. Anchoring this strip's south end are two stylish new theater complexes. The much-acclaimed **Steppenwolf** theater troupe has settled into a custom-designed complex with a 500-seat mainstage *(1650 North Halsted)*. **The Royal George Theater Center** hosts a number of companies on its two stages, complemented by a cabaret, piano bar, restaurant, and wine cellar *(1633 North Halsted)*. Charlie Trotter's, a recent darling of restaurant critics is an inventive place where diners can expect the unexpected *(816 West Armitage, just west of Halsted)*.

The Old Town School of Folk Music carries on as a steadfast Chicago treasure that gives lessons, workshops, sing-alongs, and concerts *(909 West Armitage)*. Back on Halsted, the blues talent is dependably big-league at B.L.U.E.S. and **Kingston Mines** *(2519 and 2548 Halsted, respectively)*. See pages 81-87 for more on blues clubs.

DILLINGER'S NEMESIS

It happened on a day when Chicago's temperature hit 102 degrees, and it was the city's hottest news of 1934. It drew swarms of morbidly curious onlookers to the Biograph Theater, where the shooting had taken place, and to the Cook County morgue, where the famous corpse reposed. The date was July 22, 1934, and the dead desperado was 31-year-old bank robber John Dillinger, the FBI's most-wanted fugitive and "the greatest folk hero of American crime," in the opinion of anthologist Albert Halper.

Dillinger built his tabloid fame in little more than a year during the depths of the Great Depression by planning and executing a succession of bold bank robberies and prison escapes. At the jail in Crown Point, Indiana, on March 3, 1934, he used a razor to carve a fake pistol from a piece of wood, blackened it with shoe polish, and forced his way past a dozen guards while singing, "I'm heading for the last roundup."

He was essentially a loner from a rural Indiana background. As Halper wrote, "Such a lone wolf was destined for betrayal, and a seemingly sympathetic woman in whose house he was hiding out double-crossed him by turning informer." She was a brothel madam named Anna Sage who hoped to avoid deportation to Romania as an undesirable alien by cooperating with the FBI and police. Having tipped off authorities the evening of July 22, she went with Dillinger to the Biograph, 2433 North Lincoln Avenue. Her skirt was orange, but it looked red under the marquee lights, fixing her in history as "The Lady in Red."

FBI agents and police surrounded the Biograph while Dillinger and his betrayer watched Clark Gable go to the electric chair in "Manhattan Melodrama." Emerging from the theater in a straw hat and glasses, he was ordered to halt. Instead, he reached into his right pants pocket for his Colt automatic and dashed in a partial crouch toward the alley next to the Biograph. One FBI shot tore into his left side, while another drilled through his stooped back and out his right eye. Dead on the spot, he was later buried near Indianapolis. A fable persists that some other man was shot by the FBI outside the Biograph, and that Dillinger disappeared with the aid of accomplices. If so, he may well still linger with the likes of Elvis Presley in that twilight land of the celebrated undead.

*(opposite) Arch-gangster John Dillinger posing for the camera with a machine gun
and wooden pistol at a family reunion three months before his death in 1934.
(courtesy* The Times *newspaper, Munster, Indiana)*

◆ OZ PARK   *map page 187, A/B-4*

This neighborhood got a much-needed infusion of green space in the 1970s with the creation of two-square-block Oz Park, bordering on the east side of Halsted between Dickens and Webster; its name salutes the fact that Wizard of Oz creator Frank Baum once lived nearby.

◆ SHEFFIELD HISTORIC DISTRICT   *map page 187, A-4*

West of Halsted and south of Fullerton, the Sheffield Historic District encompasses most of the DePaul University campus in another sylvan enclave where sturdy but decrepit old housing has been renovated and real-estate prices have soared.

◆ MCCORMICK ROW HOUSE DISTRICT   *map page 9, C-2*

Especially worth seeking out is McCormick Row House District, tucked into the DePaul campus just south of Fullerton and east of the rapid-transit tracks. The provenance of the privately owned three-story brick row houses, which front on Chalmers Place, dates to the 1880s, when McCormick Theological Seminary decided to augment its income by building and renting out houses. In the original plans, the house at the end of each row was a professor's home. The seminary vacated the DePaul area in the 1970s, but its row-house legacy still sounds a grace note of quiet gentility just steps from the push and shove of Lincoln Park's busy streets.

■ NORTH SIDE MOSAIC   *map page 9, B-1*

The signs still say "Andersonville," and the Swedish presence lingers in the 5200 block of North Clark Street amid this once strongly Scandinavian neighborhood on Chicago's North Side. Survivors include two delicatessens—Wikstrom's and Erickson's *(5247 and 5250 North Clark, respectively)*, where Swedish can still be heard across the counter; Ann Sather's restaurant, at No. 5207, one of the few places in Chicago where you can buy a Ringnes beer from Norway or a Nordic Wolf from Sweden *(5207 North Clark)*; and the **Swedish-American Museum Center** selling an array of handcrafted items *(map page 9, C-1; 5211 North Clark; 773-728-8111)*.

Nonetheless, these Swedish spots do share the commercial strip these days with such distinctly non-Scandinavian establishments as the Byblos I bakery-deli *(5212*

North Clark; 773-271-1005) and Reza's Persian restaurant. Although the Scandinavian and Middle Eastern cultures seem like truly odd bedfellows, they mix without evident incongruity on Clark Street. At Kopi, A Traveler's Cafe, you'll find coffee and snacks from all over the globe, as well as brochures and books on international travel destinations *(5317 North Clark; 773-989-5674).*

It's like this elsewhere around the North Side, where the city's human mosaic continues to shift away from European-Americans and toward new immigrant waves from the Middle East and southern and eastern Asia. Although it may be unsettling at times for the communities involved, this new melting-pot mix makes for fascinating hopscotch exploration (by car or public transit) from Wrigley Field north to Devon Avenue and beyond. Several enclaves of vintage architecture add extra spice to the excursion.

Wrigley Field
map page 9, C-2
Home of the Chicago Cubs, it deserves a visit during the April-September baseball season even from non-fans. It is the quintessential old-fashioned ballpark, with seating right on top of the action (but watch out for vision- obstructing posts), real grass, and outfield walls draped in ivy that occasionally snares an extra-base hit. For years, Wrigley was the only major-league park without lights, but the imperative of television ratings brought night games to the field in the late '80s. Scalpers outside the park are sometimes the only source of seats for weekend games, or you can try knocking on the doors of the three-flat apartment buildings that ring the outfield on Waveland and Sheffield, then asking politely if you might join the long-distance bleacherites on the roof. Rapid transit will deliver you directly to the ballpark from the Loop; if you drive, parking may cost as much as your box seat. *773-404-CUBS.*

Alta Vista Terrace
Tucked a block north of Wrigley Field in the Wrigleyville community is enchanting Alta Vista Terrace, an ensemble of rowhouses in varying styles that looks like a transplant from an idyllic backwater of Boston or London. Built in 1904-05, they form a tiny landmark district that abuts on Graceland Cemetery to the north.

Graceland Cemetery
map page 9, C-1
Graceland is to Chicago what Père Lachaise is to Paris: a burial ground of the rich and famous strewn with an incredible assemblage of funerary monuments. Graceland's premier attraction for grave-gazers is the Getty Tomb, designed in 1890 by Louis Sullivan with exquisitely lacy ornamentation on the upper half of the limestone mausoleum and its bronze gates. The nicely named Nuts on Clark emporium across from Graceland's southern tip stocks a cornucopia of nutmeats and candies.

(following pages) Immigrants, and Chicagoans to the core.

Maher Houses on Hutchinson Street

map page 9, C-1

Due east of Graceland, the two landmark-district blocks of Hutchinson Street between Marine Drive and Hazel Street feature five houses designed by George W. Maher, a colleague of Frank Lloyd Wright. Prairie School motifs are prominent among the more than two dozen notable residences constructed between 1894 and 1919, but there are also Queen Anne and Romanesque Revival beauties. The two-story 1902 Maher commission at 750 West Hutchinson exemplifies his Farson House style, with its low double-hip roof and stone-framed entryway.

A mile southeast at the lakefront, the **Hawthorne Place landmark district** in the Lake View neighborhood preserves a cluster of Victorian-era homes, including an Adler and Sullivan design built for insurance magnate George Harvey in 1888 at 600 West Stratford Place.

Totem Pole

Overlooking Lake Shore Drive's eight lanes opposite Addison Street stands a magnificent totem pole that is actually a replica of a century-old artifact carved by the coastal Kwakiutl Indians of British Columbia. The pole—which portrays the motifs of a sea monster, an upside-down whale with a man on its back, and a thunderbird—was bought in the 1920s by cheesemaker James L. Kraft and given to the Chicago Park District. At the urging of Native Americans from the Pacific Northwest, the original was returned to Canada and replaced by this copy in 1986.

Waveland Golf Course

North of the totem stretches the nine-hole Waveland Golf Course, with lake views only somewhat less spectacular than the ocean vistas of California's Pebble Beach, and a fieldhouse carillon lovingly restored by volunteers. A few blocks inland from the park, north-south Broadway is a main commercial axis of the city's vibrant gay and lesbian community.

◆ UPTOWN

North of Graceland Cemetery, the Uptown neighborhood has been down on its luck for decades but is showing some recent signs of rebounding. Home to the city's largest concentration of Native Americans, Uptown also boasts a bustling Little Saigon commercial strip along Argyle Street, around 5000 North just west of Lake Shore Drive.

Along with a shoulder-to-shoulder lineup of restaurants and shops run by Vietnamese and an earlier core of Chinese, the community is the site of a **Vietnam Museum** recalling that long and melancholy war *(map page 9, C-1; 954 West Carmen Ave.)*. This improving neighborhood, as Richard Lindberg puts it in *Passport's*

LINCOLN PARK &
NEAR NORTHWEST

Guide to Ethnic Chicago is a "busy, thriving retail corridor, where hard work and self-reliance carry a great weight. It is an old story with a new twist when 65-year-old refugees eagerly sign up for English classes at nearby Truman College."

◆ LINCOLN SQUARE MALL   *map page 9, B-1*

Two miles west of Broadway lies Lincoln Square Mall, around Lincoln and Lawrence Avenues, the last real vestige of a Germantown in Chicago. The commercial enclave is graced by a 96-foot-long wall mural depicting a medieval fortress and a peasant village. Teutonic-tinged shops in the area around Lincoln Square Mall include Inge's Delicatessen, the Huettenbar tavern, Merz Apothecary, and Schmid Imports gift shop. Nearby at 2458 West Montrose is the time-tested Lutz Continental Cafe and Pastry Shop, while delectably caloric treats can be found further south on Lincoln Avenue at Dinkel's Bakery.

◆ DEVON AVENUE   *map page 9, B-1*

Two or three miles north of the Lincoln Square mall are runs the east-west boulevard of Devon Avenue. No North Side thoroughfare is more of an ethnic kaleidoscope today than the mile-and-a-half of Devon Avenue running west from Ridge Boulevard. This West Rogers Park thoroughfare, at 6400 North, showed a resolutely Jewish face to the world as recently as the 1960s. Now the Indian subcontinent has the most prominent presence along Devon, but there are also Russian, Middle Eastern, Mexican, and other shops and restaurants, as well as the Croatian Cultural Center. Establishments catering to the Jewish community still keep a presence at the Devon strip's west end, which goes quiet during the Sabbath from sundown Friday to sundown Saturday.

Among the surviving stalwarts are Gitel's Kosher Pastry Shop and Chicago Hebrew Bookstore. The arrival since the 1970s of new Russian immigrants, many of them Jewish, is reflected in the Cyrillic lettering at the Three Sisters and Kashtan delicatessens, where blini and borscht are the order of the day.

Devon's shifting ethnic spectrum is marked at **California Avenue,** where the honorary street sign pointing west is Golda Meir Boulevard and the eastward name is Gandhi Marg. Popular Indian and Pakistani restaurants—where fixed-price lunch buffets are especially good value—include Viceroy of India, Gandhi, Moti Mahal, and Natraj. A profusion of shops sells videos, saris, jewelry and other imported goods to the Chicago area's 70,000 residents from the Indian subcontinent. The complexity of this South Asian weave can be gauged by the sign outside Bombay Video at 2634 West Devon: "We carry all languages of India—Hindi, Gujarati, Indi-Punjabi, Tamil, Telugu, Malayalam, Marathi, Bengali, Rajasthani, Pakistani, Pak-Punjabi, Peshto." Devon is a quick, cheap, fascinating trip halfway around the world.

■ NEAR NORTHWEST   *map page 9*

On the early stretches of its run northwest from downtown, **Milwaukee Avenue**— which long served as Main Street for Chicago's huge population of Polish descent —speaks a lot of Spanish these days. Along this commercial spine of the Wicker Park and Logan Square neighborhoods, a definite Hispanic flavor dominates the area between Diversey and Fullerton. Gentrification is making its mark as well with the rehabilitation of sturdy old homes in these communities, while hundreds of artists migrating away from the high rents of fashionable River North have set up their studios and galleries in Wicker Park and Bucktown immediately north.

(above) Ilya Rudiak offers everything Russian from matryoshka dolls to Soviet military uniforms at his store West Devon.

(opposite) East Indian textile shop on Devon.

◆ Ukrainian Village   *map page 9, B-3*

Urban pioneers are also moving into the farther-south Ukrainian Village enclave, which is graced with several splendid Orthodox churches. And there is still a Polish retail corridor on Milwaukee Avenue, concentrated in four blocks of the Avondale community between Diversey and Belmont.

The community spirit of the neighborhood's Ukrainian-Americans is captured in an incident related by Richard Lindberg in *Passport's Guide to Ethnic Chicago*. When state regulators informed a local savings and loan in 1964 that it was nearly insolvent due to $360,000 in missing assets, the association's president appealed to depositors "for help." The residents answered the appeal. Borrowing a page from the film *It's a Wonderful Life*, they streamed into his office with cash gifts, some as high as $1,000." The $300,000 infusion enabled the savings and loan to reopen three days later.

Now an independent nation, Ukraine was the breadbasket of the former Russian and Soviet empires. For a taste of the old world, stop in at **Ann's Bakery** for

The Ukrainian Village store might have been a neighborhood shop in the 19th century. Both Ukrainians and Poles can claim roots in Chicago

Ukrainian twist bread and pastries *(2158 West Chicago)* or old-line **Galans Restaurant** for a "Kozak feast" of ultra-hearty Ukranian fare *(2212 West Chicago)*.

The **Ukrainian National Museum** (west of Damen Avenue between Chicago and Diversey, 721 North Oakley Street; 312 421-8020) has fine displays of Ukranian painted Easter eggs and other folk arts. The **Ukrainian Institute of Modern Art** is at 2320 West Chicago; 773-227-5522.

◆ Polish Neighborhood   *map page 9, C-3*

A few Polish institutions remain in the old neighborhood to the south, including the **Polish Museum of America** One highlight of its substantial collection is a 13-by-27-foot stained-glass window, "Poland Reborn," that was designed in Krakow for the Polish pavilion at the 1939 New York World's Fair. *984 North Milwaukee; 773-384-3352.*

A small cluster of cooperative art galleries on the fringe of River West to the south includes ARC (Artists, Residents of Chicago) and woman-run Artemesia.

Polish neighborhoods remain to this day a large ethnic component of Chicago. This photo of an ecclesiastical goods store was taken in 1872. (Chicago Historical Society)

◆ IMPORTANT CHURCHES

Holy Trinity Orthodox Cathedral
map page 9, B-2

Chicago School master Louis Sullivan designed Holy Trinity Orthodox Cathedral in 1903 along the traditional lines of Russian churches with his own more delicate variant of that style's bulbous onion domes. The local Ukrainian congregations split in the 1960s on the matter of church calendars. *1121 North Leavitt.*

St. Volodymyr and Olha Church

Adherents of the old Julian calendar built St. Volodymyr and Olha Church on a site two blocks north in 1975. The mosaic over the main entrance portrays the conversion of the Ukraine to Christianity by St. Volodymyr in 988. Actually, Volodymyr was a warrior prince who advanced God's cause with the sword.

St. Nicholas Ukrainian Catholic Cathedral

The Gregorian calendar is still used at St. Nicholas Ukrainian Catholic Cathedral, erected in 1914 at Rice and Oakley streets on the model of Kiev's Basilica of St. Sophia with 13 copper-clad domes.

◆ WICKER PARK   *map page 9, B-2*

Wicker Park's treasure trove of Victorian homes, now much in demand, can be admired on block-long Concord Place running west off Milwaukee Avenue just north of Damen. There are handsome graystones here, and Pierce Avenue to the south boasts another block of fine homes. **Paderewski House** owes its name to the fact that the renowned Polish pianist once played there *(2138 West Pierce)*.

A Polish bakery on Milwaukee Avenue in Avondale offers many Old World delicacies.

◆ BUCKTOWN   *map page 9, B-2*

This triangular enclave just west of the Kennedy Expressway and north of Wicker Park, now draws evening visitors with a trendy assortment of restaurants, coffee shops, bars, and galleries. Goats were raised in Bucktown in the 1830s, hence the name (which derives from the male of the species).

◆ HUMBOLDT PARK   *map page 9, B-2*

West beyond Wicker Park's boundaries in a predominantly Puerto Rican neighborhood, Humboldt Park bears the pedigree of its design by William Le Baron Jenney in 1869 and its landscape improvements by Jens Jensen after the turn of the century. Expansive Humboldt Boulevard and Kedzie Avenue, with their grassy medians, were laid out as part of the green belt intended to circle Chicago in the 1870s. The towering classical column planted in Logan Square is Henry Bacon's **Illinois Centennial Monument,** dedicated in 1918 and circled at its base with sculpted reliefs portraying the state's history.

St. Mary of the Angels is the largest Roman Catholic church building in the state. Set on North Hermitage Street in the Wicker Park area, it serves a largely Polish parish.

LINCOLN PARK &
NEAR NORTHWEST

◆ AVONDALE'S LITTLE WARSAW STRIP   *map page 9, B-2*

There's no doubt of Chicago's strong Polish heritage once you're back on Milwaukee Avenue in the Avondale community's Little Warsaw strip, with its European-accented delicatessens, bakeries, markets, and gift shops. Dozens of varieties of Polish sausages with jaw-breaking names hang behind the counters of the delis. Home Bakery, operated by the Senkowski family, is among the best-regarded Polish restaurants, which include the Teresa II, Orbis, and Red Apple. Leave your cholesterol calculator at home. Tarnovia sells a weekly dinner pass and dishes up an all-you-can-eat Polish-American buffet. There's also polka-paced nightlife, or for a mellower alternative, visit one of several video shops renting Polish films. Polonia Book Store has the largest stock of Polish-language books in this country, as well as ethnic records and cassettes.

◆ CLYBOURN CORRIDOR   *map page 9, C-2*

Something very different from Milwaukee Avenue's ethnic potpourri can be found to the east of Milwaukee Avenue on Clybourn, another of Chicago's few diagonal thoroughfares. This rather faded stretch of factories and warehouses, now christened the Clybourn Corridor, has been swept by a whirlwind of retail development since the 1980s. Not all of the light industry has vanished, but shopping as a participant sport is the recreation here at a half-dozen trendy malls, some of which feature other attractions such as cinemas and a micro-brewery.

One remnant of the neighborhood's former German days, the Golden Ox restaurant, survives near the corridor's south end at North and Clybourn. Weekend nights at the Golden Ox bring zither music to accompany the perennially hearty German fare. Halsted is a warm-up act for the parade of conspicuous consumption running up Clybourn. The shopping is about what you'd expect. That's true also at Clybourn Place, Webster Place (in a former Butternut Bread factory), and other malls on the strip. Goose Island Brewing Company is a popular stop for sampling the Chicago's best-known local beer, served in restaurants throughout the city. The Clybourn Corridor speaks for the continuing commercial vitality of Chicago, as well as the fact—with apologies to P.T. Barnum—that there's a shopper born every minute.

LINCOLN PARK &
NEAR NORTHWEST

A kosher fish market on Devon in the West Rogers Park neighborhood.

SKIMMING THE SUBURBS

It has been called The Land Beyond O'Hare—a generic label hung on the sprawling expanse of suburbs that have paved over a great deal of the eight-county greater Chicago metropolitan area radiating 40 miles and more north, west, and south across northeast Illinois and into Indiana's northwest corner. Rock-ribbed city dwellers picture the suburbs as a monochromatic wasteland of crabgrass and strip malls where renting a video for the weekend may be the closest thing to live excitement. Meanwhile, suburbanites, who now make up almost two-thirds of the metropolitan population, nurse their own crime-and-grime stereotypes of the city so many have deserted—when they bother to think about Chicago at all. Particularly in the farthest exurban reaches, a trip to the Loop and Michigan Avenue may be a once-a-year (or less) expedition almost as exotic as going overseas. City and suburbs are a pair of neighboring but sometimes very distant mental planets.

In fact, the area's roughly 270 suburbs in Cook, Du Page, Lake, Will, McHenry, and Kane Counties (plus Indiana's Lake and Porter Counties) are more diverse in some ways than Chicago's 77 designated community areas. Economically, the spectrum runs the gamut from America's top "social status" suburb in a respected annual study (Kenilworth, on the North Shore) to the nation's poorest (Ford Heights, 46 miles south and a social universe away). Many suburbs are ticky-tacky bedroom subdivisions where the trees will need another generation to grow from stick figures into shade givers. But others are almost as old—and nearly as urban in feel—as Chicago itself. For short-time visitors, no single suburb falls into the don't-miss-by-any-means category, with the exception of Oak Park—if you happen to be an architecture enthusiast and particularly passionate about Frank Lloyd Wright. Still, it's worth investing a day or two, once you've seen enough of the city proper, in excursions by car west or north to expand your appreciation of mid-America's premier metropolis.

■ OAK PARK AND FRANK LLOYD WRIGHT   *map page 217, B-4*

Oak Park, just seven miles west of The Loop, boasts the world's largest trove of Frank Lloyd Wright architecture, is the core of the west-suburban itinerary. If a Wright pilgrimage is your only objective, riding rapid transit to Oak Park is feasible (although the Lake Street line does have crime problems). But driving gives

more flexibility for extending the trip to additional Wright houses in River Forest to the west, as well as taking in the sylvan 19th-century planned community of **Riverside,** impressive **Brookfield Zoo,** and (somewhat farther west) **Morton Arboretum** in Lisle and the **estate** of legendary *Chicago Tribune* publisher Colonel Robert McCormick of Cantigny near Wheaton.

Oak Park Visitors Center is a useful first stop to buy the detailed *Architectural Guide Map,* which contains photographs of the 25 Wright buildings in Oak Park and the six in River Forest, along with 49 other architecturally distinctive properties in the two suburbs. *1110 North Blvd., 708-848-1500.*

The visitors center also sells tickets for the **Wright Home and Studio Tour** and a walking tour of 13 Wright buildings along Forest Avenue. Besides the home and studio, only **Unity Temple**—his "little jewel"—is normally open to the public. It is possible see the interiors of some others, all private residences, during the annual Wright Plus Housewalk, normally held the third weekend in May.

(above) A detail of the mantel over the fireplace in Frank Lloyd Wright's Oak Park home.

(previous pages) Chicago's suburbs sprawl into the sunset.

Wright was a 22-year-old newlywed in 1889 when he built the home, only his second residential design, at 951 Chicago Avenue. His commissions before leaving Oak Park (and his wife and six children, to pursue a love affair in Europe) in 1909 provide a virtually complete record of his progress toward the revolutionary Prairie School of architecture. Observes the *Chicago on Foot* guide by Ira J. Bach and Susan Wolfson:

> *Y*ou will be surprised at the early designs, especially those before 1900. Steep gables and dormer windows have little resemblance to the style now associated with Wright's name. But the impact of the type of house he had developed by the end of that period continues to be felt today in house designs all over the world. Low roof lines, wide eaves, horizontal planes and casement windows—all are characteristics of the Prairie House.

◆ BIRTHPLACE OF ERNEST HEMINGWAY

The Wright legacy overshadows the Oak Park presence of another 20th century cultural icon who detested playing second banana during his tumultuous life. This western suburb was the birthplace of Ernest Hemingway in 1899 and the future novelist's home until he graduated from high school in 1917. Hemingway once branded Oak Park a town of "broad lawns and narrow minds," but he has been forgiven sufficiently that the Ernest Hemingway Foundation of Oak Park prints a brochure mapping out his birthplace, boyhood home, grade school, high school, and other sites with even a slender link to the future Nobel Prize winner.

◆ ERNEST HEMINGWAY MUSEUM   *map page 217, B-4*

A vivid sense of this macho maestro's formative years is conveyed at the Ernest Hemingway Museum at the **Oak Park Arts Center,** at 200 North Oak Park Avenue. The nicely arranged museum displays a copy of the famous "Ernie, dear boy" letter from nurse Agnes von Kurowsky, who tended his World War I wounds in Italy. Telling the young Hemingway she related to him "more as a mother than as a sweetheart," the nurse wrote, "I am afraid it is going to hurt you, but I'm sure it won't harm you permanently." Some critics have traced Hemingway's lifelong suspicion of women to that broken affair.

■ RIVERSIDE   *map page 217, B-5*

Four miles south of Oak Park along the Des Plaines River, Riverside was incorporated in 1875 as an early and distinctive example of planned suburbia. Principal designer Frederick Law Olmsted (most renowned for New York City's Central Park) aimed to create a community that represented "the best application of the art of civilization to which mankind has yet attained." Riverside's layout featured curving streets, then a novelty for American suburbs. As Ira J. Bach noted in an earlier edition of the *Chicago on Foot* guide, "It is a great tribute to Olmsted that the first of his suburbs has managed to maintain its rural character for over a century, despite the increase in automobiles and urban growth." The winding streets still serve, as Olmsted described them, "to suggest and imply leisure, contemplativeness, and tranquillity."

■ BROOKFIELD AND PLACES WEST

◆ BROOKFIELD ZOO   *map page 217, B-5*

There's less tranquillity to be found on a family-thronged Saturday or Sunday at Brookfield Zoo in the suburb of the same name just west across the Des Plains River from Riverside. The suburban setting allows the animals to roam in capacious enclosures, a nice complement to Chicago's skillfully designed though rather cramped Lincoln Park Zoo. *708-485-2200.*

◆ MORTON ARBORETUM   *map page 217, A-5*

It's another nine miles west to Morton Arboretum, a 1,500-acre oasis of exotic trees, shrubs, flowers, and herbs that has its prime times in April-May when the magnolias bloom and in October when fall foliage peaks. **The Schulenberg Prairie** is a 100-plus acre restoration of the area's original high prairie. The arboretum was established in 1922 by Morton Salt Company founder Jay Morton on his Lisle estate—then set amid open countryside, but now smack against busy Interstate 88. *630-434-3660.*

◆ COLONEL McCORMICK'S CANTIGNY ESTATE   *map page 217, A-5*

Colonel McCormick's Cantigny estate, four miles northwest of the arboretum off Route 38 (Roosevelt Boulevard) near Wheaton, is a revelation for its restored 35-

room mansion, superb gardens, and the Cantigny War Memorial Museum. The museums exhibits recount the tales of the Army's much-decorated First Division in four 20th-century wars. If you've meandered this far from Oak Park, the toll road will whisk you back to downtown Chicago by way of the Eisenhower Expressway. *630-668-5161.*

■ North Along the Lakeshore

One lesson of the lakeside drive up Sheridan Road from Evanston to Lake Forest is that the rich are still very different from you and me, as evidenced by the scale of their dwellings. This is one of the most expensive and exclusive residential enclaves anywhere, running through Wilmette, Kenilworth, Winnetka, Glencoe, and Highland Park. "I don't suppose there is another such extended parade of opulence on earth," wrote Jan Morris in *Locations,* a 1992 collection of essays. "Nor does it seem, like some lesser exhibitions—like Beverly Hills, California, say, or Palm Beach in Florida—in any way illusory. There is nothing flimsy to the Chicago style."

◆ Evanston   *map page 217, C-2*

A diverse community dating back to the Civil War decade, with a population 23 percent black, Evanston houses the **national headquarters of the Women's Christian Temperance Union,** without whom the United States might have been spared Prohibition and Al Capone might have stayed a small-time hoodlum.

Thanks to bluenoses of the WCTU ilk, Evanston lays claim to the invention of the ice cream sundae. The story goes that the Sunday sale of seltzer water was banned by the city council in the 1880s, taking the fizz out of ice-cream sodas on the Lord's Day. So druggists made the best of it by selling what was left—the ice cream and the syrup —as a "sundae." Although Evanston restaurants are now allowed to sell liquor, this remains a city without taverns.

As the home of **Northwestern University,** it offers an ample array of cultural activities, most notably at Pick-Staiger Hall on the lakefront campus. **Garfield Park Conservatory** is the magnificent botanic legacy of the civic-improvement flurry that accompanied the 1893 World's Columbian Exposition. *East Garfield Park, 300 North Central Park Ave.; 312-746-5100.*

◆ WILMETTE   *map page 217, C-2*

Once north of Evanston, the racial landscape is very white: the 1990 census recorded 130 African Americans among Wilmette's 26,690 residents, 45 among 12,174 in Winnetka, exactly 5 among 2,402 in ultra-posh Kenilworth.

Near the lake just across the Wilmette border looms one of the area's most eye-popping structures, the **Baha'i House of Worship**. Irreverent undergrads used to call it "the Great Orange Juice Squeezer," but Louis Bourgeois' remarkable nine-sided design (completed in 1953) evokes this ecumenical religion's 19th-century Persian origins with its soaring dome and webs of delicate stone tracery. The interior effect beneath the dome is both grand and serene. *112 Linden Ave., Wilmette; 847-853-2300, www.us.bahai.org.*

Another Wilmette attraction, **Kohl Children's Museum**, engages squirming youngsters with a diverting mix of hands-on exhibits. *Labor Day through June, Mon 9-noon, Tu-Sat 9-5, Sun noon-5, 165 Green Bay Rd., Wilmette; 847-256-6056, www.kohlchildrensmuseum.org.*

◆ CHICAGO BOTANIC GARDEN   *map page 217, B-1*

For a break from North Shore mansion-peeping, **Chicago Botanic Gardens** in the northwest corner of Glencoe shows how much beauty can be created from 300 acres of swampy soil. Developed since the mid-1960s by the Forest Preserve District of Cook County, and managed by the Chicago Horticultural Society, the gardens are scattered on landscaped islands. The varied motifs include three traditional Japanese gardens, a rose garden with 5,000 bushes, a plot designed after Europe's first scientific botanic garden (in 1545, at Italy's University of Padua), and a learning garden for the disabled. *Open 8 a.m. to sunset daily, closed Christmas Day. 1000 Lake Cook Rd., Glencoe; 847-835-5440, www.chicago-botanic.org.*

◆ HIGHLAND PARK   *map page 217, B-1*

The setting is likewise sylvan at **Ravinia**, in next-door Highland Park, the renowned open-air venue for summer concerts ranging from folk to classical. A supreme joy on a breezy July or August evening is picnicking on Ravinia's grassy lawn while the Chicago Symphony Orchestra or some other ensemble supplies the mood music. The performance season continues indoors at times of year when the lawn looks appealing only to the birds. *847-266-5100, www.ravinia.org.*

◆ LAKE FOREST

North beyond Highland Park and the former Army base of Fort Sheridan lies Lake Forest, laid out in 1856 and developed as Chicago's most exclusive suburb "the favorite resort of the better class of Chicago's inhabitants," as one 19th-century observer put it. A wistful resident in 1928 could remember when Lake Forest was a "comparatively unsuburban suburb," when few roads were paved, when "everyone kept horses and rode them," and when "there was only one country club." Just a bit of that horsey-set flavor still lingers in Lake Forest, where it's possible on the second Wednesday of each month from April through October to tour **Ragdale**, a mansion built around 1900 that serves as a retreat for artists and writers. It was originally the summer home of architect Howard Van Doren Shaw, who named it Ragdale for what he hoped would be an aura of "cultivated shabbiness." That's the closest thing to shabby in Lake Forest.

Ragdale summer home of architect Howard Van Doren Shaw circa 1900, is now a much-loved writers' colony in Lake Forest.

PRACTICAL INFORMATION

■ AREA CODES

The area code for downtown Chicago is 312. The rest of the center city area is 773. It's 708 for southern suburbs, 847 for northern suburbs, and 630 for the western suburbs.

■ WEATHER

| | TEMPERATURE | | | | PRECIPITATION | |
| | Average Daily in F | | Extremes Recorded | | Average Each Month | |
	MIN	MAX	MIN	MAX	RAIN (in.)	SNOW (in)
Jan.	18	34	-27	67	1.6	11
Feb.	20	36	-18	71	1.3	8
March	29	45	-9	89	2.6	7
Apr.	40	58	8	91	3.7	2
May	49	70	24	93	3.2	0
June	59	81	37	104	4.1	0
July	65	86	40	106	3.6	0
Aug.	65	85	41	100	3.5	0
Sept.	56	76	29	100	3.4	0
Oct.	45	65	18	91	2.3	1
Nov.	32	49	1	79	2.1	2
Dec.	22	36	-25	71	2.1	9
ANNUAL:			-27	106	33.3	39

Hit Chicago on a stormy day in midwinter, and you may logically assume that the "Windy City" label applies to the weather—rather than, as is historical fact, to the hot air of civic boosters who hustled successfully to land the 1893 world's fair. When "the Hawk"—a nickname uttered with shivers of respect here—whistles in from the north in January and February, wind-chill factors can plummet into the frostbite range. The thermometer falls to 0° F or lower on seven days in the average January, with -27° F (on January 20, 1985) the coldest ever recorded locally. So winter figures to be the least pleasant season for a Chicago pleasure trip, although it is a time of year when music, theater, museums, and restaurants are running at full steam.

Chicago summers have their occasional hot and humid blemishes: five days of 90° F or above in the average June, eight in July, five in August. The city's record high is 106° F which occurred on July 24, 1934 and again during the torrid summer of 1998. June qualifies as the rainiest month, but Chicago's annual average precipitation of 33.3 inches—less than New York's 42.8 though more than San Francisco's 19.7—is spread rather evenly around the calendar. Snowfall in the average winter adds up to 39.8 inches; in the biggest snowstorm ever, a memorable 23 inches paralyzed the city from January 26 to 27, 1967.

■ GETTING TO CHICAGO

Many visitors get their first glimpse of Chicago at O'Hare, which brags about being "the world's busiest airport"—although that may sound less like a boast than a consumer warning. More than 60 million passengers a year take off and land at O'Hare's four terminals, so brace yourself for trampling herds reminiscent of Chicago's legendary stockyards—especially when bad weather snarls air traffic and turns concourses into refugee camps.

Because O'Hare is a major hub for two of the nation's biggest airlines, American and United, it has the definite virtue of nonstop service to almost all U.S. cities of consequence and an increasing number of foreign destinations. A spanking-new international terminal opened in 1993 to replace the "temporary" facility that operated from the ground floor of a parking garage for the previous decade. The general O'Hare information number is 312-686-2200.

If you're traveling light, the least expensive way to cover the 18 miles between O'Hare International Airport and the Loop is the Chicago Transit Authority's rail service (Blue Line), which runs frequently from beneath Terminal 4 and takes 35 to 40 minutes. But you can't haul the airport's rental baggage carts onto the CTA platform, and there's no space to store luggage on the rapid-transit trains. Taxis take 40 to 60 minutes to get downtown, depending on time of day and Kennedy Expressway conditions; a share-the-ride program can cut the cost of a cab. Continental Air Transport's Airport Express, 312-454-7799, runs buses from O'Hare to hotels and other stops downtown, the Near North Side and northwest suburbs; fares are roughly half of what a taxi costs. Beware of hustlers for unlicensed cabs and limousines.

Flustered fliers may find less of a hassle at Chicago's second airport, Midway, which gets not much more than a tenth the passenger traffic of O'Hare. Midway, 312-767-0500, is located about eight miles southwest of the Loop in a bungalow neighborhood. The CTA's Orange Line provides service from Midway to downtown taking about 30 minutes.

Chicago is also a hub for Amtrak rail service from recently renovated Union Station, at Jackson and Canals streets on the western edge of the Loop. The Amtrak information number is 800-872-7245. For intercity bus riders, Greyhound's main Chicago station is at 630 West Harrison Street a bit southwest of downtown, 312-408-5970.

The tunnel connecting the United Airlines terminal at O'Hare is a public light sculpture in its own right.

MOTHER O'HARE

O Mother O'Hare, big bosom for our hungry poets, pelvic saddle for our sexologists and Open Classroom theorists—O houri O'Hare—...

Has it ever been duly noted that O'Hare, which is an airport outside Chicago, is now the intellectual center of the United States?

Curious, but true. There at O'Hare, on any day, Monday through Friday, from September to June, they sit... in row after Mies van der row of black vinyl and stainless-steel sling chairs... amid soaring walls of plate glass . . . from one tenth to one third of the literary notables of the United States. In October and April, the peak months, the figure goes up to one half.

Masters and Johnson and Erica Jong, Kozol and Rifkin and Hacker and Kael, Steinem and Nader, Marks, Hayden and Mailer, Galbraith and Heilbroner, and your bearmarket brothers in the PopEco business, Lekachman & Others—which of you has not hunkered down lately in the prodigious lap of Mother O'Hare!

And why? Because they're heading out into the land to give lectures . . . . Giving lectures in the heartland is one of the lucrative dividends of being a noted writer in America. . . . All the skyways to Lectureland lead through O'Hare Airport. In short, up to one half of our intellectual establishment sits outside Chicago between planes.

. . . I . . . ran into a poet who is noted for his verse celebrating the ecology, née Nature. He lives in a dramatic house nailed together completely from uncut pieces of hickory driftwood, perched on a bluff overlooking the crashing ocean. . . . I remarked that this must be the ideal setting in which to write about the ecological wonders.

"I wouldn't know," he said. "I do all my writing in O'Hare."

—Tom Wolfe, "The Intelligent Coed's Guide to America"
in *Mauve Gloves and Madmen, Clutter and Vine,* 1976

■ CHICAGO TRANSIT AUTHORITY OFFICIAL ROUTE MAP

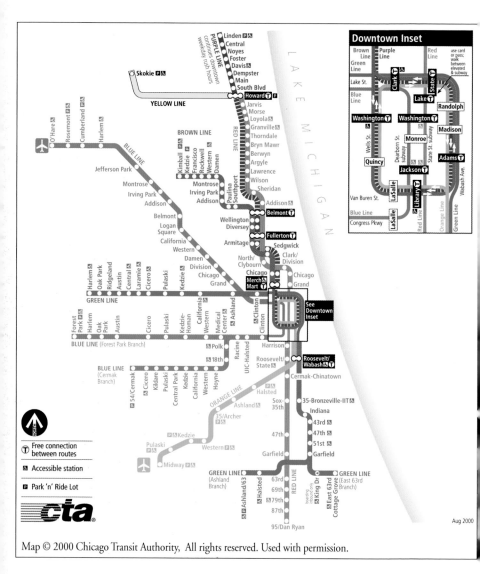

■ GETTING AROUND TOWN

The Chicago Transit Authority has recently added more services and more buses. Visitors from the many U.S. cities less well-endowed with public transportation are likely to marvel at the CTA's extensive network of buses and trains. The rapid-transit segment, which celebrated its centennial in 1992, is known as the "L"—short for elevated, even though parts of some lines run in subways or down the middle of expressways.

Many CTA routes operate 24 hours a day, crisscrossing the city and serving a number of bordering suburbs. Riding the L and buses at night can be risky if you are unfamiliar with high-crime neighborhoods. For a different slant on the city, a daytime ride on the Brown Line L circles the Loop's skyscrapers before heading north and west through a variety of commercial and residential neighborhoods to the end of the line at Lawrence and Kimball.

CTA buses require exact change (with $1 bills accepted). A fare card system is also used for all buses and rapid transit lines. Fare cards can be obtained at CTA rail line stations, currency exchanges, Jewel and Dominck's food stores, as well as the internet. In addition, CTA offers several types of Visitor Passes, providing convenience and economy in traveling around the city. For CTA fare information, visit cta's website at *www.transitchicago.com* or call 1-888-YOUR-CTA or call 312-836-7000 for trip planning and route maps.

It's usually easy to find a taxi in Chicago—except during wretched weather when you really need one. In the central city, simply hail an unoccupied cab on the street; to call for a pickup from outlying neighborhoods, the main companies include Checker/Yellow, 312-829-4222; Flash, 312-561-1444; and American United, 312-248-7600. Fares rise periodically, and all cabs are metered.

Whether you'll want a car in Chicago depends on your itinerary. In the central city, trying to negotiate dense traffic jams and find a parking spot for less than a prince's ransom is sure to have you cursing the invention of the internal-combustion engine. The best means of private transportation in the Loop and environs is your own two feet. To visit outlying neighborhoods or suburbs, however, an automobile is often the only practicable way to go. All major and many off-brand rental-car agencies operate in Chicago; you're likely to get a better rate by reserving in advance through the toll-free numbers in your Yellow Pages. Taxes on rental cars total at least 18 percent.

TOURS

■ TOURS

There are plenty of Chicago enterprises eager to give visitors a guided overview of the city or a focused look at some special subject. Here's a sampler:

Chicago Architecture Foundation
Wide-ranging selection of authoritative architecture tours by foot, bus, and boat. 312-922-3432

Friends of the Chicago River
Docent-led walking tours along various stretches of the river. 312-939-0490

Mercury Skyline Cruises
Ninety-minute sightseeing voyages on the lake and river. 312-332-1353

Shoreline Marine Sightseeing
Departures from the Shedd Aquarium/Field Museum dock for half-hour Lake Michigan cruises. 312-222-9328

Untouchable Tours
Two-hour bus circuit of Prohibition-era gangster sites. 312-881-1195

Wendella Sightseeing Boats
River and lake cruises of one to two hours, by a company founded in 1935. 312-337-1446

Chicago Trolley Company
Total tour 1 and 1/2 hours, but can get on and off. 773-648-5000

Many of Chicago's tours are focused on Lake Michigan boating opportunities.
Kayaks may also be rented off navy pier (above).

■ INFORMATION SOURCES

The **Chicago Office of Tourism** distributes free brochures and other information at visitor centers in the Historic Water Tower (806 North Michigan Avenue) and the Chicago Cultural Center (77 East Randolph Street). To call the Office of Tourism, dial 312-744-2400; from outside Illinois, 800-487-2446. Another agency, the **Chicago Convention and Tourism Bureau,** is headquartered at Mc-Cormick Place Convention Hall, 312-567-8500. Help for foreign travelers is available at the **International Visitors Center,** Merchandise Mart, Suite 930, 312-645-1836.

For current recorded information on events, call the **Mayor's Office of Special Events Hotline,** 312-744-3370; **Chicago Fine Arts Hotline** (free exhibits and performances), 312-346-3278; **Dance Hotline,** 312-419-8383; **Jazz Hotline,** 312-427-3300.

Both of Chicago's metropolitan daily newspapers, the *Sun-Times* and the *Tribune,* are filled with information on events and activities of interest—particularly in the weekend sections published as part of the Friday editions and the arts-and-entertainment sections on Sunday. Exhaustive weekly cultural and nightlife listings can be found in the free *Reader* newspaper, distributed each Thursday. The monthly *Chicago* magazine lists a host of performances and exhibits, as well as capsule reviews of numerous recommended restaurants. The *Chicago Daily Defender* has a long history as the city's principal African-American newspaper. The free *Windy City Times* focuses on the gay and lesbian communities.

■ RADIO STATIONS

Popular Chicago radio stations on the AM band (with frequency and format) include: WIND (560, Spanish language); WMAQ (670, news, sports); WGN (720, variety, talk, sports); WBBM (780, news); WSCR (820, sports, talk); WLS (890, talk); WMVP (1000, sports); WJJD (1160, talk).

Among major stations on the FM band are: WBEZ (91.5, National Public Radio daytime, jazz at night); WXRT (93.1, rock); WLIT (93.9, adult contemporary); WLS (94.7, talk); WNUA (95.5, jazz); WBBM (96.3, Top 40); WNIB (97.1, classical); WLUP (97.9, comedy talk); WFMT (98.7, classical); WUSN (99.5, country); WPNT (100.3, adult contemporary); WKQX (101.1, rock); WTMX (101.9, adult contemporary); WRCX (103.5, rock); WJMK (104.3, oldies); WOJO (105.1, Spanish language); WCKG (105.9, rock); WGCI (107.5, urban contemporary).

■ MUSEUM LISTINGS

Art Institute of Chicago
Loop 111 S. Michigan Ave. at Adams
St.; 312-443-3600. www.artic.com
(see page 120 for details)

Balzekas Museum of Lithuanian Culture.
Marquette Park 6500 S. Pulaski Rd.;
773-582-6500

Chicago Children's Museum
Streeterville 700 E. Grand Ave.;
312-527-1000 *(see page 164 for details)*

Chicago Historical Society Museum
Old Town 1601 N.Clark St.;
312-642-4600. *(see page 193 for details)*

**Du Sable Museum of African American
History** *Hyde Park* 740 E. 56th Place;
773-947-0600, dusablemuseum.org
(see page 143 for details)

Field Museum of Natural History
South Loop S. Lake Shore Dr. at
Roosevelt Rd.; 312-922-9410
www.fmnh.org *(see page 126 for details)*

Garfield Park Conservatory
East Garfield Park 300 N. Central Park
Blvd.; 312-746-5100

Museum of Contemporary Art
Streeterville 220 E. Chicago Ave.;
312-280-2660 *(see page 167 for details)*

Museum of Contemporary Photography
South Loop 600 S. Michigan Ave.;
312-663-5554 *(see page 124 for details)*

Museum of Holography
Near West Side 1134 W. Washington
St. *(see page 148 for details)*

Museum of Science and Industry
Hyde Park S. 57th St. at Lake Shore
Dr.; 773-684-1414 ww.msichicago.org
(see page 140 for details)

Oriental Institute Museum
Hyde Park 1155 E. 58th St.;
773-702-9520 *(see page 139 for details)*

Peace Museum *Near North*
350 West Ontario. 773-638-6450

Peggy Notebaert Nature Museum
Streeterville 435 E. Illinois St.;
312-871-2668 *(see page 193 for details)*

Polish Museum of America
River West 984 N. Milwaukee Ave.;
773-384-3352 *(see page 213 for details)*

Shedd Aquarium
South Loop 1200 S. Lake Shore Dr.,
312-939-2438 www.sheddnet.org
(see page 127 for details)

Smart Museum of Art
Hyde Park 5550 S. Greenwood Ave.;
773-702-0200 *(see page 139 for details)*

**Smith Museum of Stained Glass
Windows,** *Streeterville* Navy Pier,
312-595-7437 *(see page 164 for details)*

Spertus Museum
South Loop 618 S. Michigan Ave.;
312-922-9012 *(see page 124 for details)*

Swedish American Museum Center
Andersonville 5211 N. Clark St.,
773-728-8111, www.samac.org
(see page 204 for details)

Terra Museum of American Art
Magnificent Mile 666 N. Michigan
Ave.; 312-664-3939 *(see page 170 for
details)*

Ukrainian Institute of Modern Art
2320 W. Chicago; 773-227-5522

Ukrainian National Museum *Ukrainian
Village* 721 N. Oakley St.;
312-421-8020 *(see page 213 for details)*

The Shedd Aquarium.

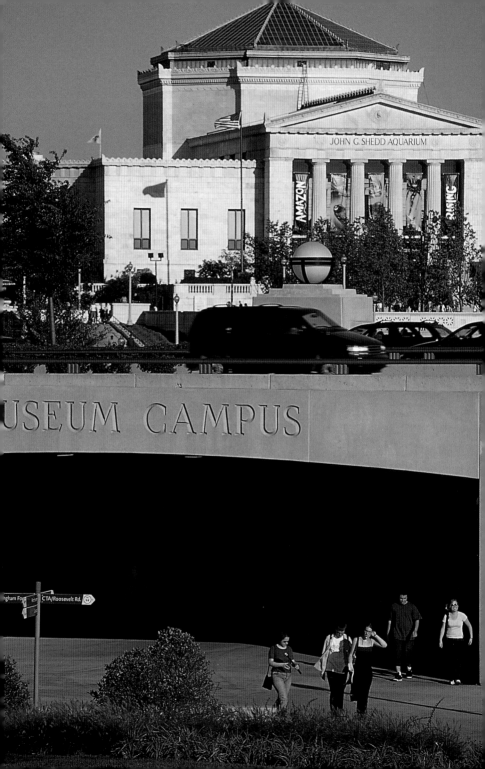

HOTELS & INNS

■ ABOUT CHICAGO LODGING

YOU CAN SEARCH A LONG TIME in Chicago without finding the hotel hunter's dream of an elegant and intimate hideaway centrally located and charging a mere pittance. This is a high-priced metropolis, after all, not a fantasyland.

Many of Chicago's most vaunted (and most expensive) hotels are located within an easy walk of the Magnificent Mile. The Loop and its southern fringe contain a number of older properties that have benefited greatly from renovation over the past decade. Motels along commercial strips in outlying city neighborhoods are a less expensive option for visitors with a car. And the suburbs offer budget lodging down to the barebones motel level—if you don't mind daily commuting as part of your vacation.

B&Bs: Chicago lacks the network of commercial bed-and-breakfast inns that enrich the tourist fabric of cities like San Francisco. But it is possible to book a room in a private home or apartment through time-tested Bed and Breakfast Chicago 773-248-0005, which represents about 70 properties. Rates start around $65 a night including breakfast, while a self-contained apartment goes for $85 and up; there's a two-night minimum stay.

Bargains: You can get a lot more hotel room for your dollars, as in most big cities, by scheduling your visit over a weekend and shopping around via toll-free 800 numbers for the best deals (as much as 50 percent off rack rates—with breakfast, champagne, parking, or other amenities sometimes thrown in). Both the Chicago Office of Tourism *(312-744-2400)* and the Hotel-Motel Association of Illinois *(www.hmai.org)* publish brochures listing weekend and other discounts. Cut-rate bets may be off on weeks of the half-dozen biggest annual conventions.

Hostels: On the city's North Side, two hostels offer a frugal option for the young-at-heart: **Chicago International Hostel**, at 6318 North Winthrop Avenue near Loyola University, 773-262-1011, and **Arlington House International Hostel**, 616 West Arlington Place in the Lincoln Park neighborhood, 773-929-5380.

Our Listings: Because hotels are a matter of personal taste and budget, any short list of top bets is a risky undertaking subject to debate. Each of the two dozen places that follow has some special virtue—whether that be beautiful antique furnishings, live music, or a particularly good value for the location. There are dozens of other commendable lodgings. Keep in mind that advance reservations almost always make sense.

The coding at the end of each listing that indicates the property's price range (note that the plague of occupancy and other local taxes will add 12.4 percent or more to the bill).

Chain Lodging: Should you prefer a particular chain lodging, use the chart below to select the location; however, usually it's best to use a local number when booking your final reservation. (A person at the front desk of the Chicago Hyatt on Printers Row will certainly be able to help you more than will a reservationist sitting at a Hyatt's 800-reservations center.)

Hotel and Motel Chains			
Best Western	800-528-1234	Motel 6	800-466-8356
Days Inn	800-325-2525	Omni	800-843-6664
Doubletree	800-222-8733	Radisson Suites	800-333-3333
Embassy Suites	800-362-2779	Ramada	800-228-2828
Hilton	800-445-8667	Sheraton	800-325-3535
Holiday Inn	800-465-4329	Stouffer Renaissance	800-468-3571
Hyatt	800-233-1234	Travel Lodge	800-578-7878
Inter-Continental	800-327-0200	Westin	800-228-3000
Marriott	800-228-9290		

Note: COMPASS AMERICAN GUIDES makes every effort to ensure the accuracy of its information; however, as conditions and prices change frequently, we recommend that readers also contact local sources for the most up-to-date information. Typing in www.chicago.com leads to several useful sites including news both local and outside; tours of the city and its neighborhoods; restaurant reviews; and arts and event listings.

BEST WESTERN RIVER NORTH

CHICAGO ESSEX INN

BEST WESTERN RIVER NORTH
map page 243, B-4
125 West Ohio St.
312-467-0800 or 800-727-0800
www.bestwestern.com
$-$$$$
Free parking is a bonus at this recently refurbished motel-style spot handily located for River North's galleries and Michigan Avenue's shops. Kids' rates.

Neighborhood: *River North*
Number of Rooms: 122 rooms, 26 suites
Gym/Spa Facilities: fitness center, pool
Parking: Free
Pets allowed: No
Business Services: in-room data ports, meeting rooms
Restaurants: Pizzeria Ora
Bar: Pizzeria Ora Lounge

CHICAGO ESSEX INN
map page 241, C-3
800 South Michigan Ave.
312-939-2800 or 800-621-6909
www.essexinn.com
$$
Located across from Grant Park, within walking distance to the Museum Campus, and near downtown shopping.

Neighborhood: *South Loop*
Number of Rooms: 254
Gym/Spa Facilities: year round pool and fitness center
Parking: valet $16 per night
Pets allowed: no
Business Services: in-room data port, fax, and voice mail
Restaurants: Savoy Bar and Grill

Loop, South Loop
and Chinatown
Lodging & Restaurants

CHICAGO HILTON AND TOWERS

CITY SUITES CHICAGO

CHICAGO HILTON AND TOWERS
map page 241, C-3
720 South Michigan Ave. (Balboa)
312-922-4400 or 800-445-8667
www.hilton.com
$$$$

This massive hotel attracts its share of convention crowds, but makes a good base for families who want to explore the nearby Museum Campus (many rooms have two bathrooms). The impressive Grand Stair Lobby, with its lavish rococo touches, makes a stunning first impression. The upper-level rooms on Michigan Avenue offer sweeping views of the lake and Grant Park.

Neighborhood: *South Loop*
Number of Rooms: 1,544 rooms
Gym/Spa Facilities: fitness center, pool
Parking: valet, $24 per night
Pets allowed: yes
Business Services: business center
Restaurants: Buckingham's (steakhouse), Pavilion
Bar: Kitty O'Shea's (Irish pub)

CITY SUITES CHICAGO
map page 245, A-1
933 W. Belmont Ave.
773-404-3400 or 800-CITY-108
www.cityinns.com
$$-$$$

Good value in an interesting neighborhood, the 1920s hotel houses Art Deco interiors with upgraded amenities for business and pleasure travellers alike. Elegant continental breakfast is served in the warm and welcoming lobby. "Steps away" from the front door are Chicago's best dining, theater and nightlife, as well as easy access to the L.

Neighborhood: *Lincoln Park*
Number of Rooms: 16 rooms, 29 suites
Gym/Spa Facilities: near by
Parking: self parking $17
Pets allowed: no
Business Services: in-room dataport, spacious work desks, concierge
Restaurant/Bar: none in house

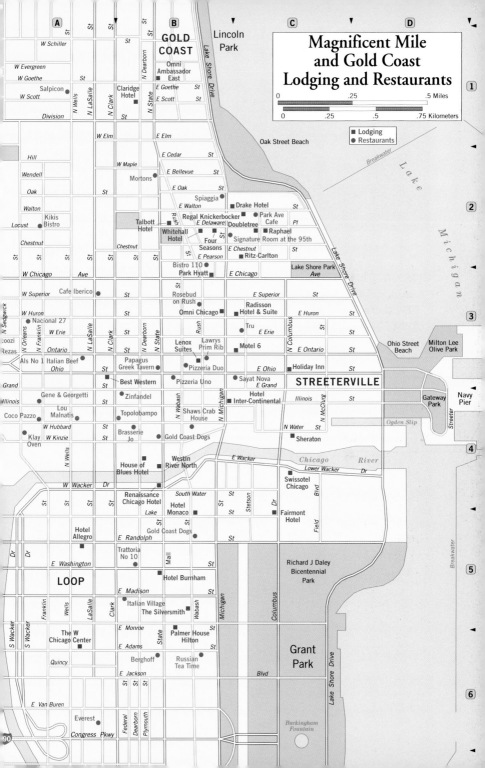

CLARIDGE HOTEL

CLARIDGE HOTEL
map page 243, B-1
1244 North Dearborn Pkwy.
312-787-4980 or 800-245-1258
www.claridgehotel.com
$$

Reasonable rates and European gentility commend this 172-room hotel, in a 1930s building on a tree-shaded Gold Coast street, close to shopping. Continental breakfast.

Neighborhood: *Gold Coast*
Number of Rooms: 163 rooms, 2 suites
Gym/Spa Facilities: none
Parking: self park next door, $28 day
Pets allowed: yes
Business Services: in-room dataport, conference service, limo service

COMFORT INN CHICAGO
map page 245, B-2
601 West Diversey Pkwy.
773-348-2810 or 800-228-5151
www.comfortinn.com
$-$$$$

Reliable comfort, a value-hunter's best bet along a bustling commercial strip four miles north of the Loop.

Neighborhood: *Lincoln Park*
Number of Rooms: 71 rooms, 3 suites
Gym/Spa Facilities: nearby
Parking: self park $8
Pets allowed: no
Business Services: conference room
Restaurant/Bar: none in house

*CROWNE PLAZA CHICAGO
THE SILVERSMITH*

CROWNE PLAZA CHICAGO
THE SILVERSMITH
map page 241, C-1
10 South Wabash St. (Madison)
312-372-7696 or 800-2 CROWNE
www.crowneplaza.com
$$$$

A converted National Historic Landmark, this deluxe hotel has both stylish rooms and 21st-century business amenities in a welcoming, comfortable Old World setting. Complimentary dessert served in the lobby at 9 P.M. Monday through Thursday. All rooms have 12-foot ceilings, 10-foot windows, CD players, and desks with ergonomic chairs.

(continues page 246)

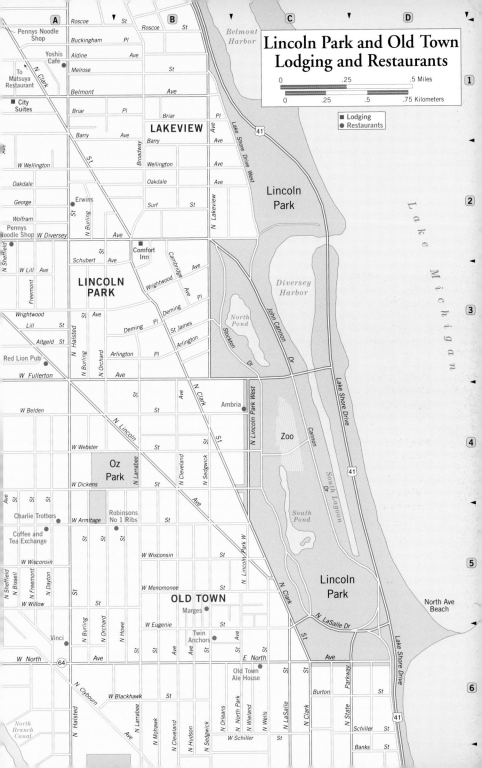

Lincoln Park and Old Town
Lodging and Restaurants

Lodging
Restaurants

A **B** **C** **D**

Pennys Noodle Shop
Yoshis Cafe
To Matsuya Restaurant
City Suites
Erwins
Pennys Noodle Shop
Comfort Inn
Red Lion Pub
Ambria
Charlie Trotters
Coffee and Tea Exchange
Robinsons No 1 Ribs
Vinci
Marges
Twin Anchors
Old Town Ale House

Roscoe St
Buckingham Pl
Aldine Ave
Melrose St
Belmont Ave
Briar Pl
Briar Pl
Barry Ave
Barry
Wellington Ave
Oakdale Ave
Oakdale Ave
George
Surf St
Wolfram
W Diversey Ave
Schubert Ave
Wrightwood Ave
Deming Pl
Deming Pl
St James
Arlington
Arlington Pl
W Fullerton Ave
W Belden
W Webster
W Dickens
W Armitage
W Wisconsin
W Wisconsin
W Menomonee
W Eugenie
W North Ave
W Blackhawk
W Schiller

LAKEVIEW
LINCOLN PARK
Oz Park
OLD TOWN

Lincoln Park
Belmont Harbor
Diversey Harbor
North Pond
Zoo
South Pond
South Lagoon
Lincoln Park
North Ave Beach

Lake Michigan

N Clark St
Broadway
N Lakeview
N Burling St
N Sheffield
N Halsted St
N Burling St
N Orchard St
N Clark St
N Lincoln Ave
N Larrabee St
N Cleveland
N Sedgwick St
N Lincoln Park West
John Cannon Dr
Stockton Dr
Lake Shore Drive West
Lake Shore Drive
Cannon Dr
South Lagoon Dr

41
64
41
41

1
2
3
4
5
6

0 .25 .5 Miles
0 .25 .5 .75 Kilometers

North Branch Canal
N Clybourn
N Halsted St
N Larrabee Ave
N Mohawk
N Cleveland
N Hudson
N Sedgwick St
N Orleans
N North Park
N Wieland
N Wells St
N LaSalle
N Clark St
N State Pkwy
Parkway
Burton
Schiller
Banks

W Wellington
Wellington
Freemont St
W Lill Ave
W Willow
W Wisconsin
N Bissell
N Freemont
N Dayton
Altgeld St
Lill St
Wrightwood St
Cambridge Ave
N Lincoln Park W
N LaSalle Dr
E North Ave

Neighborhood: *Loop*
Number of Rooms: 143 rooms,
63 suites
Gym/Spa Facilities: fitness room
Parking: valet $25 per night
Pets allowed: no
Business Services: business center,
secretarial services, in-room dataports
and voice mail
Restaurants: Ada's (upscale deli)
Bar: Lobby Lounge

DOUBLETREE GUEST SUITES

DOUBLETREE GUEST SUITES
map page 243, C-2
198 East Delaware Place
312-664-1100 or 800-222-TREE
www.doubletreehotels.com
$$$$

The lobby is sophisticated, but the overall feeling is welcoming at this all-suites hotel (maybe it's the fresh-baked chocolate-chip cookies they hand out at the front desk). Each suite includes a separate living room with a sofabed. Pay more for a room with a lake view, or check out the skyline from the 30th floor fitness room.

Neighborhood: *Magnificent Mile*
Number of Rooms: 345 suites
Gym/Spa Facilities: health club
Parking: valet $23 per night
Pets allowed: no
Business Services: business center with
secretarial services, in-room dataports,
meeting rooms
Restaurants: Park Avenue Cafe (New
American), Mrs. Park's Tavern (Traditional American)
Bar: Blenz Coffee Bar

THE DRAKE
map page 243, C-2
140 East Walton Pl. (Michigan)
312-787-2200 or 800-55-DRAKE
www.drakehotel.com
$$$$

Since 1920, this hotel has been a landmark of the city's skyline. The glamour may have faded a bit with time, but that's part of the charm. The Italian Renaissance– inspired lobby still exudes luxury, and the elegant Palm Court is the perfect setting for afternoon tea. The rooms have been nicely updated; many have two bathrooms.

Neighborhood: *Magnificent Mile*
Number of Rooms: 480 rooms, 55 suites
Gym/Spa Facilities: fitness center, in-room
massage
Parking: valet $25 per night
Pets allowed: no
Business Services: business center, in-room
dataports
Restaurants: Oak Terrace *(American),*
Cape Cod Room *(seafood)*
Bars: Coq d'Or (piano bar), Palm Court

FAIRMONT HOTEL

FOUR SEASONS

FAIRMONT HOTEL
map page 241, D-1
$$$$
200 N. Columbus Dr. (Lake)
312-565-8000 or 800-527-4727
www.fairmont.com

A bit removed from the downtown bustle, the Fairmont lures visitors with luxury amenities such as custom-made beds, high-end sheets, and feather pillows. The elegant and comfortable rooms all have separate sitting areas feature stereo systems and TVs in the extra-large bathrooms.

Neighborhood: *Loop*
Number of Rooms: 626 rooms, 66 suites
Gym/Spa Facilities: health club with pool and spa
Parking : valet $28 per night
Pets allowed: yes
Business Services: business center, in-room dataports and fax
Restaurants: Entre Nous (French), Primavera Ristorante (Italian)
Bars: Metropole, Lobby Bar

FOUR SEASONS
map page 243, B-2
$$$$
120 East Delaware Pl. (Michigan)
312-280-8800 or 800-332-3442
www.fourseasons.com/chicagofs

A star of Chicago's hotel scene and consistently rated one of the top hotels in the world for its top-notch service (experts at handling special requests), the Four Seasons is located on the upper floors of an upscale vertical mall. Elegant design but intimate just the same. The English-style rooms feature hand-crafted woodwork and custom-woven rugs and tapestries.

Neighborhood: *Magnificent Mile*
Address: Number of Rooms: 190 rooms, 153 suites
Gym/Spa Facilities: fitness center with pool and spa
Parking: valet $29 per night; self-park $20
Pets allowed: yes
Business Services: business center, in-room dataports, meeting rooms
Restaurants: Seasons (New American), Seasons Cafe
Bars: Seasons Lounge and Bar

HOLIDAY INN CHICAGO CITY CENTRE

HOTEL ALLEGRO

HOLIDAY INN–CHICAGO CITY CENTRE
map page 243, C-3
$$$$
300 East Ohio St. (Fairbanks/
North Columbus)
312-787-6100 or 800-HOLIDAY
www.holiday-inn.com
One look at the sophisticated lobby will banish the chain hotel stereotype. The Holiday Inn is an excellent choice for families: kids under 18 stay free, and beach, a lakefront park, and the Children's Museum on Navy Pier are all within walking distance. Request a room with a view of the Hancock Building or of Monroe Harbor.

Neighborhood: *Magnificent Mile*
Number of Rooms: 491 rooms, 9 suites
Gym/Spa Facilities: free access to next-door health club, outdoor pool
Parking: valet $20
Pets allowed: no
Business Services: business center
Restaurants: Centre Cafe *(American)*, Corner Copia
Bars: Winner's Lounge

HOTEL ALLEGRO
map page 241, B-1
$$$ - $$$$
171 W. Randolph St. (LaSalle)
312-236-0123 or 800-643-1500
www.chicago.citysearch.com
The bright colors that fill the lobby set the tone: this is a hotel that wants its guests to have fun. Jazz and pop songs play in public areas, and guests are directed to bowls of tootsie rolls by attractive staff in funky uniforms. The whimsical theme extends to the rooms, decorated in shades of coral, yellow and green.

Neighborhood: *Loop*
Number of Rooms: 452 rooms, 31 suites
Gym/Spa Facilities: exercise room, access to nearby health club
Parking: valet $28 per day, in/out privileges
Pets allowed: yes
Business Services: business center; in-room voice mail, dataports, and fax, high-speed internet service, meeting rooms
Restaurants: 312 Chicago *(Italian)*, Encore Lunch Club
Bar: Liquid Lounge

HOTEL BURNHAM

HOTEL INTER-CONTINENTAL

HOTEL BURNHAM
map page 241, C-1
1 West Washington St. (State)
312-782-1111 or 877-294-9712
www.burnhamhotel.com
$$$$

The Reliance Building, one of the first skyscrapers ever built, now houses an elegant hotel guaranteed to draw architecture buffs. The original grillwork and marble have been restored, and the hallways have retained the look of an early 20th-century office building. Rooms are decorated in a sophisticated colors —midnight blue, cream, and gold. Floor-to-ceiling windows overlook bustling downtown.

Neighborhood: *Loop*
Number of Rooms: 103 rooms, 19 suites
Gym/Spa Facilities: exercise room
Parking: self-park $19 per night
Pets allowed: no
Business Services: business services, in-room dataports
Restaurant/Bar: Atwood Café *(New American)*

HOTEL INTER-CONTINENTAL CHICAGO
map page 243, C-4
505 North Michigan Ave. (Grand)
312-944-4100 or 800-327-0200
www.interconti.com
$$$$

The original Inter-Continental (one of Chicago's premier hotels in the 1920s and '30s) has been combined with a modern addition that lacks the original's charm. Request a room in the south tower if you want the vintage feel (the views are better, too). Take a peek at the lavish ballrooms and the 10th-floor Venetian-style indoor pool.

Neighborhood: *Magnificent Mile*
Number of Rooms: 765 rooms, 35 suites
Gym/Spa Facilities: health club
Parking: valet $32 per night
Pets allowed: no
Business Services: business center, in-room dataport and fax, meeting rooms
Restaurants: Amber *(Mediterranean)*
Bar: Salon Lounge

HOTEL MONACO

HOUSE OF BLUES HOTEL

HOTEL MONACO

map page 241, C-1
225 North Wabash St. (Wacker)
312-960-8500 or 800-397-7661
www.monaco-chicago.com
$$$-$$$$

One of Chicago's first boutique hotels, the Monaco sets itself apart from the chain hotel crowd with a funky atmosphere and offbeat props (Derby hats on the doormen, goldfish in the rooms). The Art Deco–inspired furnishings are amusingly eclectic, and the bathrooms come stocked with aromatherapy oils. The hotel hosts a nightly wine reception.

Neighborhood: *Loop*
Number of Rooms: 170 rooms, 22 suites
Gym/Spa Facilities: fitness room, access to nearby health club
Parking: valet $28 per night
Pets allowed: no
Business Services: business center, secretarial services, in-room dataports voice mail and fax, meeting rooms
Restaurants: Mossant (French)
Bar: Lobby Lounge

HOUSE OF BLUES HOTEL

map page 243, B-4
333 North Dearborn Ave. (Kinzie)
312-245-0333 or 800-23-LOEWS
www.loewshotels.com
$$$$

An extension of the club/restaurant next door, this dramatic hotel has a crimson-and-blue interior; elaborate carvings and statues (even a gold Buddha) and a tented seating area worthy of *The Sheik* spice up the lobby; weekend nights there are tarot card readings and blues bands in the lobby. The funky guest rooms feature Southern folk art and high-tech amenities (CD players, VCRs, web TV).

Neighborhood: *River North*
Number of Rooms: 345 rooms, 21 suites
Gym/Spa Facilities: Crunch Fitness Center
Parking: valet $28 per night
Pets allowed: yes
Business Services: in-room fax, voice mail, dataports, meeting rooms
Restaurant: Bin 36, House of Blues Restaurant *(Southern)* known for its Gospel Sunday brunch
Bar: Kaz Bar

HYATT ON PRINTERS ROW
map page 241, B-2
500 South Dearborn St. (Congress)
312-986-1234 or 800-233-1234
www.hyatt.com
$$$$

This tasteful, quiet hotel will appeal to Frank Lloyd Wright fans; his Prairie style served as inspiration for the understated yet sophisticated decor. The location, in a neighborhood of rehabbed former industrial buildings, is peaceful but within easy walking distance of museums and down-town sites. Guest rooms are good-sized and offer high-end amenities.

Neighborhood: *Loop*
Number of Rooms: 158 rooms, 3 suites
Gym/Spa Facilities: small fitness room, access to nearby health club
Parking: valet $29 per night
Pets allowed: no
Business Services: business center, in-room dataports
Restaurant: Prairie *(Contemporary Midwestern)*
Bar: Lobby Bar

LENOX SUITES HOTEL CHICAGO
map page 243, B-3
616 North Rush St. (East Ontario St.)
312-337-1000 or 800-44-LENOX
www.lenoxsuites.com
$$$$

Convenient to shopping, fine dining, cultural activities, and Magnificent Mile. Complimentary continental breakfast is served in each suite along with the morning paper. Special Disney Quest, American Girl, museum, and romance packages.

LENOX SUITES HOTEL

Neighborhood: *Magnificent Mile*
Number of Rooms: 325 suites
Gym/Spa Facilities: fitness center
Parking: valet $30 per night
Pets allowed: no
Business Services: in-room dataport, fax, business center
Restaurants/Bars: Houston's, Andrew's

MOTEL 6 CHICAGO DOWNTOWN
map page 243, C-3
162 East Ontario (St. Clair)
312-787-3580 or 800-4 MOTEL 6
www.motel6.com
$

Budget kingpin's city-slicker outpost just off North Michigan Avenue. Children stay free. One of the best values in Chicago and therefore usually full. Reserve well in advance.

Neighborhood: *Magnificent Mile*
Number of Rooms: 191 rooms
Parking: self-park at Ohio and St. Clair Sts.
Pets allowed: Yes
Restaurant/Bar: Coco Pazzo *(Italian)*

OMNI AMBASSADOR EAST

OMNI CHICAGO HOTEL

OMNI AMBASSADOR EAST
map page 243, B-1
1301 State Pkwy.
312-787-7200 or 800-843-6664
www.omnihotels.com
$$$$

As simply the Ambassador East, this hotel played host to Hollywood royalty (Frank Sinatra, Humphrey Bogart, etc.). Booth One in its famous Pump Room was the place to see the latest celebrity passing through town. The lobby retains its timeless elegance, and the overall feeling of understated luxury fits in well with the neighborhood of multi-million-dollar homes surrounding the building. Member of Historic Hotels of America.

Neighborhood: *Gold Coast*
Number of Rooms: 285 rooms, 55 suites including 5 ADA
Gym/Spa Facilities: fitness room, access to nearby health club
Parking: valet $33 per night
Pets allowed: no
Business Services: business center, in-room dataports
Restaurants: Pump Room (New French)
Bar: Byfields Lounge

OMNI CHICAGO HOTEL
map page 243, B-3
676 North Michigan Ave. (Huron)
312-944-6664 or 800-843-6664
www.omnihotels.com
$$$$

The chandeliers, marble floors, and lavish flower arrangements make the Omni a notch above the standard business hotel. All of the rooms are suites with separate sitting and dining areas, wet bars, and refridgerators. Ask for a corner suite to get a view down Michigan Avenue). Talk-show guests of Oprah Winfrey stay here so you may spot some celebrities in the lobby.

Neighborhood: *Magnificent Mile*
Number of Rooms: 347 suites, including 12 ADA
Gym/Spa Facilities: health club with pool
Parking: valet, $32 per night
Pets allowed: no
Business Services: business center, high-speed internet access in all rooms, courtesy car for trips in downtown area
Restaurants: Cielo's (Italian)
Bar: Cielo's Lounge

PALMER HOUSE HILTON

PARK HYATT

PALMER HOUSE HILTON
map page 241, C-2
17 East Monroe St. (State)
312-726-7500 or 800-HILTONS
ww.hilton.com
$$-$$$$

Don't be fooled by the shopping mall entrance; it's not until you reach the palatial second-floor foyer that the Palmer House reveals its heritage as Chicago's first luxury hotel. With its gilded, mural-covered ceiling, the lobby feels like a piece of Europe transported. The guest rooms are large but don't retain the historical feel of the lobby, but many doubles have two renovated bathrooms.

Neighborhood: *Loop*
Number of Rooms: 1,551 rooms, 88 suites
Gym/Spa Facilities: health club with indoor swimming pool
Parking: valet $25 per night; self-park $19
Pets allowed: no
Business Services: business center, two executive floors for business travelers, in-room dataport
Restaurants: Trader Vic's *(Polynesian),* French Quarter *(Creole/Cajun),* The Big Downtown *(American)*
Bar: Windsor's Lobby Bar

PARK HYATT
map page 243, B-3
800 North Michigan Ave.
312-335-1234 or 800-233-1234
www.hyatt.com
$$$$

Located just west of the Old Chicago Water Tower, the 255-room Park Hyatt is elegant in an understated way.

Neighborhood: *Magnificent Mile*
Number of Rooms: 196 rooms, 7 suites
Gym/Spa Facilities: health club
Parking: valet $35 per night
Pets allowed: no
Business Services: in-room data ports, business center, meeting rooms
Restaurant/Bar: Nomi *(French)*

RADISSON HOTEL & SUITES - DOWNTOWN CHICAGO
map page 243, C-3
160 East Huron St.
312-787-2900 or 800-333-3333
www.radisson.com
$$$
New identity, spruced-up facilities for this former condo complex. Children's rates.

Neighborhood: *Magnificent Mile*
Number of Rooms: 350 rooms, 90 suites
Gym/Spa Facilities: fitness center, pool
Parking: valet $28
Pets allowed: yes
Business Services: business center, in-room dataport
Restaurant/Bar: Becco D'Oro

RADISSON SUITES HOTEL O'HARE
map page 217, A-3
6810 North Mannheim Rd.
847-297-1234 or 800-333-3333
www.radisson.com/rosemontil
$-$$$
At this recently renovated hotel, the spacious rooms, business center, and gym facilities are the major selling points for choosing the Radisson over other hotels near O'Hare orbit.

Neighborhood: *O'Hare*
Number of Rooms: 467 rooms, 13 suites
Gym/Spa Facilities: fitness center, pool
Parking: yes
Pets allowed: no
Business Services: business center, in-room dataport
Restaurants: Barley's *(Steakhouse)*
Bar: Maxie's Sports Bar *(Pub)*, lobby lounge

RAPHAEL
map page 243, C-2
201 East Delaware St.
312-983-7870 or 800-695-8284
$$-$$$
It's hardly a country inn, but this neighbor of the skyscraping John Hancock Center gives guests a bracing taste of European intimacy and charm at sensible prices.

Neighborhood: *Magnificent Mile*
Number of Rooms: 172 rooms, 99 suites
Gym/Spa Facilities: no
Parking: valet $28 per night
Pets allowed: no
Business Services: in-room dataport
Restaurant/Bar: none in house

REGAL KNICKERBOCKER HOTEL
map page 243, C-2
163 East Walton St.
312-751-8100 or 800-222-8888
www.regal-hotels.com/chicago
$$$$
The Knickerbocker's colorful past includes underworld links during the Capone era and a stint as a *Playboy* hangout in the 1970s. A recent renovation brought back the 1920s style. The rooms are done in a rich, European decor, but most have views only of the surrounding buildings.

Neighborhood: *Magnificent Mile*
Number of Rooms: 290 rooms, 15 suites
Gym/Spa Facilities: fitness room
Parking: valet $30 per night
Pets allowed: no
Business Services: business center, in-room dataports
Restaurants: Nix *(Fusion cuisine)*
Bar: Martini Bar

RENAISSANCE CHICAGO HOTEL
map page 241, C-1
One West Wacker Dr. (State)
312-372-7200 or 800-HOTELS-1
www.renaissancehotels.com
$$$-$$$$
Bay windows in the rooms of this sleek high-rise allow stunning views of the Chicago River and of North Michigan Avenue. Comfortably decorated with rich tapestries, chandeliers, and thick carpets.Near several Loop theaters; the hotel frequently offers theater packages.

Neighborhood: *Loop*
Number of Rooms: 553 rooms, 40 suites
Gym/Spa Facilities: indoor pool, gym
Parking: valet $30; self-park $18 per night
Pets allowed: yes
Business Services: business center, in-room dataports and fax
Restaurants: Great Street *(Contemporary American);* Cuisines *(Mediterranean)*
Bar: Lobby Court *(Cocktails and Tea)*

RITZ-CARLTON FOUR SEASONS

RITZ-CARLTON FOUR SEASONS
map page 243, C-2
160 E. Pearson St.
312-266-1000 or 800-621-6906
$$$$

Tucked away on the 12th floor of the Water Tower shopping center, this hotel has been ranked among the world's best by frequent travelers. An elegant and sunny lobby with marble floor, sophisticated floral arrangements, and fountain has views of the lake. Rooms are furnished with classic pieces and cheery fabrics. The Ritz prides itself on its service, and the dining room chef is known nationally for her creative cooking.

Neighborhood: *Magnificent Mile*
Number of Rooms: 344 rooms, 91 suites
Gym/Spa Facilities: health club with pool
Parking: valet $32 per night; self-park $24
Pets allowed: yes
Business Services: business center, in-room fax and dataports, "comp-cierge" for computer troubleshooting
Restaurants: The Dining Room *(French)*
Bar: The Greenhouse

ROSEMONT SUITES AT O'HARE
map page 217, A-3
5500 North River Rd.
847-678-4000 or 800-4-ROSEMONT
www.rosemontsuites.com
$-$$$$
Breakfast included; great choice for families.

Neighborhood: *O'Hare/Rosemont*
Number of Rooms: 296 suites
Gym/Spa Facilities: gym, pool, tennis
Parking: $10 day
Pets allowed: yes, maximum 20 pounds
Business Services: business center
Restaurants: The Prairie Grill
Bar: The Bar

SOFITEL CHICAGO

SOFITEL CHICAGO
map page 217, A-3
5550 North River Rd., Rosemont
847-678-4488 or 800-233-5959
www.sofitelchicagoohare.com
$$$

This Midwest outpost of the upscale French chain has the most distinctive character of any O'Hare hotel.

Neighborhood: *O'Hare*
Number of Rooms: 300
Gym/Spa Facilities: gym, indoor pool, sauna free for guests
Parking: $16 valet; $12 self park
Pets allowed: yes
Business Services: business center
Restaurants: Chez Collette *(French)*
Bar: Le Barp

SWISSOTEL CHICAGO
map page 241, D-1
323 East Wacker Dr. (Columbus)
312-565-0565 or 800-73 SWISS
www.swissotel.com
$$$-$$$$

An all-glass, triangular Swissotel, designed by noted Chicago architect Harry Weese, delivers

with sweeping views and luxuriously oversized rooms and suites. Even if you're not a fitness fanatic, stop by the Penthouse Health Spa on the 42nd floor for a panoramic view.

SWISSOTEL CHICAGO

Neighborhood: *Loop*
Number of Rooms: 632 rooms, 36 suites
Gym/Spa Facilities: health club, pool
Parking: valet $33 per night
Pets allowed: no
Business Services: business center, in-room data ports and fax machines
Restaurants: Cafe Suisse *(European Bistro)*, Palm Restaurant *(Steak and Seafood)*
Bar: Hideaway Lounge

TALBOTT HOTEL
map page 243, B-2
20 East Delaware Place
312-944-4970 or 800-TALBOTT
www.talbotthotel.com
$$$$

Built in 1927, the family-owned Talbott draws loyal guests who appreciate its homey feel. The welcoming wood-paneled lobby has leather sofas, velvet armchairs, and fireplaces; the modern rooms are livened up with art work and antique. Continental breakfast.

Neighborhood: *Magnificent Mile*
Number of Rooms: 116 rooms, 32 suites
Gym/Spa Facilities: access to nearby club
Parking: self-park $19
Pets allowed: no
Business Services: business center, in-room voice mail and dataports, meeting rooms
Restaurant/Bar: Basil's

THE W CHICAGO CITY CENTER
map page 241, B-2
172 West Adams St.
312-332-1200 or 800-621-2360
www.whotels.com
$$$-$$$$
This newly and handsomely renovated heart-of-town hotel stands in the shadow of the Sears Tower.

Neighborhood: *Loop*
Number of Rooms: 390 rooms
Gym/Spa Facilities: fitness center
Parking: valet $30 night
Pets allowed: no
Business Services: business center, in-room dataports
Restaurants: Ticker Tape Bar & Bistro, Gigi's W Cafe
Bar: Whiskey Blue

WESTIN RIVER NORTH
map page 243, B-4
320 North Dearborn St.
312-744-1900 or 800-WESTIN1
www.westin.com
$$$$
This upscale hotel was previously the Hotel Nikko, and traces of the Japanese design

linger. Sushi is served in the lounge lobby and the rooms are decorated in soft tones of gold and brown. Catering mainly to a well-heeled business clientele, the Westin offers all the amenities frequent travelers demand.

Neighborhood: *River North*
Number of Rooms: 424 rooms, 17 suites
Gym/Spa Facilities: fitness center, sauna
Parking: valet $30 per night; self-park $15
Pets allowed: no
Business Services: business center, in-room voice mail and fax, in-room dataport
Restaurant: Celebrity Cafe *(American)*
Bar: Hana Lounge

WHITEHALL HOTEL
map page 243, B-2
105 East Delaware Place (Michigan)
312-944-6300 or 800-323-7500
www.whitehallhotel.com
$$$$
This small luxury hotel welcomes guests with a cozy lobby decorated in the style of an English country home. The rooms feature traditional furniture (some rooms have four-poster beds) are livened up with Asian accents. But the Whitehall is not lost in the past: you can play video games on the rooms' TV sets.

Neighborhood: *Magnificent Mile*
Number of Rooms: 213 rooms, 8 suites
Gym/Spa Facilities: exercise room
Parking: valet $24 per night
Pets allowed: no
Business Services: business center
Restaurants: Whitehall Place *(Bistro)*
Bar: Lobby Lounge

RESTAURANTS

MOST CHICAGOANS DO KNOW HOW to use a knife and fork, although you might wonder from watching them tuck into the city's trademark delicacies. Deep-dish pizza, Chicago's most heralded contribution to the American gastronomic lexicon, is best savored as a hands-on experience. Even more so are some other grasp-and-chew foods—hot dogs, barbecued ribs, Italian beef sandwiches—for which Chicagoans take inordinate pride in doing it their way. Getting a Chicago-style hot dog just right—down to the poppy-seed bun and the celery salt (but never, ever, catsup)—is a matter of no small skill and artistry. Nathan's, that hot dog hall-of-famer from New York, couldn't cut the mustard here.

Finger food may be a local headline act, performed with gargantuan gusto by two million or more frenzied feeders at the start of each summer during the Taste of Chicago festival in Grant Park. But the real story of Chicago dining in the 1990s was the ever-expanding depth and breadth of ethnic diversity simmering among the 7,000 restaurants in this melting-pot metropolis. From Afghan to Vietnamese with dozens of nationalities in between, Chicago dishes up a culinary global tour as exhaustive and rewarding as you'll find anywhere in North America. It's an astonishing transformation for the erstwhile meat-and-potatoes bastion of the Midwest, where the ingrained beef bias was captured deliciously in Lucius Beebe's 1951 *Holiday* magazine article headlined "Name Your Cut!" Beebe, a trencherman as well as railroad buff, branded Chicago "the beef citadel of the world." The city, he wrote, "lives by beef, and the best food you can get in any Chicago restaurant, with few exceptions, is some part of a steer raised on the distant ranges of Texas, Colorado, or Nebraska."

Longtime mecca for carnivores was the legendary Stock Yard Inn, "a temple of T-bone," as Beebe called it. Patrons at the inn's Sirloin Room selected their cut from a great ice-filled altar in the center of the restaurant, stamped the steak with one of the miniature branding irons from the nearby charcoal brazier, and dispatched it to the kitchen. That marked the summit of Chicago gourmet dining two generations ago, when seldom was heard a discouraging word about cholesterol. The Stock Yard Inn, like the South Side yards themselves, is merely a

Chicago memory today. And while it is still possible to get a slab of grilled meat in the City of the Big Shoulders, the decline and fall of beef can be gauged by comparative figures from two useful diners' resources: in a typical recent month, *Chicago* magazine's restaurant guide recommended five places for vegetarian dishes, seven for seafood, a mere eight for steaks, ten for Japanese and 26 for French. Top steak venues, if you care to indulge, include Morton's (four locations), Gene & Georgetti, and the Palm.

Thanks in part to all the storefront ethnic fare, Chicago dining tends to be light on the wallet—if not always light on the stomach. Zagat, which bases its ratings on reports from thousands of volunteer gourmets, ranks this as the most fair-valued of major U.S. dining markets: an average customer tab of $23 for the nearly 800 Chicago area places covered. Comparative figures are $35 for New York, $28 for Los Angeles, $26 for San Francisco and Miami. "There's no question that Chicago leads all Zagat big cities in unadorned, salt-of-the-earth eating," says the guide. Heading Zagat's Top 100 "Bangs for the Buck" list is Walker Bros., a local-institution pancake house with three north suburban locations. Whatever your budget, a blossoming summer delight is the scores of Chicago restaurants that set up their gardens or sidewalks for outdoor dining, a pleasure almost unheard of during the red-meat era.

This selective menu of recommended Chicago restaurants merely nibbles at the banquet of possibilities in one of America's richest and most varied cities for dining. Each month's *Chicago* magazine contains incisive reviews of about 150 area restaurants. The *Zagat Chicago Restaurant Survey* pocket guide digests opinions of frequent diners on several hundred places. Dining reviews appear in the Friday activities sections of the *Chicago Sun-Times* and *Chicago Tribune,* as well as the Sunday *Sun-Times.*

Reservations are always a good idea at restaurants that accept them. A call ahead also can confirm opening hours and credit-card policy. Restaurants do change chefs and go out of business, so no set of listings can be entirely up-to-date. Price categories are coded at the end of each listing:

Abril   *Logan Square*
2607 North Milwaukee Ave.;
773-227-7252 $–$$ *Mexican*
This family-filled taqueria serves up huge portions of Mexican standards plus some less-expected menu items. It's a great spot to take kids and it's also a good late-night spot for night-owl revelers. The food here is always good and the service is always friendly.

Addis Abeba [sic]   *Lake View*
3521 North Clark St.; 773-929-9383
$$ *Ethiopian*
This could be Chicago's premier purveyor of Ethiopia's exotic cuisine, which uses the tangy *injera* pancake bread as an eating utensil. There are many combination platters here making it easy to share and allowing diners to simply give in to the urge to just reach across and grab something desirable off their neighbor's plate.

Al's No. 1 Italian Beef
Little Italy 1079 West Taylor St.;
312-226-4017
River North, map page 243, A-3
169 West Ontario St.; 312-943-3222
$ *American*
This stuff, along with hot dogs and deep-dish pizza, is real Chicago food. Neighborhood food. Al's serves chin-dripping beef sliced paper thin, heaped onto soft Italian bread and slathered with juice. You've seen the Superfans on Saturday Night Live? They would have stock in this place.

Ambria   *Lincoln Park, map page 245, C-4*
2300 North Lincoln Park West;
773-472-5959 $$$$ *French*
A night at Ambria is a grand-night-out amid an Art Nouveau setting and featuring Spanish-and-French-inspired cuisine courtesy of chef-owner Gabino Sotelino. The menu features different selections daily, perhaps including an appetizer of seared sea scallops with navy beans and beet vinaigrette or caviar with traditional garni. Entrees might include rack of lamb, veal tenderloin, medallions of venison or grilled salmon, all complemented by perfectly suited vegetables and sauces. And the wine list at Ambria is superb.

Ann Sather
Andersonville 5207 North Clark;
773-271-6677
Lake View 929 West Belmont;
773-348-2378
$-$$ *Swedish*
Swedish dishes from fruit soup to meatballs dot the menu of this homespun favorite with two North Side locations and several other scaled-down outposts. The signature item here is the venerable cinnamon roll—buy them by the box—and the can't-miss meal here is breakfast.

Army & Lou's   *Grand Crossing*
422 East 75th St.; 773-483-3100
$$ *American*
A genuine soul food destination, this spacious South Side spot is renowned for its gumbos, short ribs, fried chicken and cornbread—all the stuff to keep you warm on a chilly afternoon or evening.

Arun's   *Irving Park*
   4156 North Kedzie Ave.;
   773-539-1909
   $$$$ *Asian/Thai*
This place tucked away in a North Side neighborhood is consistently voted not only one of the nation's best Thai restaurants, but also one the nation's best restaurants. Period. Dining here takes a huge leap above typical storefront Thai restaurants with well-informed service and exquisite presentations. Try steamed rice dumplings, three-flavored red snapper and for dessert, poached pears or the tasting platter of four assorted Thai custards, which makes a splendid shared dessert.

Berghoff   *Loop, map page 243, B/C-2*
   17 West Adams St.; 312-427-3170
   $$ *German*
Your crusty waiter is as likely to be Hispanic as Teutonic these days, but the Berghoff soldiers on as a century-old stalwart of German heartiness. Try wiener schnitzel, sauerbraten, red cabbage, seafood brochette, chicken Dijon and Dortmunder-style beer. Adjoining the restaurant, but also with its own street entrance, is a stand-up bar where deli sandwiches are served.

Bistro 110   *Magnificent Mile*
   map page 243, B-2/3
   110 East Pearson St.; 312-266-3110
   $$-$$$ *French Eclectic*
It's not pure Paris, but here's a fashionably bustling spot for a break from all the nearby shopping. The wood-burning oven plays a starring role in the preparation of the restaurant's not-to-be-missed wood-roasted entrees such as the tuna "filet mignon," Prince Edward Island mussels, steak au poivre, and rack of lamb with dauphine potatoes. Garlic is a key ingredient here. Try the creme brulee for dessert.

Le Bouchon   *Bucktown*
   1958 North Damen; 773-862-6600
   $$ *French*
Best-buy bistro fare draws throngs to Lyonnaise lair of chef Jean-Claude Poilevey, where the onion tart is the signature dish. Also, try the roast duck for two; after all this is a tiny place in the artsy Bucktown neighborhood but alas, it is also a cramped and loud place. Devotees could care less, though. It's that good..

Brasserie Jo   *River North*
   map page 243, B-4
   59 West Hubbard St.; 312-595-0800
   $$$ *French*
Chef/owner Jean Joho's less formal alternative to his popular and elegant Everest is modeled after an early 1900s French brasserie and boasts wonderful service. Menu favorites include coq au vin, rack of lamb, Hangar steak, bouillabaisse and frisee salad. Try the profiteroles for dessert. A trendy crowd tends to frequent this airy and open space

Cafe Iberico   *River North*
   map page 243, A-3
   739 North LaSalle St.; 312-573-1510
   $$ *Spanish*
This sprawling two-story place started as a tiny four-table place, but the popularity of the tapas genre and the deftness with which

Cafe Iberico prepares them has caused it to grow exponentially. A loud, fun crowd frequents this place, which is convenient to River North galleries and tons of nightlife and shopping. Prepare to wait for an hour for a table on weekends. The baked goat cheese is terrific, as are the grilled sea scallops and the beef tenderloin skewers. Also, don't forget to order a pitcher of Sangria.

Carlos' *North Shore*
  429 Temple Ave., Highland Park;
  847-432-0770 $$$$ *French*
Nouvelle French flies high at this small but firmly entrenched north suburban temple of lighter-is-better gastronomy. Carlos' is a gracious, intimate and romantic spot. Try the roasted vegetable terrine, a New York strip steak in a cabernet wine reduction, Atlantic salmon or tuna with a California pistachio crust. A restaurant that is very serious about food and the dining experience, Carlos' gracefully lacks the pretentiousness of other spots on par with it.

Charlie Trotter's *Lincoln Park*
  map page 245, A-5
  816 West Armitage Ave.; 773-248-6228
  $$$$ *Eclectic*
The eponymous chef-owner of this much-praised townhouse restaurant stirs Asian flavors into European recipes for an experimental American cuisine superbly on target all of the time. Trotter's infused oils add depth to dishes that appear on the nightly-changing menus. The service here is meticulous and the wine list is one of the best in the country.

Coco Pazzo *River North*
  map page 243, A-4
  300 W. Hubbard; 312-836-0900
  $$$ *Italian*
New York City export does deft work in a dramatic loft setting, with an exposed kitchen and Tuscan staples at the menu's core. Fish of the day is done *aqua pazza* (crazy water) in a white-wine broth with garlic, tomatoes, and pepper. Also consider calamari al forno, ravioli di spinach, risotto del giorno and chocolate fondonte for dessert.

Costa's *Near West Side, map page 241, A-2*
  340 South Halsted St.; 312-263-0767
  $$ *Greek*
Ambiance a cut above the Greektown crowd is matched by Greek cooking that goes a step beyond the typical. The menu at this well-appointed spot features broiled octopus, red snapper and sea bass, lamb chops and angel hair pasta with artichokes. Sokolatina, a chocolate tart, is a fine dessert selection.

Dixie Kitchen & Bait Shop
  Hyde Park 5225 S. Harper Ave.;
  773-363-4943
  North Shore 825 Church St., Evanston,
  847-773-9030 $—$$ *American*
Cajun, along with other Southern genres, is still the rage in these friendly spots with the jumbled decor of flea markets. Try fried green tomatoes, first-rate jambalaya, oyster po' boys. It ain't N'awlins, but it's close.

Emperor's Choice *Chinatown*
map page 241, B-6
2238 S. Wentworth Ave.;
312-225-8800 **$$** *Asian/Chinese*
Cantonese classics, especially seafood, are at
the top of their form here. Many call it the
best Chinese restaurant in town. The mini-
malist dark decor gives way to wonderful
dishes, all of which are splendid, but just to
name a few names, try the Peking lobster
(or any of the other lobster preparations),
deep-fried soft shell crab, poached shrimp
or steamed fish. There are also great non-
fish dishes centered on duck and ostrich.

Erwin *Lake View, map page 245, A-2*
2925 N. Halsted St.; 773-528-7200
$$-$$$ *American*
Dining room windows provide peeks into
the kitchen, where chef Erwin Drechsler
devises an array of inventive American
dishes on an ever-changing menu. The
whitefish—however prepared—is an excel-
lent choice.

Everest *South Loop, map page 241, B-2*
440 S. La Salle St.; 312-663-8920
$$$$ *French*
Ambrosial Alsatian-accented fare from chef
Jean Joho puts this 40th-story aerie in
Chicago's financial district at the pinnacle
of the city's dining pyramid. Maine lobster
acquires new heights when it's roasted with
gewurztraminer and ginger. Consider a
seven-course tasting or pre-theater menu.
And savor the simply gorgeous view.

Gene & Georgetti *River North*
map page 243, A-4
500 N. Franklin; 312-527-3718
$$$ *American*
Carnivores and spaghetti hounds keep the
faith at this longtime steakhouse where
brusque service is considered part of the
charm. If you're looking for a quiet dining
experience at a secluded table, this place is
not for you. If you're looking for a quality
steak in a lively historic joint, it probably is.

Gin Go Gae *Ravenswood*
5433 N. Lincoln Ave.; 773-334-3895
$$ *Asian/Korean*
The large number of Korean diners in this
two-room storefront testifies to the quality
of the cuisine at this ethnic stalwart. If
you're new to Korean cooking, try the vast
all-you-can-eat buffet and have a taste of
everything.

Gladys' Luncheonette *Grand Boulevard*
4527 S. Indiana Ave.; 773-548-4566
$ *American*
Bustling soul-food diner dishes up top
value along with rib-sticking fare. All the
staple dishes are here. And they're all good,
especially the peach cobbler. There's noth-
ing fancy about the decor and it's a bit of a
hike from downtown, but legions of serious
eaters would swear by it. And have been
swearing by it for 25 years. Sunday is a big
day after church but Monday is a day of
rest when Gladys' is closed.

Gladys' Luncheonette   *Grand Boulevard*
4527 South Indiana Ave.;
773-548-4566
$ *American*
Bustling soul-food diner dishes up top value along with rib-sticking fare. All the staple dishes are here. And they're all good, especially the peach cobbler. There's nothing fancy about the decor and it's a bit of a hike from downtown, but legions of serious eaters would swear by it. And have been swearing by it for 25 years. Sunday is a big day after church but Monday is a day of rest when Gladys' is closed.

Greek Islands   *Near West Side*
map page 241, A-2
200 S. Halsted St.; 312-782-9855
$$ *Greek*
This long-time favorite does a high-spirited—almost kitschy—job at dispensing good-value Hellenic fare including fresh seafood, lamb forno and some low-cholesterol dishes. Naturally, saganaki, the famous flaming cheese, is a staple here. *Opaa!* A Greek cake called nogatina is the best dessert.

Hashalom   *West Rogers Park*
2905 W. Devon Ave.; 773-465-5675
$-$$ *Middle Eastern/North African*
This Israeli-Moroccan hybrid is a melting pot of Middle Eastern and North African flavors. Try the great soups, Cornish hens and couscous. It's a good hike north from downtown but where else are you going to get Israeli-Moroccan combinations?

Hau Giang   *Uptown*
1104 West Argyle St.; 773-275-8691
$-$$ *Asian/Vietnamese*
A top choice among the Vietnamese spots clustered in a North Side Asian enclave, Hau Giang does wonderfully filling noodle soups. Easily accessible by the Howard/Dan Ryan Red Line "L," a stroll through this area could easily put your mind in a far away place.

Hong Min   *Chinatown*
map page 241, B-5/6
221 West Cermak Rd.; 312-842-5026
$-$$ *Asian/Cantonese*
The dim sum lunch is a prime draw at this no-frills Cantonese mainstay. This is not a pretty place to look at, but it just might have the best dim sum in the city and the rest of the menu is extensive. The service is not great either, but you can bring in your own booze.

Indian Garden   *West Rogers Park*
2548 West Devon Ave.; 773-338-2929
$$ *Indian*
The huge menu here includes dishes cooked on the *tawa* (a griddle-like iron plate) and in the *kadhai* (an iron wok). A whole leg of lamb makes for a stupendous tandoori entree. The waitstaff is consistently friendly and the dishes are magnificently spiced. *Also location in Schaumburg.*

Italian Village   *Loop, map page 241, B-2*
71 West Monroe St.; 312-332-4040
$$-$$$ *Italian*
Owned and operated by the Capitanini

family since 1927, Italian Village is comprised of three outposts exuding Italian charm. **The Village** (upstairs) is known for Northern Italian cuisine in an Old World atmosphere; **La Cantina** (downstairs) for Italian seafood dishes (check out the aquariums); and **Vivere** for New Italian cuisine in a Postmodern space designed by Jordan Mozer. All three restaurants share Italian Village's 30,000-bottle wine list, which has received *Wine Spectator's* Grand Award annually since 1984.

Kiki's Bistro   *River North*
   map page 243, A-2
   900 North Franklin St.; 312-335-5454
   $$-$$$ *French*
Good value for French country fare lures crowds who savor such standards as gloriously rare roast leg of lamb or steak frites. Also try roasted chicken marinated in olive oil and garlic. For dessert, try creme brulee with chocolate. Kiki's is a charming place with light wood in the decor reminding one of a Provencial inn.

Klay Oven   *River North*
   map page 243, A-4
   414 N. Orleans St.; 312-527-3999
   $$-$$$ *Indian/Mogul*
Upscale quality distinguishes the intricately seasoned Indian Mogul cooking here. This is a huge step above any Indian restaurant on Devon Avenue and the prices reflect that. Fine Indian textiles on the walls and private alcoves set the tone here. An innovative menu, with foods prepared in a clay oven or Indian wok, makes it a special dining experience. The Mulligatawny soup, tiger prawns, lobster, and quail are all reliably good; accompany your dinner with a selection from the fine wine list.

Lawry's The Prime Rib
   Magnificent Mile, map page 243, B-4
   100 East Ontario St.; 312-787-5000
   $$$ *American/Steakhouse*
Enjoy the ornate setting in a former McCormick mansion while making the only basic menu decision— which cut of the excellent prime rib to order. Noteworthy, as it is in many steakhouses, is the creamed spinach side dish. There's also lobster and the daily fish special. After the hearty stuff, chef Jackie Shen's famous chocolate bag dessert is a can't-miss. Lawry's is a notorious "special-event" place for birthdays and anniversaries. It also sees its share of business-types and tourists.

Le Francais   *Northwest Suburbs*
   map page 217, A-1
   269 South Milwaukee Ave., Wheeling; 847-541-7470
   $$$$ *French*
Master chef Jean Banchet has returned to the kitchen of his nationally renowned bastion of culinary excellence and it is certainly worth a trip north to see what he is preparing. Le Francais features tradition with modern overtones. Try confit tomatoes and celery root salad with avocado sorbet; salmon pave on roasted cauliflower with cucumber-caviar sauce; or, for dessert, a lemon souffle crisp with sweet basil ice cream.

RESTAURANTS

Le Titi de Paris   *Northwest Suburbs*
1015 W. Dundee Rd.,
Arlington Heights; 847-506-0222
$$$-$$$$ *French*
Popular items on the boldly contemporary menu at this northwest suburban mainstay include tuna tartare with a coulis of avocado veal sweetbreads; antelope medallions; and grilled swordfish with orzo in a shrimp, basil, butter and wine sauce. Any grilled fish or robust game dishes here are highly recommended. For dessert, try the "chocolate symphony."

Lou Malnati's   *River North*
map page 243, A-4
439 North Wells St.; 312-828-9800
$—$$ *American*
Deep dish pizza is serious business in Chicago. And even though most of the Malnati's locations are in the suburbs, they're still a contender and a legitimate choice for a nice pizza pie.

Marge's   *Old Town, map page 245, B-5*
1758 North Sedgwick, 312-787-3900
$-$$ *American*
Established as a saloon more than a century ago. It prospers today as an admirably old-fashioned tavern, even if the neighborhood yuppies are sometimes a bit thick on the ground. Good pub grub.

Matsuya   *Lake View*
3469 North Clark St.; 312-248-2677
$$ *Japanese*
Sushi plays a starring role at Matsuya, but the rest of the good-value Japanese menu also sparkles.

Metro Club   *Lake View*
3032 North Lincoln Ave.; 773-929-0622 $$ *Austrian*
Don't confuse this place with Chicago's premier rock and roll venue, the Metro, on Clark Street near Wrigley Field. The Metro Club is a tiny Austrian restaurant with only a few tables and a tiny bar. It's so intimate, customers must be buzzed in. Stand by the front door and let the bartender get a good look at you, then enter when you hear the buzz and enjoy authentic Austrian fare and super-fresh BBK beer on tap.

Morton's   *Gold Coast, map page 243, B-2*
1050 North State St.; 312-266-4820
$$$—$$$$ *American*
The elite meet to eat meat in this time-tried spot that gets tons of votes as Chicago's best steakhouse. Perhaps the decor could use an update, but the service is first-rate. As is the case at most steakhouses, the portions are huge and side dishes easily serve two people. *Also suburban locations in Schaumburg, Rosemont, Westchester.*

Nacional 27   *River North*
map page 243, A-3
325 West Huron St.; 312-664-2727
$$ *Latin American fusion*
This restaurant/club features the cuisine of the 27 nations in the South and Central Americas—don't forget the islands. There's a contemporary twist on traditional Latin dishes like Chimichuri Churasco steak with roasted peppers and papas fritas, or Chilean sea bass Zarzuela poached with shellfish broth and served with spicy tomato stew

and annato rice. Nacional 27 also boasts decent rum and tequila collections.

Papagus Greek Taverna   *River North*
   map page 243, B-3
   620 North State St.; 312-642-8450
   $$ *Greek*
Papagus, in all its faux-rustic glory, offers less heavy Greek food in a non-Greektown location. The restaurant offers an array of *mezedes,* the Aegean equivalent of small-portion tapas. The spanakopita, the Greeks' spinach and feta cheese pie in phyllo pastry, is exceptional. Also, try spit-roasted Greek chicken or braised lamb with orzo. For dessert, what else? Baklava.

Park Avenue Cafe   *Gold Coast*
   map page 243, C-2
   199 East Walton St.; 312-944-4414
   $$$$ *American*
Name and concept of super-chef David Burke's New York City restaurant are cloned to well-earned applause on the second floor of Doubletree Guest Suites. Try the chef's trademark swordfish chop or pastrami salmon in a warm corn pancake. The wine list here (a good one) features mainly American bottlings.

Parthenon   *Near West Side*
   map page 241, A-2
   314 South Halsted St.; 312-726-2407
   $-$$ *Greek*
One of the oldest and most reliable Greektown competitors, featuring an 11-course family-style feed for serious diners.

Penny's Noodle Shop   *Wrigleyville*
   map page 245, A-1

3400 North Sheffield Ave.;
773-281-8222
Lake View (map page 245, A-2)
950 W. Diversey Ave.; 773-281-8448
   $ *Pan Asian fusion*
You'll see a lot of pretty young faces in these bright and cheery no-nonsense noodle houses. Even a student could afford the dishes here, but someone with a little more money would do well to make a visit to Penny's because the simple food is really quite good. Selections hail from Thailand, Vietnam, China and Japan. You can't go wrong with any of the vegetable dishes here.

Pizzeria Uno/Pizzeria Due
   Magnificent Mile/River North
   map page 243, B-3/4
   Uno: 29 East Ohio St., 312-321-1000
   Due: 619 North Wabash Ave.,
   312-943-2400
   $-$$ *American*
Both are Chicago staples and the birthplace of the Chicago deep-dish pizza—and just a block apart from each other, so just choose the one with the shorter wait. Bring patience to both places or dine at an off-hour. Or be content to have a few drinks amid a high-energy downtown clientele.

Prairie   *South Loop, map page 241, B-2*
   500 South Dearborn St.; 312-663-1143
   $$$ *American*
A personal favorite, Prairie features ingredients from America's heartland creatively prepared and served in a dining room that evokes Frank Lloyd Wright's Prairie Style. Get it? Other notable dishes include lamb loin salad with bleu cheese dressing and

honey-coated Wisconsin duck breast. Convenient to downtown theaters, Grant Park and the Museum Campus.

Printer's Row   *South Loop*
   map page 241, B-2
   550 South Dearborn St.; 312-461-0780
   $$$ *American*
Down the block from Prairie, chef-owner Michael Foley's neighborhood pioneer likewise does inventive cooking in Midwestern ways. Try venison, duck or rosemary-infused grilled sturgeon over red-wine mashed potatoes with baby bok choy, or Moroccan-spiced cured salmon. An upscale eatery like Prairie, this restaurant named for the neighborhood it's in is convenient to downtown theaters, Grant Park and the Museum Campus.

Red Lion Pub   *Lincoln Park*
   map page 245, A-3
   2446 N. Lincoln Ave.;
   773-348-2695 $$ *British*
You'll have a bit of the all right here. Authentic British fare ranges from fish and chips to bangers and mash (sausages and potatoes) to kidney pie. Great British and Irish beers on tap, too. And it's right across the street from the Biograph theater, where John Dillinger, Public Enemy No. 1, was shot.

Reza's   *two locations:*
   Andersonville
   5255 North Clark St.; 773-561-1898
   River North, map page 243, A-3
   432 West Ontario St.; 312-664-4500
   $-$$ *Persian*
These large and lively Persian storefronts

dispense vast portions of authentic Iranian fare, including succulent quail, dill rice, lamb shank and plenty of great vegetarian dishes, and a decent wine selection.

Rinconcito Sudamericano   *Bucktown*
   1954 West Armitage Ave.;
   773-489-3126
   $$ *Peruvian*
Seafood stands out at this Peruvian storefront, but so do intriguing Andean dishes like beef heart and tripe stew. This is a place to which you don't have to bring a lot of money, but you do have to bring a sense of adventure. There's virtually no decor, but the food is consistently good.

Robinson's No. 1 Ribs   *Lincoln Park*
   map page 245, B-5
   655 West Armitage Ave.;
   312-337-1399
   $-$$ *American*
This barbecue front-runner: uses a slow-smoking process that lowers fat content. Neither location is anything fancy to look at, but it's the 'cue that brings people back. From full slabs to pork sandwiches and chickens, barbecue lovers rave about this place. *Suburban location in Oak Park.*

Rosebud on Rush   *Magnificent Mile,*
   map page 243, B-3
   55 East Superior; 312-266-6444
   $$$ *Italian*
This crowded and noisy red-sauce celebrity hangout features homemade pastas, chicken Vesuvio and the standard tiramisu for dessert. The service can be rushed but if you're looking for a belly buster of a meal, the portions are huge.

Russian Tea Time *Loop*
map page 241, C-2
77 East Adams St.; 312-360-0000
$$ *Russian/Ukrainian*
Tashkent carrot salad and other exotic dishes dot the pan-Soviet menu of this antique-decorated eatery run by mother-son team from Uzbekistan. Delight in the dense pumpernickel bread and try a bowl of Ukrainian borscht, all within steps from the Art Institute of Chicago and Grant Park. And the vodka choices are many.

¡Salpicon! *Old Town*
map page 243, A-1
1252 North Wells St.; 312-988-7811
$$ *Regional Mexican*
Storefront festooned with colorful art purveys deftly prepared Mexican regional fare that goes beyond the clichés thanks to chef Priscila Satkoff. The quesadillas Tres Marias pack three different fillings into golden mesa dumplings. Fresh fish and meat dishes also stand out. For dessert, oranges poached in cinnamon-orange syrup or flan. There's also an award-winning wine list and much tequila.

Santorini *Near West Side*
138 South Halsted St.; 312-829-8820
$$ *Greek*
Accent on seafood in whitewashed Greektown setting with a touch of class. Cod takes on Aegean airs as a crusty bacalao (salted cod) with garlic-potato purée.

Sayat Nova *Magnificent Mile*
map page 243, B/C-3
157 East Ohio St.; 312-644-9159
$$ *Armenian*

A tried-and-true Armenian spot that dependably does the standards, from hummus, baba ghannouj and stuffed grape leaves to borek, kebabs, and couscous. The cozy setting inside the restaurant takes you a million miles from North Michigan Avenue, which is just steps away.

Scoozi! *River North, map page 243, A-3*
410 West Huron St.; 312-943-5900
$$-$$$ *Italian*
It's easy to imagine Fellini filming the jam-packed seekers of la dolce vita who flock to the trendy but tasty country-Italian menu. This huge place has an open loft feel about it and was one of the first fashionable Italian joints in town when it opened in 1986 to rave reviews from local yuppies and tourists. The food here is quite good; the atmosphere, bright and loud and fun. Popular selections are the wood-roasted dishes, half-moon raviolis and the antipasti bar.

Shaw's Crab House
Magnificent Mile/River North
map page 243, B-4
21 East Hubbard St.; 312-527-2722
$$$ *Seafood*
The bounty of superlative seafood in this bustling place starts with such basics as exemplary oysters on the half shell and Maryland crab cakes, plus excellent seasonal offerings. The main room has a 1940s East Coast feel to it, but there's also an adjoining Blue Crab Lounge featuring a raw bar and a full menu, plus live jazz and blues. The music next door at Andy's is probably better, though, if you're in for a serious jazz fix. *Suburban location in Deerfield.*

RESTAURANTS

Siam Cafe   *Uptown*
4712 N. Sheridan Rd.; 773-769-6602
$—$$ *Asian/Thai*
Chicago is filled with budget-minded Thai restaurants and most are very good, but this time-tested spot is among the oldest and the best. Coconut-milk curry dishes here are fantastic. Service is hot and cold, but a Siam Cafe's prices, no one is complaining.

Signature Room at the 95th
Magnificent Mile, map page 243, B/C-2
875 N. Michigan Ave.; 312-787-9596
$$$$ *American*
That's 95th as in 95th floor. Happily, the quality of the regional American food is not inversely proportional to the view from 1,000 feet up in the John Hancock Center. Floor-to-ceiling windows assure a dazzling look at the city or the lake. As for the food, try the shrimp and brie baked in phyllo pastry garnished with scallions and ginger soy sauce, and the filet of sauteed salmon with spinach and a merlot butter sauce. One floor below is a cocktail lounge—a great spot for a late-night drink.

Spiaggia   *Magnificent Mile*
map page 243, B/C-20
980 North Michigan Ave.;
312-280-2750 $$$$ *Italian*
The high-end Italian food matches the exquisite setting at this expense-account favorite. Try chef Paul Bartolotta's pastas—specifically stuffed pastas, such as the tortel-lini with potatoes and leeks in a pesto sauce—or roasted meats, specifically wood-roasted guinea hen with pancetta, porcini, and Savoy cabbage. The formal, romantic room and the views of Michigan Avenue and the lake (thanks to the restaurant's second-floor location) are spectacular. And if you're not in the mood (or financially equipped) for fancy-schmancy, try the Spiaggia Cafe down the hall.

Tango Sur   *Wrigleyville*
3763 North Southport.; 773-477-5466
$$ *Argentinean*
This Argentinean storefront is stylishly located in a trendy row of newer restaurants a couple blocks west of the Cubs' home field. The steaks here are good and so is the budget-priced parrillada of short ribs, sweetbreads and sausages served sizzling on a tabletop grill.

Topolobampo/Frontera Grill
River North, map page 243, B-4
445 North Clark St.; 312-661-1434
$$ - $$$ *Regional Mexican*
Serious regional Mexican fare sparkles in these same-kitchen siblings steered by the genius of chef-owner Rick Bayless, who has turned the rooms into mini museums of Mexican art. Both offer sophisticated Mexican fare, but Topolobampo is the more upscale of the two. For dessert, check out a slice of chocolate pecan pie or one of many rare tequilas.

Trattoria No. 10   *Loop*
 map page 241, B-1
 10 North Dearborn; 312-984-1718
 $$$ *Italian*
An erstwhile downtown boiler room has been transformed into a fair imitation of a time-seasoned trattoria, where pastas are among the top choices. Also try grilled portobello mushrooms baked with aged goat cheese, polenta and pomegranate molasses; risotto with roasted venison loin; or osso bucco.

Trio   *Evanston/North Shore*
 1625 Hinman Ave.; 847-733-8746
 $$$$ *Eclectic*
Trio offers French cuisine with Asian and Italian influences and consistently provides a wonderful dining experience, courtesy of chef Shawn McClain. Try smoked salmon and ahi Napoleon with crispy potatoes and wasabi creme; grilled venison and pine nut and herb-crusted rack of lamb; roasted scallops; or smoked beef tenderloin on gnocchi with a Gorgonzola and port wine reduction. Dinner at the kitchen table is offered for an extra fee.

Tru   *Magnificent Mile,* *map page 239, C-3*
 676 N. St. Clair; 312-202-0001
 $$$$ *Eclectic*
Spousal chefs Rick Tramonto and Gale Gand have fun with the preparations at this very serious eatery. Food often is plated on granite slabs, panes of glass, mirrors or artist palettes. To wit: roasted lobster with truffle mashed potatoes served in a martini glass and garnished with a tiny lobster claw or antenna. The menu changes constantly here, but the service is always first-rate. Turn off your cell phones and prepare for a long meal, possibly in the three- to four-hour range. The kitchen table must be reserved two months in advance..

Twin Anchors   *Old Town*
 map page 245, B-6
 1655 North Sedgwick St.;
 312-266-1616
 $$ *American*
Many patrons, including Frank Sinatra, have deemed the barbecued ribs at this nononsense neighborhood tavern the best in Chicago. Start with the fabulous dark rye bread basket and a salad, then move into a meaty slab of baby backs, which are always cooked to perfection. And speaking of always, there's always a wait at Twin Anchors in the evening—a testament to quality of the food. The jukebox is a good one, but take note of the conspicuous sign in this tiny place that reads "Positively *No* Dancing."

Viceroy of India   *West Rogers Park*
 2520 W. Devon Ave.; 773-743-4100
 $$ *Indian & Pakistani*
Here's a reliable winner among the welter of Indian/Pakistani storefront eateries along West Devon Avenue. Most are good, but Viceroy of India gets raves for its tasty tandoori and its consistency of quality.

Vinci *Lincoln Park, map page 245, A-6*
   1732 North Halsted St.; 312-266-1199
   $$—$$$ *Italian*
This top-flight trattoria dishes up glorious grills among its robust offerings, which also include polenta con funghi and spinach and cheese ravioli with brown-butter sauce. Hazelnut cheesecake for dessert. Vinci is convenient to both Steppenwolf and Royal George theaters, and to the post-performance watering hole O'Rourke's, where you can get a glimpse of an actor you just saw perform and listen to some great jazz on the jukebox.

Walker Bros. Original Pancake House
   North Shore
   153 Green Bay Rd., Wilmette;
   847-251-6000 $ *American*
The delectably fresh, cholesterol-count-be-damned breakfast fare brings legions of flapjack fans to this north suburban institution famous for serving up its legendary cinnamon apple pancake, plus waffles, omelets and German and Dutch baby pancakes. There's also standard lunch and dinner diner fare here, but you to to Walker Brothers for breakfast. *Other locations in Arlington Heights, Glenview, Highland Park and Lincolnshire.*

Yoshi's Cafe *Lake View*
   map pager 241, A-1
   3257 North Halsted; 773-248-6160
   $$$—$$$$ *Eclectic*
West and East meld marvelously at chef-owner Yoshi Katsumura's cozy Pacific Rim restaurant where subtlety is the hallmark. Lots of low-fat options are available on the vast Japanese/French-inspired menu, including grilled baby octopus and daikon salad drizzled with ponzu, a citrus-flavored soy sauce. The staff here is quite knowledgeable.

Zinfandel *River North*
   map page 243, B-4
   59 West Grand Ave.; 312-527-1818
   $$—$$$ *American*
Revived recipes from the past, updated and featuring native ingredients, are the trademark of a regional American menu served in craft-filled setting. Try the dry-rub barbecued rib sampler. There's a regular menu here, monthly regional specials and daily specials. And of course, there are many, many zinfandels on the wine list.

RECOMMENDED READING

■ NON-FICTION

Addams, Jane. *Twenty Years at Hull-House.* Insightful memoirs of the Hull House founder. New York: Macmillan, 1910.

Asbury, Herbert. *Gem of the Prairie.* Gangsters and the rest of Chicago's demi-monde. New York: Alfred A. Knopf, 1940.

Condit, Carl. *The Chicago School of Architecture.* Definitive work on the 1875-1925 architectural golden era here. Chicago: University of Chicago Press, 1964.

Cromie, Robert. *A Short History of Chicago.* Brisk waltz through two centuries. San Francisco: Lexikos, 1984.

Cronon, William. *Nature's Metropolis: Chicago and the Great West.* How Chicago shaped America's mid-continent and in turn was defined by the wide-open spaces to the west. New York: W. W. Norton, 1991.

Dedmon, Emmett. *Fabulous Chicago: A Great City's History and People.* Lively spin on larger-than-life personalities, by a redoubtable newspaperman. New York: Atheneum, 1981.

Farber, David. *Chicago '68.* Portrait of a tumultuous watershed year. Chicago: University of Chicago Press, 1988.

Granger, Bill and Lori. *Fighting Jane: Mayor Jane Byrne and the Chicago Machine.* Life and times of the city's first woman mayor. New York: Dial, 1980.

Hayner, Don, and Tom McNamee. *Metro Chicago Almanac.* Irresistible smorgasbord of everything you always wanted to know about the Second City. Chicago: Chicago Sun-Times/Bonus Books, 1993.

Hayner, Don, and Tom McNamee. *Streetwise Chicago: A History of Chicago Street Names.* More delicious facts. Chicago: Loyola University Press, 1988.

Heise, Kenan, and Ed Baumann. *Chicago Originals.* Colorful characters, decade by decade. Chicago: Bonus Books, 1990.

Honig, Donald, and Lawrence S. Ritter. *The Image of Their Greatness: An Illustrated History of Baseball from 1900 to the Present.* Play-by-play history of America's legend-filled sport, with great old black-and-whites. New York: Crown, 1992.

James, Henry. *Letters of Henry James.* New York: Scribner, 1920.

Kaufman, Mervyn. *Father of Skyscrapers, a Biography of Louis Sullivan.* The tempestuous life of the Chicago School genius. Boston: Little, Brown, 1969.

■ NON-FICTION *(continued)*

Kipling, Rudyard. "From Sea to Sea," *Letters of Travel.* New York: Scribner, 1889.

Kleppner, Paul. *Chicago Divided: The Making of a Black Mayor.* How Harold Washington won the 1983 mayoral election. De Kalb, Illinois: Northern Illinois University Press, 1985.

Lewis, Lloyd, and Henry Justin Smith. *Chicago, the History of Its Reputation.* Sweet story from two legendary *Chicago Daily News* men. New York: Harcourt Brace, 1929.

Lowe, David. *Lost Chicago.* Vivid photographic look at the heritage that has been torn down. Boston: Houghton Mifflin, 1975.

Mayer, Harold M., and Richard C. Wade. *Chicago: Growth of a Metropolis.* Magisterial illustrated survey of the city's development. Chicago: University of Chicago Press, 1969.

McPhaul, John J. *Deadlines and Monkeyshines, the Fabled World of Chicago Journalism.* Tales from the Front Page Era. Englewood Cliffs, New Jersey: Prentice Hall, 1962.

Rakove, Milton L. *Don't Make No Waves, Don't Back No Losers: An Insider's Analysis of the Daley Machine.* Behind the scenes of Hizzoner's empire. Bloomington: Indiana University Press, 1975.

Rowe, Mike. *Chicago Blues: The City and the Music.* The evolution of a Chicago trademark. New York: Da Capo Press, 1975.

Royko, Mike. *Boss: Richard J. Daley and His Era.* Superlative model of what an urban biography should be. Chicago: Dutton, 1971.

Schoenberg, Robert J. *Mr. Capone: The Real—and Complete—Story of Al Capone.* The latest look at Scarface Al. New York: William Morrow, 1992.

Spear, Allan H. *Black Chicago: The Making of a Negro Ghetto, 1890-1920.* The roots of the city's racial anguish. Chicago: University of Chicago Press, 1967.

Terkel, Studs. *Division Street: America.* Chicagoans talk to the master listener. New York: Pantheon, 1967.

Travis, Dempsey J. *An Autobiography of Black Chicago.* Stirring account of African-American community life here by an civic-minded real-estate man. Chicago: Urban Research Institute, 1981.

Wille, Lois. *Forever Open, Clear and Free: The Struggle for Chicago's Lakefront.* Engaging history of a vital and ongoing battle. Chicago: University of Chicago Press, 1972, 1991.

Wolfe, Tom. *Mauve Gloves and Mad Men, Clutter and Vine.* Commentary on American cities, including essays on Chicago. New York: Farrar, Strauss & Giroux, 1976.

■ FICTION

Ade, George. *Fables in Slang.* Satirical parables by a pioneering Chicago newspaper columnist born in Indiana. Chicago: H. S. Stone, 1900.

Algren, Nelson. *The Man With the Golden Arm.* Poetry and humor in novel of West Division Street saloon life by a writer who loved and hated his Chicago. Garden City, New York: Doubleday, 1950.

Bellow, Saul. *Humboldt's Gift.* Closest thing to Chicago novel in oeuvre of city's most famous post-World War II writer, a Nobel Prize laureate. New York: Viking, 1975.

Brooks, Gwendolyn. *Annie Allen.* Pulitzer Prize volume of poetry by leader of city's literary Black Renaissance in 1960s and '70s. New York: Harper, 1949.

Dreiser, Theodore. *Sister Carrie.* Early Chicago-set novel by the relentless social realist. New York: Doubleday, 1900.

Dunne, Finley Peter. *Mr. Dooley in Peace and War.* Chicago-Irish saloon wit of a century ago, collected from Dunne's famous newspaper columns. Boston: Small, Maynard, 1898.

Farrell, James T. *Young Lonigan.* First and most forceful volume of Farrell's South Side Irish trilogy. New York: Vanguard, 1932.

Ferber, Edna. *The Girls.* Three-generation novel spanning Chicago history from 1840s into twentieth century. Garden City, New York: Doubleday, 1921.

Lardner, Ring. *You Know Me Al.* Letters to a friend back home from a major-league baseball naif in the wicked big city of Chicago. New York: Doran, 1916.

Maugham, W. Somerset. *Stories of Hawaii and the South Seas.* Honolulu: Mutual Publishing, 1921.

Sandburg, Carl. *Chicago Poems.* City of the Big Shoulders, and much, much more. New York: Holt, 1916.

Sinclair, Upton. *The Jungle.* Muckraking classic that exposed exploitation of immigrant Chicago stockyard workers— and vile sanitary conditions of the slaughtering process. New York: Doubleday, Page, 1906

Smith, Patricia. *Life According to Motown.* Award-winning Chicago poet writes about growing up in Chicago. Chicago: Tia Chucha Press, 1991.

Wright, Richard. *Native Son.* New American tragedy of Bigger Thomas, a black man "whipped before you were born." New York: Harper, 1940.

■ GUIDEBOOKS

Bach, Ira J., and Susan Wolfson, revised and updated by James Cornelius. *Chicago on Foot.* An array of walking tours with an architectural focus. Chicago: Chicago Review Press, 1994.

Dale, Alzina Stone. *Mystery Reader's Walking Guide: Chicago.* Tailing the haunts of fictional sleuths spun by Sara Paretsky and others who favor Chicago settings. Lincolnwood, Illinois: Passport Books, 1995

Lindberg, Richard. *Passport's Guide to Ethnic Chicago.* History and attractions, from Irish to Native American. Lincolnwood, Illinois: Passport Books, 1993.

Phalen, Lane. *The Book Lover's Guide to Chicagoland.* Where the bookstores are. Hoffman Estates, Illinois: Brigadoon Bay Books, 1995.

Schulze, Franz, and Kevin Harrington, editors. *Chicago's Famous Buildings.* Illustrated briefs on nearly 200 landmarks and notable buildings. Chicago: University of Chicago Press, 1993.

Sinkevitch, Alice, editor. *AIA Guide to Chicago.* Exhaustive and erudite survey sponsored by American Institute of Architects Chicago, the Chicago Architecture Foundation, and the Landmarks Preservation Council of Illinois. San Diego: Harvest Original/Harcourt Brace, 1993.

Sirefman, Susanna. *Chicago: A Guide to Recent Architecture.* Pocket-sized gloss on 100 buildings erected between 1983 and 1993. London: Artemis, 1994.

Vettel, Phil, and Carolyn McGuire, editors. *Zagat Chicago Restaurants Survey.* Meaty frequent-diner consensus on hundreds of city and suburban eateries. New York: Zagat, 2000.

I N D E X